A BOOK OF CHRISTIAN FAITH

A BOOK OF CHRISTIAN FAITH

Questions and Answers for the 20th Century

JOHANN CHRISTOPH HAMPE

AUGSBURG Publishing House • Minneapolis

A BOOK OF CHRISTIAN FAITH

Contents

Introduction

This is a book for people who are sympathetic to the Christian faith but have many questions about its intellectual integrity and the example of those who call themselves Christians. It faces up to those questions honestly, and takes both young and old readers into a developing encounter with Christ. It could be called a "catechism," because it outlines the questions of the Christian faith and gives answers to those questions. But it is much more than a catechism. It is a spiritual pilgrimage from doubt to faith. It begins with a man named Archimedes crying out for "one firm place to stand." All the doubts and confusions of today—with their uncertainty about our human origins, our purpose in life, and our destiny—are heard in that cry.

This book tries to give a "firm place to stand." But it gives no cheap answers. The questions of our day are taken seriously and explored carefully; the weaknesses of the church and the foolishness of some of its cherished teachings are freely admitted. But progress through the book soon shows flashes of light, leading to an affirmation of faith soundly based on clear thought and true experience. A critical examination of church history, clarification of obscure doctrine, and a rejection of what has not stood the test of time or the disciplined methods of science enable the author to come out at the end with a statement of faith all Christians can affirm.

Each of the six main sections of the book follows the same pattern. First the main questions are dealt with, then comes a survey of what has been said by the church, followed by a summary. Affirmations of faith are found in these last paragraphs of each section. Beginning with a place on which to stand, the book examines our origins, our motivations, our redemption, and our way of life, and looks courageously into the nature of our destiny—"the goal of our calling." The last section closes with a note of triumph:

I believe in the glory of the future world.
I believe that the church of Christ in all its brokenness, as we see it today, yet bears the stamp of this glory already on its body, and that the Christ who is to come is already in its midst when it hears, confesses, and celebrates the gospel of his good news and authenticates it by its love. That is what I believe. Amen.

Anyone who reads this book with care will come to grips with the heart of Christian tradition; but more than that, he or she will experience a real discussion with those who believe, and will be taken more deeply into the church's own questioning about its most basic teachings. Readers may not always find the answers given convincing, but they will find them to be honest and offered with respect. The author has given his mind to each question, admitting much that is usually thought to be unquestioned in the church, and then affirming his own faith and the reasons for it. Sufficient information is provided for discussion of both the questions and the author's answers. There is a remarkable openness even in the treatment of central issues of the Christian faith, and a readiness to be done with doctrines that became untenable after the arrival of modern science.

The author and the committee he worked with have broad ecumenical sympathies and have dealt with the Christian faith in terms relevant to all denominations. An example is the treatment of Baptism. The explanation of infant baptism is accompanied by a sympathetic understanding of the Baptist position and an exhortation to learn from the 16th-century Anabaptists. The discussion of the sacraments shows an understanding of the Roman Catholic position as well as that of the less sacramental churches. The treatment of "faith and order" shows a clear understanding of the issues facing the ecumenical movement and makes a contribution to the debate on the mutual recognition of ministries and sacraments. This book should be read through to catch the sense of pilgrimage (indeed to join in it), but once read it will be a reference book of continuing importance.

About the author

Johann Christoph Hampe is a well-known writer and theologian. He served with the German army in Russia during World War II, and emerged from that experience with an inner calling to the ministry. He studied in Göttingen at a time when one of the principal problems of the British occupation forces was finding enough food for the students. Help eventually came through a generous gift from the Southern Baptist Convention in the United States. Hampe continued his studies in Geneva, where the World Council of Churches was young and ably led by General Secretary Visser 't

Hooft, and where Hendrik Kraemer was building Bossey as an ecumenical institute. From there he went to Tübingen for further study, becoming a Lutheran pastor in 1953. Already recognized as a writer, he soon became editor of the Hamburg church paper *Sonntagsblatt*. Hampe remained editor for ten years, during which time he became a full-time writer and broadcaster. Since 1962 he has been what could be called a "theological journalist." It is in that role that he wrote this book. He is widely known far beyond his own church, and his books, articles, and broadcasts have stimulated ecumenical discussion about the Christian faith.

Communicating the faith

The origins of this book can be traced at least as far back as Martin Luther, who was deeply concerned that both parents and children learn the basic truths of the Christian faith. Luther himself tried to meet this need with two catechisms that were widely used and remain influential to this day. Lutheran churches have continued to place high importance on teaching the faith in terms understandable to everyday people. In 1969 a commission established by the German Lutheran churches began five years of intensive work on a new catechism, which was intended to identify and address the realities of life in the modern world from the perspective of Christian faith. This was to be a cooperative effort by not only pastors and theologians, but also other professionals. There were 17 members of the commission and more than 200 consultants, representing such fields as medicine, commerce, law, and sociology. The text of the emerging book was read by 35 groups of people that represented those who would be using the new catechism.

Out of this process developed a large and excellent book, based on experience and the living discussion of pastoral problems and intellectual difficulties in many fields. Its German title is *Evangelischer Erwachsenenkatechismus*, and its broad understanding, attention to accurate detail, and awareness of modern thought make it an excellent reference book. What was needed in addition to this large volume was a way to communicate its material to a wider audience. Another book was needed for serious lay enquirers, who could then read for themselves the answers the church offers to questions about modern life and the Christian faith.

With this intention in mind the catechism committee brought Johann Christoph Hampe into their meetings in 1973. He kept close to the work of the committee over the final two years. Then, in cooperation with the four major authors, he began this book, bringing together the material from the larger work in a style and format that can be appreciated by any serious reader. Its German title is *Was Wir Glauben.*

This translation and adaptation of *Was Wir Glauben* makes this important work available to the English-speaking world. It will be an invaluable aid to Christian groups and individuals desiring a serious and contemporary discussion of the faith.

Using this book

The arrangement of material in this book makes it very suitable for class use. It can be used as a basic text on Christian teachings in both churches and schools. Young and old readers alike will find it more attractive than the historical treatment of Christianity or literary study of the Bible which so often passes for "religious instruction."

The material is progressive, which means that the book should be taken in the order in which it has been written. Courses of varying lengths could use it, depending on frequency of meeting. There are six sections, each having six subsections, that could serve as convenient division points. It would not be possible to handle more than one subsection at any one meeting. In any case they are complete in themselves and provide a satisfying amount of material.

An appropriate method would be questions and discussion. Each subsection has six questions, and a convenient session could consist of reading a question (which is usually self-explanatory), encouraging discussion of it, and then presenting the material Hampe has provided for further discussion. What will emerge in such a plan is that the author's closing material will lead at once to the next question.

The church's common faith

Throughout the book there are references to divisions among Christians ("the church in its brokenness"). But the overall impression is that we are dealing with one church and not many. This is exemplified in the last section, which brings together under the title "What Unites Us" creeds and confessions that are generally accepted by the whole church. Here are statements from the Old and New Testaments, the Apostles' and Nicene Creeds, documents from the Lutheran Reformation, the Thirty-Nine Articles of the Church of England, the Second Vatican Council, and various ecumenical gatherings. The final part of this section contains quotations from the Church Fathers, medieval writers, the Reformers, and on up to modern theologians. These are the voices of great Christian souls who still speak to us and are read without controversy.

Both the large new German catechism and the New Testament end with the prayer, "Come, Lord Jesus!" All forms of Christian piety, whatever shape they take in different times and places, come from this prayer. All Christians want to be with Jesus Christ, follow him, carry his burden in the midst of life, at its beginning and end, with him and never without him. We cannot see or experience God, humanity, the ups and downs of life, or the universe itself without him. Therefore we pray,

Come, Lord Jesus!
Come into our thoughts and our hearts!
Come into our houses and our families!
Come to us when we work and when we rest!
Come in our joy and in our sorrow!
Come to those who do not know or understand you!
Come to all who live in terror and despair!
Come into our congregations and churches!
Come to the weak and to the strong!
Come in our time!
Come to us in eternity!
Come, Lord Jesus!

And the response to this prayer is his words, "I will not leave you desolate; I will come to you" (John 14:18).

EDWIN ROBERTSON

1

WHERE WE STAND

**We Question,
We Seek,
We Believe:**

Human Beings

1. A Human Being Is an Open Question

Where do we stand?

"Give me just one firm place to stand, and I will move the world." These were the proud words of the ancient Greek scientist Archimedes. We still have not found that one firm place. We are in motion. We have no security; we seek it. Everything swims around us. So often we become disappointed; so often we lose what we already have. And no one will guarantee us anything. From all sides we are told to take a stand and join a party. But all we see is that the peace of the world, of nations, and of families suffers because people will not yield to other points of view. Where do we stand? Can we stand at all?

Are we driven?

Many people today feel driven. They feel powerless in their world. "We can't change anything," they say. "Things have a will of their own, and the powers-that-be do whatever they want to us." It is useless to resist. Every morning I make a new effort, reach for my tools, and accept my drudgery once again. But what is the use? Happiness, if it comes at all, is short-lived. I get older every year and still haven't found it. It's like swimming in a raging river: I want to reach the safety of a raft, which moves away from me as I swim toward it. But it moves faster than I do. Happiness is always faster than I am, and the best I can do is thrash the water behind it.

Who drives us?

Our concerns about where we stand raise questions about where we came from, who we are, and where we're going. There is great uncertainty today. Anyone who is awake can see that. And even if we feel secure within our four walls, with people we trust because they understand us, all we have to do is open our windows. One glance at the nations of the world and into books on the future tells us that the ground we live on is reeling. And yet it is not true that we have nothing to help us. We have not arrived at this point with empty pockets. Our past has a claim on us; it drives us toward the future. We cannot be completely stifled by the things we use to make our everyday lives tolerable. We humans are a rare kind, unique on the face of the earth: we must ask questions. We cannot rest until we have found that "one firm place" we now lack. If we are driven, it is something in ourselves which drives us. What is it? Who is it?

What questions do we ask?

We cannot escape from them. Whether thrust into bitter misfortune, the height of luxury, or the hell of human illness, whether unjustly imprisoned or in a state of blissful well-being, whether beaten down or pampered by life, we always have clear moments when we wake up and ask questions. What is the meaning of life? What is it all about? And the longer we ask, the more our questions become sharpened into this one question: *Who in fact are we?* Who are we human beings, that we must ask? Who are we that all this should happen to us? Who are we that we are driven and yet don't want to be? Who are we that we must have a firm place to stand?

Is there one answer?

It would be wonderful if there were one formula which gave one simple answer to our questions, one key which opened the door to us once and for all, revealing life's secrets. From earliest times people have tried many keys, but the rooms they open always lead to more closed doors. We human beings cannot be reduced to a formula. We are limitless. Once we have been found, we must be pursued further. Our greatness and destiny comes from the fact that we do not end. As Pascal said, we are "made for eternity." This book offers a key. But do not imagine that all of life's problems will be solved if you simply turn it three times in the lock. It will be of use to you if the door it opens leads into a large hall, not a small room. After you have heard the answers in this book you will have to ask further. You will only see ever-greater questions. But you will have a place from which you can go out and to which you can return.

Who am I? Who calls me?

There are times when we suddenly break away from our familiar surroundings and search for something. That is our nature, because we are persons. We question all that surrounds us—even ourselves. We are curious. We are curious above all about where we actually came from, who we really are, and where in fact we are going. In asking, we take a risk. A word may startle us—or a glance from a friend, the cry of a bird at night, the morning alarm clock, or news that hundreds of people have died in a crash. We may sense an answer to our questions in the movement of a leaf, or in a sentence someone wrote down 3000 years ago. And however much we shut ourselves in, our hearts will burst out, because we are persons—open questions, made for eternity. And the reverse is true as well: the less we question, the less we are persons.

Where we have come

As children we asked mostly about the reasons for things and their origin. Why is a field green and not red? Why can birds fly when cats can't? As we grow up we ask more about meaning and the future. What will tomorrow bring? What should I do with my life? Who am I? Where should I go? But we do not get finished answers now any more than when we were children. We must learn as we question and as we let ourselves be questioned. It will not be made easy for us. We are not finished beings. We have not inherited our standpoints in the world in the same way as our faces and limbs. We must seek them, capture them, defend them, lose them, and win them again. We question in order to question some more. That is the unending human task. As we grow more mature we discover that not only the world but we ourselves are full of mysteries, both good and evil. We become open questions to ourselves. That is why it is so difficult to stand on our own two feet.

2. A Human Being Is an Open Ear

Is questioning and seeking enough?

Anyone who asks questions but doesn't listen is a fool. We are rational beings; we should listen and learn from the questions we ask and the answers we are given. It is true that the less we *question*, the less we are persons, but it is also true that our personhood is diminished when we do not *listen*. Isn't it through hearing things that we break out of our familiar surroundings and ask questions? Something or someone startles us and ends our isolation. That a human being can be called an incessant questioner, and in fact an open question, is only half the truth. The other half is that we must go beyond our doubts and questions, turning more and more toward the answers that can be heard.

Does the best lie in ourselves?

We are not blank pages. There are answers that we bring with us. Within each of us is a voice that knows sense and nonsense, and knows that nonsense cannot be right. Our hearts instinctively know the correct solutions to many things. The human heart cannot be shaken in its conviction that there is right and wrong. It is not always certain where the dividing line is, but that there *is* a line is indisputable. All attempts by people and nations to deny this, from earliest times to the present, have been shattered. The consequences of evil always overtake us.

Can science help?

We can go wrong if we listen only to ourselves. There are so many voices within us, and decisions without other points of reference can be costly. Today we naturally accept the help that science gives, appreciating its history of incredible efforts of the human spirit. Science has changed our lives, illuminated the past, and made the present more comfortable. It thinks of tomorrow and the day after tomorrow, calculating rockets' paths to the stars. It constantly offers new answers to our questions. The human race has worked together in this. We accept this work; we listen day by day to its voice and its endless information; we will learn from it wherever it leads. We see that in science the dignity of the human spirit can come to the fore, compelling us to *think*—to measure step-by-step one phenomenon after another—and at the same time not to lose sight of hypotheses, those auguries of things to come.

Does art give an answer?

In great works of art we find the reality of our lives, the burden of our questions; the color of our dreams, the visions of our joy, the games of our youth, and our agonies and hopes. The answers art gives cannot be encompassed by words. Art takes us further than anything we can experience in daily life. By means of it we are moved at a level far deeper than feeling or thinking. Here is a voice which discovers us at our roots and seeks to illuminate the meaning of life. Great works of art are a challenge. At the sight of one ancient masterpiece Rainer Maria Rilke said, "You must change your life."

Can science or art set us free?

In response to many of our questions (indeed, to the most important ones), science and art are silent. They do not tell us what to do. I am informed about the world by science, and am astounded by the beauty of things through art—but neither has anything to say to my troubled conscience. They express truths, but not the whole truth. Science can study and measure me, but it cannot tell me who I am. Art can make me serene or shatter me, but when I have been unjustly imprisoned it seems like a mockery. Science turns the world—and me—into an object. Its ambition is to be as objective as possible. Through art I can express myself; it wants to be as subjective as possible. But there is a third voice that I long for, one that will call to me as a person. Neither science nor art can rescue me from my loneliness. The laws of science survey my house, and the parables of art illuminate my existence; but when a flood hits or my father dies, they are no comfort.

What about the world's religions?

Questioning persons do not seek answers that will quiet them, but that will set them free. Answers that simply say yes or no, this is right and that is wrong, may be informative, but are not liberating. To be human is to seek answers which encompass us, that totally involve and encounter us. Throughout the continuing human search for answers there have been many offers. Those made by religions are bound up with demands. Every religion has its own. Some demand keeping laws, others require following a long ascetic path toward enlightenment. This is not to demean religions, but only to show where they lead. In the West today, religions lie side by side in a kind of marketplace. New religions are being added to the old, like Marxism, whose distinctive teachings offer salvation no longer to individuals or to a specific nation, but to society as a whole. And the number of sects grows day by day, with many finding their answers there.

Where we have come

We must learn not only to question, but also to listen. We will be able to perceive what is reasonable and good; we can hear within ourselves a voice that knows both good and evil. We cannot ignore this voice. As human beings we are taught by science and enthralled by art. But there remain questions which they cannot answer. These questions are the most important ones: Who am I? Why am I the way I am? Why must I die? What is the meaning of suffering? We have many questions about existence itself, and about our own nature—which is both our glory and our poverty. The religions of the world have sought answers and offered solutions without end. Today these lie spread out before us. But can I find *my* answer?

3. Our Questions

Why are the basic questions always the same?

Everywhere people seek answers to the same questions. Throughout history the question of suffering has been raised. We are told just to accept it. Even as children we always asked, "Whose fault is that?" Today we ask how we can remain innocent. Why must we become guilty? Who is responsible for suffering in the world? And whoever talks about happiness asks the same question in different words. After all, isn't happiness the absence of suffering and guilt? If both were not hopelessly intertwined throughout our lives, their giant shadows would not stretch over us year after year. Without them we would be truly happy, whatever life brings, because what we really want is to be at peace with ourselves. But we must continue to ask questions because we are *not* at peace with ourselves. We hear ready-made explanations from all sides, but who knows the answer?

What does it all mean?

From early morning until late at night people talk at us. It is
impossible to remember it all. What should we pay attention to?
There is so much talking, and yet so little is really said. Most
everything seems interesting. I want to listen, but what is important
to me? Wouldn't one statement be better than many? Voices from
all sides make me unsure. There are some things I would really like
to know, like answers to a few questions: Why am I here? What
does my life mean? I don't always ask such big questions. Perhaps
at the end of a year, or at the beginning of a new one, or when I
have a birthday and think about myself. On an ordinary day the
important questions seem simpler: What has this day really brought?
Who needs my work? What does my labor mean? But it is in these
little questions that the big ones are hidden. I want to know the
meaning of my life. Like any human being, I cannot live and remain
healthy in body and spirit unless I know the point to it all. If anyone
could tell me that, I would pay attention.

Freedom? What's that?

Our strength holds out for eight hours. And in between we must
rest. Our life lasts 50, 60, or 70 years; with luck maybe a little longer.
But we want to live forever. We start many things as though they
will never end. We build houses to last a hundred years, we enter
professions and sketch plans as though we will have many decades
to labor on them. We prepare ourselves to last, because we are
hungry for continuity. When the morning is beautiful, when the year
has just begun, or when we travel out into the country, all of time
and space seem to be ours. When we have had a good night's rest
and begin the day, no task seems too great, no distance too far. But
all too often when we return we realize our limitations. We want to
do so much, but we bring so little to completion. We are prisoners
of our very narrow possibilities. In every little sigh a greater longing
is hidden: Oh, if I could only be free! As human beings we cannot
live and remain healthy in body and spirit unless we are promised
freedom. We suffer under our limitations, both outer and inner. A
voice calls us to freedom. Our best efforts come from freedom and
belong to freedom.

What should I do?

So many people tell us what to do. We are supposed to live by a mass of regulations, often under threat of punishment. I don't always see the point of them, but I obey. They have force behind them. They mostly concern practical questions of life together and various professions. I hear and obey because it is necessary and useful to me. But in the big questions, which can unexpectedly change my whole life, I get either too little or too *much* advice. What should I do? Suddenly the freedom to choose becomes a burden. There must be a standard I can use. What is good for me and for others in this situation? How can I balance our different interests in such a way that no injustice is done? The old recommendation to "do what's right and fear no one" is hardly enough in this difficult situation. Aren't both sides right to a degree? Haven't I already wrestled in the night with this question? So many people today are over-conscientious. I'm always under pressure. Too much is expected of me. I can't handle it. I don't know what to do. Like any human being, I can't live and remain healthy in body and spirit unles I am given courage in what I do.

Are we really satisfied?

Meaning, freedom, and *action* give birth to our three great questions: What power surrounds our lives? Who will set us free from our prison, our limitations, and the bonds we feel every day? Who will tell us what we should do? Some people are easily satisfied; others question and seek further. Some may say that a little happiness on a vacation, the freedom of going out Saturday nights, and obeying the law is enough. But some are not satisfied with that. There is something in them that needs bigger answers. And then there is the failure that enters into each person's life. Suddenly the autumn air blows cold. Perhaps my child or my partner for life, on whom I had set my whole heart, leaves me. What is left? Doesn't life as a whole have any meaning? What is my real task? And what if, when I am in the fullness of my strength, no one wants anything from me? Is that freedom? Those who are unemployed know their thirst for freedom is too great to be satisfied that way. Don't I need to be freed from myself before I venture out into the world? Yes, but even then, where will I go? In my freedom I know the things that I don't want to do, and yet must do. *Meaning, freedom,* and *action*—these are the three forms of our longing. As endless, open questions, we humans ask: What is the meaning of life? Who will set us free? What should we do?

What will this book do?

Together with you this book will seek an answer to these questions. It is a book concerned with the Christian faith in our time. For Christians these questions take a particular form, and any answers that are given are based on a particular presupposition: *faith.* Therefore we must first make clear what faith means to Christians. We will do this in the rest of this chapter.

Whatever human questions are concerned with, Christians must take them further. To seek the meaning of one's own life, the meaning of the world, and the meaning of all existence is to ask about God. God is the *Creator* of all that exists. The following chapter discusses God as the Creator.

When Christians in our day see how the longing for freedom breaks out so violently, they ask about the frustrations, pressures, and burdens of slavery which cause this longing. Why do these pressures come upon us, and from where? Why can't we simply live as we please? The root of the trouble must lie in ourselves. God's greatest creation, the human race, is not only damaged but has *damaged itself.* We will discuss this in the third chapter.

But whoever in the weakness of their own bondage asks for and seeks after freedom is already on the road toward liberation. Rather than freedom, Christians have traditionally talked about *redemption.* Our fourth chapter asks about the form this redemption takes in the Savior of the world, Jesus of Nazareth.

In the fifth chapter we will show the way contemporary life can be assessed by the traditions of this Jesus and his church, and find out how those who are redeemed *live* in our time and in the light of their new freedom.

Finally, this book will set *hope* before our eyes in both its forms. One kind of hope can already be lived in the symbols of the Christian community. We are called into this community, the church. Its life proclaims to us our coming redemption. The other kind of hope is turned toward the end of the world in a final sense, which God has revealed through the prophets of the Bible and the Christian story.

Where we have come

There is unrest in us, driving us to ask about sorrow and pain, joy, feelings, and guilt. We question anew every day, for we are restless. But we cannot find peace, because we cannot live without answers. We trace our boundaries. We want to be free, to be more able, and to know more. We have to make decisions every day, and we don't know how. We are open questions to ourselves, and never stop questioning. But we do have ears to hear. In this book we will repeat afresh those answers Christians have learned over the centuries. They are ancient, and yet as we think on them anew every day they become as fresh as the morning dew. This book will speak of God, humanity, and our redemption. It will tell us where our freedom and hope lie and what we should do so that we can live—together with thankful and hopeful persons of faith—with all creation and with the generations of those God has redeemed.

4. Faith Which Questions and Understands

What are the presuppositions?

This book is written for mature people. A mature person will question and understand. This book speaks from the presupposition of faith. In dialog with mature people it will introduce the Christian faith as a response to our ultimate questions and search for final understanding. It will question, inform, and consolidate what understanding has been gained. This already shows that faith in the Christian sense is the opposite of what we mean by the word in common speech. When we say someone "just has faith," we usually mean they don't know. But if you have faith in the sense that Christians use the word, you know something about both ultimate questions and final understanding. Your seeking and understanding have been validated as faith.

How does knowledge by faith differ
from knowledge through science?

The understanding of science comes through our senses of sight, hearing, touch, taste, and smell, and through the work of our minds. It is related to the world through our senses and scientific instruments, and to our minds and spirits as they construct a conceptual model of the world. The knowledge of faith is related to the whole person and to the whole world. Science informs and observes; faith orients and gives direction. If I *believe* with all my heart and soul and mind, and also with all the spirit of my understanding, then I *know*. Faith is knowledge, but a different kind of knowledge than science. It is different in content, purpose, weight, and function.

Where is faith to be found?

Faith and science are locked together. Human beings have been compared to the ancient temple of the Jews. In front of the temple was the forecourt, open to the heavens. Here is where people see, feel, and comprehend all that can be experienced in the full light of day. Inside was the holy place, the sanctuary. Here we find understanding and the possibility of differentiating what is experienced outside (science). But the innermost part of the temple was the Holy of Holies. Here is where Christians dwell (in the spirit). This is the place where experiences, knowledge, understanding, and the power to differentiate are all locked together to give direction to existence in the world. Both the Holy of Holies in the temple and the holy of holies in persons (their spirits) are places left free for God.

Where can we stand?

Faith does not simply give an answer to ultimate questions. It is not only a map or pointer. It is the way itself. It is not only an orientation but a destination. We ask where we can stand. Faith answers, "Here." Faith offers not only a standpoint from which we can debate, but ground on which we can camp, a house in which we can be at peace. It not only gives certainty in life's troubled waters, but is itself trust and confidence—a means of remaining firm and enduring in the conviction that we shall not be lost. Faith challenges us to do the works of faith. We must commit ourselves to the way of faith if we are to experience it. It will cost our entire life. Faith is both an understanding and a life lived. It is therefore a path that is a goal and a goal that is a path. It is a path because we can only learn faith by believing, and it is a goal because the first act of faith already has its reward in understanding and preparation for yet greater questions.

Where does faith come from?

According to Christian teaching, faith has a still wider meaning. It is the trust we put in God and God's truth. But it is also the trust God puts in us. And it is this trust that first and ultimately makes it possible for us to trust. We who question, hunger, and are either poor or happy in spirit are called and accepted in faith. As we listen to its call, faith becomes a trust that we must fulfill. Faith is not a skill but a *gift*. In it a clear voice calls us to the fulfillment we have always longed for. So we do not so much learn or achieve faith, but are rather *called* to faith. The deeper we believe, the better we know that faith can never be our possession or property.

Where do we find faith?

Faith does not sit somewhere waiting to be "found." It is not discovered. It finds us. It must find us anew every day. Nevertheless we live it and know it. The world does not believe; it mistrusts. It has no peace. It is torn apart by divisions, differences, violence, and greed. It creates iron curtains because it is afraid, and lives by the law of fear. The world knows that peace is necessary for its survival, but it cannot accomplish it. I need only glance inside myself to feel the world's fear. But because I am accepted, I have protection against fear. I cannot be afraid anymore when faith has received me. I have been accepted, and given over into other hands. Therefore if I am afraid, I must let myself be found again. Faith is not my possession—it possesses me.

Where we have come

To have Christian faith does not mean to not know. To believe means to be sure in oneself. Yet faith offers a different kind of certainty than science. Faith does not want to study the world or human beings in minute detail, but as a whole. What faith knows is comprehended and grasped by believers with their whole hearts. They take possession of their spirits, the places God has prepared. Faith opens a way for us, giving us standards and a grip on our lives. It is solid ground on which we can stand. We can be converted to faith. Faith demands commitment, trust, and faithfulness. There is no deeper and therefore no surer knowledge than that of faith. We cannot acquire it as we do a table or a house. We must give ourselves for it. We cannot learn it; we must be called to it. Therefore faith brings more than all that can be acquired or learned. Faith frees us from *fear,* which fills us and all the world. Faith gives *peace* which unbelief does not.

5. The Origin of Faith: Revelation

Can we prove God's existence?

In the same way that faith as power for life is both a call and a gift, so faith as content is *revelation*. What does that mean? It means that God, in whom we believe, has personally communicated with us. When we speak of the faith of Christians, we presuppose that this has happened. Put another way, this means we do not believe because clever persons have "proved" the existence of God—in the way Euclid proved his theorems. God has always been inaccessible to proofs. God does not depend on them. God does not come near to us because we have logically deduced from the origin of things that he must have existed first; from the motion of the world that he must have been there at its beginning; from the development and order of nature that he must be the supernatural authority behind it all; or that from the very being of things he must be the source of all being. Even the voice of conscience, and the fact that there have never been peoples that have not acknowledged a god, does not amount to proof. That could simply be wishful thinking, a challenging image of our imagination, the longing of our soul.

Can we speak if God does not speak?

Because of God's very identity he is not in the world, but the world is in him. Therefore we can make no statement about God which he has not already spoken. If the curious ask, "Does God exist?" the answer is silence. My hand and this table exist, rhinoceros and sacred cows exist—all the objects which science studies and art celebrates exist, but God is not numbered among these. God is not in us so that we can know him, but we are in *him*. When we speak and question, seek and believe, it is God who has done this in us. We have nothing to communicate about God. Rather, God comes to us, revealing himself. That is the presupposition of the Christian faith.

When does God speak to us?

Out of either curiosity or criticism, we can ask if God really exists. We can ask further why God doesn't come forward and show himself. But if we ask in that way we will get no answers. Yet if we ask in a way that puts ourselves into our questions (Where can I stand? Who am I? What should I do?), we will learn about God. When we are in despair from suffering or guilt, when we ask about the meaning of it all and cry out for liberation from the entanglements of our lives and the vengeance of those who persecute us, then God is not far away. For God was already present in our questions. In those questions lie our longing for eternity which can never be stilled, not by anyone on earth: not by the closeness of a loved one, the promise of happiness, or by a dictator. Those questions are the voice of God in us, even when we do not know it and would never call them that. In this way God makes himself understood by us and in us. What does God say? Does God say something different to each person? We must understand God's voice, and we cannot do that on our own. Christian faith says that God has clearly spoken in order that we might understand what he says.

Who can speak reliably about God?

What we experience has been experienced by people from earliest times. We know of God simply through our own experience, but what we know is nothing precise—not much more than presentiments which we have allowed to come out. For there is much in our lives that leads us to the limits where we can see God, who is unlimited, underived, and unconditional. But what can we say about God? Christian faith teaches that we can know very little about God from ourselves, but that God has in fact said who he is. God has said this in what he has done and continues to do with those who believe in him. God has indicated what he is doing with the world, with its very foundation, origin, history, future, and end. God has allowed prophets, witnesses, disciples, and apostles to speak his word to people and nations. God has shown himself in the history of his people, in whom we can read his will. And finally God has revealed himself in Jesus of Nazareth, who suffered and died for us as the preeminent one who was, is, and will be forever. This self-revelation of God has been attested for us in the Bible, the Holy Scriptures of the Old and New Testaments. We can be sure that we will encounter the very word and will of God whenever we approach the Scriptures with an open mind and readiness to understand. The Bible speaks reliably of God; it is authentic; it speaks clearly with the force and power of its author.

What does God say in the Bible?

This book will constantly refer to the Bible. It will get its content from the Bible even when the relationship is not clearly stated. For Christian faith comes through the Bible and is constantly nourished by this unique book of God's revelation. Yet anyone who tries to tackle the Bible may well become confused. The Bible is not just one book, but contains 39 books in an "Old Testament" and 27 books in a "New Testament"; many of these books were written by not one, but several authors; these authors who witnessed to the will of God did not all live in the same time period, but were separated from one another by centuries; historical writings, stories, poems, prayers, theological exhortations—there are so many different forms, ways of thinking, and languages; in the Bible a whole world confronts us. We might well ask what holds it together and what the key to understanding it is. That key is *faith*. Faith has been nourished and assured by the Bible for many generations. Faith's center is the "gospel" (or "evangel," from the Greek *euangelion*), the good news of God's love and compassion for his people. Faith draws its red thread through all the biblical stories and witnesses, and beats in them as the pulse of their proclamation, speaking the first and last word of God's message to us.

What does God say today?

This book does not repeat and explain the Bible. It presupposes interpretation. Its task, then, is in the name of the church to set down the Christian gospel in plain words so that it can be appropriated and retained. In doing this it will relate the gospel to the Bible as the church does that today. The Bible is always the same. Its oldest parts are nearly 3000 years old, and its most recent parts are 1800 years old. It is the most widely distributed, translated, and read book in the world. The text of the Bible is also the best preserved of any piece of ancient literature. It is this ancient text which today waits to come alive in us. And today we cry out for answers to its old but familiar questions about the origin and goal of the world, and about our human survival and uncertainty. What does the "evangelical" faith, taught by the message of the Bible, have to say to us today, so that we might also believe, love, and hope?

Where we have come

Christian faith is directed toward God. It does not express an idea *about* God, but comes from God's self-communication and self-revelation. God comes to us and opens our mouths so that we can speak of him and bear witness to him. God is present already in our questions, and gives answers through revelation. So we must look for God's revelation in the Bible, in the books of the Old and New Testaments. At the same time faith will open up these books for us. The key is the good news of God's love for us and for all creatures. When this love encounters us we become freed from the many terrible traits people have given to their gods. We see God's love and compassion, trust and help—even in those places where God appears to be hidden behind threatening "masks." Step by step faith discovers the true face of God in the Bible, as in life. God becomes real both through the Scriptures and in the realities of daily living. Faith sees God as the life of all lives, the heart of all things, the power of all powers, and the varied and inexhaustible Word of revelation to all people.

6. The Responses of Faith

Can we understand without listening?

In this book we want to present the will of God for our world today as seen by the Christian faith. Therefore we must examine again the questions we have already looked at, tracing their roots more carefully. But one thing must be made clear at the outset. There is another presupposition of both this book and the Christian faith: whenever we know that God has spoken and given answers to us and our questions, behind that knowledge lies an experience. We hear God's answers only as *we ourselves respond*. It is not that our words in any way qualify the word of God. But we hear God's word only if we let it be spoken to us. Our first response is listening.

Can we listen?

But can we listen? We know the mass of information and advice that presses in on us from every side. We are confused. We have to be selective about what to listen to. But we also know that we have an open ear for that which is within us. We cannot ignore what our conscience says without a sense of shame. This is a different kind of listening than listening to a weather forecast. And what is in us—that bit of eternity, that remarkable longing for breadth, depth, and fulfillment—speaks to us from great paintings and music, and from the world's religions. The kind of listening meant here is difficult. We cannot learn it like a language. Jesus pointed this out when he said over and over again, "He who has ears to hear, let him hear." All have ears, but not all have learned to use them and to hear in this way. And many other statements by Jesus make clear what has not always been recognized: in the end, whether we listen or not does not depend on our wills or practice. God himself must make us able to listen.

Do we want to listen?

When we begin to speak about the revelation to which the Christian faith bears witness, we confront a mystery. The opening prayer of Jewish services of worship to this very day is "Hear, O Israel . . . ," the call with which Moses introduced the message he brought from

God on Mount Sinai. But the Bible is full of reports indicating that Israel did not hear God. The mystery of *hardness of heart*, that we do not *want* to hear and therefore *cannot* hear, sadly accompanies the whole history of faith. God's word is offered, but not received; the gospel can be heard and God has given us ears to hear, but few listen. Where salvation is found, the absence of salvation is also to be found. Even as we make our way to the biblical message, asking how we should read the Bible, the threatening question raises its head: Will the Bible fail to tell us of a good God? We already begin to feel that the door is locked. We must hold fast to Paul's statement that ". . . faith comes from what is heard" (Rom. 10:17).

Is the Bible for everyone?

Some of the first witnesses of faith wrote down what they heard from God. We have these testimonies in the Bible. Our listening, then, consists first of reading and studying the Bible. It should not be the property only of certain studious people in the church, but rather a living book in the hands of every Christian. It is by reading this book that we prove ourselves to be listeners and attentive readers. It often seems to us that the Bible cannot be the voice of God, for so much at first glance is dim and disturbs us. But we must remember how old these texts are. We must translate them from their time into our own—not only their words, but also their language, thoughts, and images. So much has changed in the world since they were written. But those things the Bible is concerned with have not changed. We ourselves are still open questions, and we still have a mighty longing for redemption. The red thread of the Bible—its main theme, the good news—still touches our hearts today as much as ever. We may at first pass over obscure passages we meet. Later we can employ many aids, laying different translations and commentaries side by side, so that we can understand. Christians know they must press on to the very end, always growing in their understanding of the Bible. It is inexhaustible. We will continue to find new things as we faithfully listen to it.

Can we believe without praying?

Many people today think they can be Christians without going to church. But if they say they have given up praying, then they show by those very words that they no longer believe. Prayer answers God with praise, thanks, confession, and intercession. God is not restricted by the answers of our lips; he does not cease to speak. But if our heart rejects God, then God says no more to us. When we see a praying person whose life does not conform to his or her confession, we quickly recognize that hypocritical babbler Jesus warned about. But such examples show a misunderstanding of prayer. Martin Luther described how Christians should pray: "The way is that there be few words used, but much and profound intention and meaning. The fewer words, the better the prayer; the more words, the worse the prayer. . . . (Pray) with the worship of the heart. Then the appearance will be drawn into the truth, and the outward into inwardness. Yes, the interior truth breaks out and lights up the outward appearance. But it is not possible that the one who prays with many words can pray profoundly and in the spirit. For the soul, if it is to be true to what it says, and think upon the words and their meaning, must let the words go and hang onto the meaning . . . (*Commentary on the Lord's Prayer for Plain People*, 1519). It is an old Christian exercise to study the Bible in close association with prayer. Only if we learn from our faith will we pray aright, not simply expressing our wishes, but seeking God's will. Prayer is the answer to God's word; the "amen" at its end is the beginning of new perception. *Amen* means "Yes, it is true!"

Can we believe without loving?

If we seriously seek God's will as our faith finds it in the Bible, then we will desire to be changed. Those who believe do not want to remain as they are. Hearing, learning, and understanding are all works of the intellect, but faith is a work of the heart and the will. Certainly human nature is such that actions follow insights; but it is the mystery of faith to *understand once one has acted.* "But he who does what is true comes to the light" (John 3:21). We do not listen in order to remain who we are. Faith comes from hearing, but becomes real in love. Only then do we understand ourselves in our ultimate depths. Just as we first truly understand a person only when we love them, so our ears remain closed to the message of faith if we simply hear its words but deny its love in our lives. We must go beyond what we have heard. God wants to come not only to us, but to all people. The more love we exercise in our words and deeds, the better we understand God's love.

Where we have come

Faith brings three responses. The first is *listening*. But the listening of faith is more than receiving information. Of course we must also be informed about God's revelation, and theology must continue to test whether the information we receive from the Bible has been properly understood. We should understand what we read. But we truly listen in faith only when we receive, perceive, and acknowledge—when we submit to what is heard. Faith involves this kind of listening in our hearts. The Bible constantly tells of the enigma of hardness of heart among those who hear. Faithful listening will be rewarded by better listening. For it is not true that we know and experience once and for all. The more we listen in faith, the more we will hear. The more we persevere in believing, the stronger our faith grows. If we lose our faith, God will find us again. The second response of faith is *praying*. In prayer we affirm God, unite ourselves with him, put ourselves under the protection of his power, and bind ourselves to all who pray with us. The third response of faith is our *actions*. We cannot believe without loving. These three responses brought by faith, which are really only one, are then obedient listening, praying in community, and loving here and now.

Summary

I experience

I experience myself as a *stranger*. I feel alienated from myself. What seems most important lies beyond my grasp. I often feel rejected, as though this world of technical progress and cold competition is not the world I was born in. I can't resign myself to a merely functional existence. I experience myself as more than just what is on the surface.

I experience myself as a *disturbance* of my life. Like a wolf in its cage, I am driven to and fro by my wishes, desires, and dreams. I want to do so much at the same time, and I have no idea who is driving me. I am not only ravenous for food like a beast, but for good and for evil, for both the great and terrible moments of life— I am hungry for everything that I *have not* and *am not,* that I might become more than I am. And in all of this I sense my longing for continuity and permanence.

I would like to be strong, but I experience my *weakness.* I cannot be completely satisfied with anything. I am bored, anxious, and drunk with desire. I covet appearance, power, love, honor, happiness, and fulfillment. I see my days running out. I suffer under much that is meaningless, and under powerful people, most of them nameless and faceless. And most of all I suffer under the past, which I must leave behind me and yet can never quite get rid of.

I question

I ask about the reason for this *unrest.* Day by day it tosses new questions out from inside me. Not only my words, which are thrown out into the wind, but also much that I do or don't do becomes a cry for help, an appeal. All that I experience and encounter becomes a question. And I see that for everyone else it is the same. That is what it's like to be human. We are human to the extent that we ask questions.

I ask about the reason for *suffering,* for *ecstasy,* and for *guilt.* What does it all mean? I long for freedom from carrying the burden of decisions for my life. And all my questions come down to myself: Who am I? I question within at the same time that I ask about the world around me. Fear of the old and hunger for something new are only two different sides to my search for unity within myself.

When I reach out from myself, I seek others. Each day I ask myself why this *tension* must exist: Why do I long for unity when it escapes me? Why can't I live without community when I can't achieve it? As I ask who I am, I also ask who others are. Do we become ourselves only when we are with each other?

I believe

I believe I am called to something eternal, just as I am called to unity. I believe that the meaning I do not yet see will be revealed to me, and that suffering in the world will find comfort and redemption. I believe there is an order to replace my disorder, a fulfillment of my legitimate longings, an answer to my questions, and direction and guidance on my way. I believe there is a place where I can stand.

I believe that faith cannot come from myself, but is sent to me by God. It must be renewed daily through trust, obedience, and living interaction with God. My faith does not come from a general knowledge of God, but is based on what God has revealed to me. This is set forth in the Holy Scriptures of the Bible, which bear witness to God's saving acts on behalf of his people—those he loves and who love him. In the Bible we have God's first and last Word, and by our living appropriation of this book we have God's word for our daily life.

I believe I am called to respond to God's revelation. I believe I should examine all my seeking and questioning in the light of this message, while I let the word of God speak to me. Yet I am not called to hear with blind acceptance, but to freely test and decide. God does not wish to overpower me in my weakness and ignorance, but to meet me at the center of my being. My first response is *hearing* God; my second is *praying* to God; my third is *acting* out of obedience to God. These three together are the basis of informed trust and proven faithfulness. These three together form my response of faith.

2

OUR ORIGINS

God Comes to Us:

Creation

1. The Living God

Who is God?

God is not a concept, formula, plan, or object. We cannot see, hear, or describe God. There are no facts to prove God. God does not have the same kind of reality as a person standing at my side. God is neither nature nor our human inwardness. God is his own reality, withheld from us. We cannot grasp that reality. We say this not simply because we know it, but because God has said it: "I am who I am" (Exod. 3:14).

We cannot see God, yet God shows himself. We cannot hear God, yet God speaks. We cannot find the right words, and our arguments are weak; yet so long as there have been people on the earth, God has been near to them as the source of all wisdom in their lives. This is still true today, and will remain true forever. God impresses himself on us more than everything we experience through our eyes and ears. God is hidden, and yet lies open to the day like broad land beneath a cloudless sky. Hour by hour we encounter God's open arms, and day by day God holds us firmly by the hand. Our lives are often dark, but as we look back we see that our path was also God's path, even though we may not have realized it. God has now revealed this to us, for he has emerged from the ambiguity in which ancient peoples knew him in order to be a word for our ears, light for our eyes, a measure for our consciences, and hope for our despair.

Can we escape from God?

We cannot grasp God's reality. But God grasps us: he works in us, on us, with us, and even against us (though even then *for* us). Among many other attempts to describe God, the Bible uses the image of a *father*. Of course we do not live together with God as in a human family, but even so, people have experienced God dealing with them as a father deals with his children. A good father loves without end and will not forget to warn and punish his children for the sake of their future; in fact in his anger he will often have to become a puzzle to them. He gives his children freedom in order that they may grow up and achieve selfhood. He allows them to run away, but he receives them in his arms again when they return. He wants them to grow up, and they want to become more like him.

In this way God reveals himself to us. We do not see him, but we experience his work. We can turn away from God, but he still looks into our eyes. We can run away from God like the prophet Jonah— even to the end of the world—but God has already gone before us to meet us. We can give up in disappointment over others and despair over the meaning of our lives; yet God rescues us. This book is about the many such ways God continues to work.

Who can name God?

The name "Father" is one of the many names the Bible uses for God. Jesus gave this to us as the principal name of God. He taught us to pray, "Our Father in heaven. . . ." The Lord's Prayer stands for God's never-ending goodness. Other names tell of other characteristics of God's actions. The names "Lord of Lords," "King," and "Judge" speak of God's unlimited power. "Stronghold," "Mighty Rock," "Shield," and "Safeguard" tell how people have experienced this power as protection. And when those who pray to God call him "My Light," "My Salvation," or "My Deliverer," they confess that God has led them and given them new life. A special favorite of Old Testament writers (who always regarded the nomadic period as the idyllic period of their people's past) was "Shepherd." With this name Jesus designated his own role as one who fulfilled the will of God for all people: "I am the good shepherd" (John 10:11). For it was the old biblical hope that God himself would lead his people through the dark valley of their existence, protecting them from the wickedness of evil persons and keeping them secure forever in the safety and fullness of life with him. "He will feed his flock like a shepherd," declared the prophet Isaiah (40:11).

What is a name?

We must remember what a name is and what it is intended to do. Names are very important to us; we give them not only to our children but also to pets and inanimate objects. We give names for several reasons. One is to see the qualities of a name in the person or thing named. Another reason is to gain authority, ownership, and power over what we have named. This is what Adam ("man") was doing in the ancient biblical story about the first human being. God had given the earth into Adam's care, and God watched as Adam took responsibility for it by giving each creature and thing its name (Gen. 2:19).

Yet of all the reasons why we give names, the most important is that by doing so we can address, implore, and call upon those we name. We call our children by name, and they hear even when they don't want to. If I do not know the name of a person I love, then I cannot personally approach them. A person without a name is in a very real sense not there. But God wants to be both present and present *for us*. God wants to be the living one, our life and life-giver. Since we need to call on him, he bears a name for us to use. We are permitted to name the distant God so that he can become very near to our lives, nearer even than our closest friends.

Does God accept our names?

There is no human name, word, image, or concept of the world that can comprehend God. No one can make God clear but God himself. No human thought can equal his glory and power, the depth of his love, his unfathomable ways, and the breadth of his eternity. The same God who wants to have a name among us so that we may call on him is ultimately beyond all human names. When Moses heard God speak from a burning bush, calling him to lead the people of Israel out of their Egyptian slavery, he asked God to reveal his name. God replied, "I am who I am" (Exod. 3:14). In Hebrew this is *Yahweh*. God always remains the same, for even the name he gave to Moses means one who is eternal. No name can capture God. It is true that we can only speak of God by using names and images, but his reality does not consist in these. They are only reflections of our encounters with God and his dealings with us. To this day pious Jews show their reverence for the mystery of God's holy name by never pronouncing the name *Yahweh*.

Where is God in space and time?

God wants us to enter into a relationship with him. The first thing we can do is recognize that God is already the ground of our existence and the source of our very life. God's first command is that we acknowledge this and have no other gods. The Bible repeats this command continually. The only people who really believe in God are those who make his uniqueness the basis of their understanding of the world and the plumbline of their lives.

The Bible tells us the dramatic story of a people who came face to face with nations who did not share such a faith in God. It tells of their experiences of faith, doubt, temptation, failure, and turning away from the one God of heaven and earth. The Bible bears witness that those who trust themselves to the one God—not looking back, but recognizing him as the source and goal of their lives—will experience God in the stillness of the present moment. They will receive guidance which today is gentle, but tomorrow will be full of power. They will experience God's never-ending watchfulness and care.

There can be no dwelling place for this God:

If I take the wings of the morning
    and dwell in the uttermost parts of the sea,
even there thy hand shall lead me,
    and thy right hand shall hold me.
If I say, "Let only darkness cover me,
    and the light about me be night,"
even the darkness is not dark to thee,
    the night is bright as the day;
    for darkness is as light with thee (Ps. 139:9-12).

This God cannot be contained by time, for space and time are his creation:

For a thousand years in thy sight
    are but as yesterday when it is past,
    or as a watch in the night (Ps. 90:4).

Thy eyes beheld my unformed substance;
    in thy book were written, every one of them,
the days that were formed for me,
    when as yet there was none of them (Ps. 139:16).

The living God who is our contemporary speaks through the witnesses, reports, stories, prayers, songs, and confessions which together make up the books of the Bible. This has been the experience of faithful people from generation to generation. It is in connection with these witnesses that persons of faith experience the life of God: his continuous presence and invincible power. It is a common experience to become ever closer to God even as he appears to be moving farther and farther away. The better we know ourselves, the greater

God becomes. He increases as we decrease. But there is also a growth in our awareness that God is love and faithfulness. Even in separation from us God remains our contemporary, giving life and daily creating anew. This pursuing love takes ultimate form in Jesus, who is the eternal mediator between God and human beings. He came and continues to come to those who are lost and separated from God, and it is through the cross on which he was crucified that the gulf between God and human beings is overcome.

Where we have come

We are commanded not to make an image of God (Exod. 20:4; Deut. 5:8). And we can't. Christian faith begins with the reality of God. If we think of that which shatters us, which suddenly takes possession of our whole beings, or which constrains us from within to hold to our life's purpose, then we have experienced God. More than all the theories about God, it is *dealing with God* that brings us close to him. "The Lord is near to all who call upon him" (Ps. 145:18). The believers we meet in the Bible have given God many names, but he is greater than any name. If we call God "Father," as Jesus did, then we have a name we can hold onto. In the Bible God is often called "the living God." That means God is always contemporary, the one who is at work creating and renewing. Christians are committed to this contemporary God. We can and should call on him. But in God's answers to us he remains himself—we cannot constrain him. We find that among those who speak to us in the Bible God is experienced as an inescapable presence and at the same time one who is beyond reach, as concrete reality and at the same time the power our finitude cannot contain. For God is the Lord of our finite world.

2. Other Gods

Do we need religion?

The Bible repeatedly calls the God who cannot be described but can only reveal himself the *one God*. Beginning with the first biblical books we find the commandment "I am the Lord your God. . . . You shall have no other gods before me" (Exod. 20:2-3). Only by the faith which God gives and by trust in him will we be saved and guided. Today, as then, this statement has a polemical edge to it. The tiny nation of Israel was constantly tempted to build altars to the seemingly more powerful gods of neighboring near-eastern nations. Today we also are faced with a colorful market of religious and ideological goods. What links us with other religions, and what divides us from them?

Many people today have withdrawn from organized religion because of its authoritarianism and inflexible dogmas. Yet religious longings are growing and finding new forms of expression. "Holy men" and gurus make their appeal and attract disciples. The gods that were pronounced dead have returned in the form of new religions, confessions, and ideologies.

Most of us have been fascinated by one or another of these gods. Many of them sound less demanding than the God of the Bible. At the time the Old and New Testaments were written the great temptation was polytheism. It is attractive to see each of our needs satisfied by a different power: to give every anxiety another name and to entrust each hope—be it for the body, soul, children, or the state—to a different lord of heaven. That could ease our overly complicated lives. There were almost 3000 gods and goddesses in the world of the late Roman Empire. Of course even at that time educated people hoped and believed that all these gods were only different expressions of one God. Ancient mythology saw in God the overriding principle and general concept of the world, united with the power of fate. This could be much the same assumption that our own contemporaries make.

Do eastern religions entice us?

Today we live in an open world. Anything is accessible if we are willing to be informed. The Christian faith appears old-fashioned and complicated. Hasn't it served its purpose? Aren't other religions much more attractive? Islam seems as simple as a mosque. One single thought is dominant: we must submit ourselves to Allah, the one God, and follow the precepts given by his prophet Muhammad. We are to pray, give alms, fast, and make a pilgrimage to Mecca. If we do good, our destiny is assured in this world and the next.

And the good is this one thing: to submit to Allah and accept his will. That is what it means to be a Muslim ("one who submits"). The apparent simplicity of Islam has great appeal for many of us who live in a complicated world that demands too many decisions.

Hinduism is also attractive, and comes in innumerable forms. It offers eternal bliss when our souls become blended with the soul of the world. We could take upon ourselves the difficult exercises which would lead us toward that blissful goal: asceticism and yoga—the training of our souls through the discipline of our bodies. The inner world to which our souls would be united has no name, and the many gods and spirits, half-gods and gradations between the human and the divine are only an expression of the ultimate oneness of all things. Hinduism is attractive, for we suffer from the unrest of our own lives and of a society which is concerned most about the protection of property and the keeping of little laws. Meditation offers a path into a realm of pure spirit.

There is also Buddhism, which was originally a reform movement within Hinduism. By following its teachings we could learn to know the radical insufficiency of this changing world, and how to look on our own personal self-awareness as an illusion. It is this illusion which Buddhism calls us to overcome through severe exercises, removing step-by-step the deception of our senses, and finally escaping the suffering of existence.

Today these world religions (not to mention many others) are in dialog with Christian faith. They present for discussion their respective understandings of reality, the meaning of life, and the significance of good and evil. We need to know that our response to them is not of little importance, for we are given no option. We should indeed recognize the sincere search for truth in eastern religions. But we must clearly see that the faith of Christians in God—who communicates himself to us, takes us seriously as irreplaceable persons, and remains the same through all eternity—rests on quite different foundations.

What divides us and what unites us?

Some people look only at what Christians and followers of other religions have in common; others look only at what divides them. Wisdom requires that we do both. We should note the common features, and yet not keep silent about differences, especially where these differences have to do with the means of our salvation. We are united with followers of other religions to the extent that together we know our lives are more than we can discern with our eyes—that the world has a dimension which our senses cannot comprehend. We are human, and in order to remain human we must hold this dimension open. Together with Islam, Hinduism, and Buddhism we feel deeply the human longing for the fulfillment of life, the redemption of the world, and a paradise which endures. Like them we look forward to the full development of the human race and liberation from the fetters which bind us.

But we Christians are not free to simply select an ideology. In faith our whole beings respond to the word of God that comes to us. We have come to faith neither through our own thinking and enlightenment (as with Buddha) nor through a vision (as with Muhammad), but by the word of God which Jesus of Nazareth proclaimed and in fact is. At this point of comparison, Christian faith does not qualify as a religion. It is not an attempt by people to find God, but the amazing, unexplainable experience of the Word of God in history. In the Christian faith we do not put God in question, but rather God has put *us* into question.

What about Judaism?

Among all the world religions, Judaism has a special place. Jews belong not only to a community of faith but to a community of destiny, a covenant community which God established in ancient times and honors to this day. The Jews were chosen by God. This means they are under the constraint of a special history, a special responsibility, and a special promise. There is no other religion with which Christian faith has so much in common as Judaism. Christians accept the Hebrew Bible as Holy Scripture. The assumptions about God are the same, as are the understandings of revelation and faith and many elements of tradition and practice. There is also a great and sad common history of Christians and Jews living together—often in hostility, though sometimes in friendship.

What has most divided Jews and Christians is the enmity of two siblings who are very similar to each other. Martin Buber has put it this way: "The Christian cannot understand the Jew, because he is stubborn and will not see what he has entered into. The Jew cannot understand the Christian because he is insolent and asserts his full redemption in an unredeemed world." Jews and Christians are divided in particular by the name which for Christians means salvation: Jesus Christ. Today Jews and Christians are learning to speak together about what divides them. In the light of their common faith, the fact that Jews reject faith in a particular Jew—Jesus—should constrain Christians to test, understand, and develop ever more clearly what this faith means.

Is God out of date?

Most of our neighbors are likely to ask, "Why do we need God at all? Don't we live much better when we throw God overboard? Aren't we self-sufficient? Is God anything more than a figment of our imagination?"

Today atheism has become the faith of many. They say religion can be explained psychologically, from what we now know about the human psyche. Freud believed religion to be nothing more than the assertion of our self-conscious against the threats of existence. Since we wish that a God would exist, we therefore invent one. We pray to a God we dreamed up ourselves. Yet the Bible itself rejects all gods that people invent for themselves.

We are informed that as a result of modern science the "God hypothesis" has been superfluous and unnecessary for 200 years. What we don't know today we will discover tomorrow. But among many leading scientists such brash statements are a thing of the past. All our knowledge is leading us only toward greater mystery. The more we understand, the more we come into contact with that we *don't* understand. The dream of the Enlightenment still haunts many minds, but it is an illusion. Even if our knowledge about the world were tremendously expanded, the riddle of existence would still not have disappeared. Where do we come from? Where are we going? What should we do? Who are we? What is the meaning of life? Why does the world exist? These are not questions that can be answered by science. They are on a different level.

There are politicians in both the East and West who either openly declare or imply through their actions that God is unnecessary, and even destructive to social progress. Whether they hold the "collec-

tive" or an ever-rising standard of living to be of ultimate importance, there is no place for God. They say that humanity cannot
progress as long as it has a master, and cannot truly serve its own
development until it sees itself as the highest form of existence. Yet
a single objective glance at the present social situation reveals that
people have made no progress at all toward freeing themselves.
Most of us are not inclined to believe that those who have put their
faith in Communism will soon acquire great appreciation for freedom and human values. Neither do we expect that those who put
their faith in capitalism will soon escape from their slavery to
"progress." God may have been rejected, but his place is not likely
to be filled soon.

Do we need God?

We would be poor Christians if we had only contempt for atheists,
for those who want nothing to do with God. Atheism can challenge
us to better understand our faith. There are Christian thinkers who
have used the insights and standards of the Enlightenment to evaluate the faith of past generations. They agree with much of the modern criticism of religion, acknowledging that any god *we need* is one
we can do without. A god who does only what we want is an idol,
a mirror of ourselves. Such a god exists only in our heads; it is an
image we have created. We do not need such idols. They destroy us,
warp us, and rob us of our freedom.

Nonetheless we do need *God,* the real God who is truly God. God
gives us freedom. We who are mortal cannot live without this
immortal one. We are made for eternity, and without God we are
like fish out of water. Here is where atheism—in any of its forms,
ancient or modern—is all wrong. It speaks falsely of God and of
human beings. Whoever attempts to destroy God succeeds only in
destroying humanity. For anyone who robs us of God pulls away
the ground on which we stand, the goal of the passion that sustains
us through life, the breath of life, the blood in our hearts, and the
voice which speaks to us in nights of sorrow and death. Without
God we are trapped in deep loneliness; our senses leave us and
things become hostile. It is God who gives life meaning and carries
us through the days and years. We are no longer ourselves without
God; we are not capable of saying, "I am who I am." We cannot

establish our own identity, but can only share in the identity of the
one who calls himself *Yahweh*.

Where we have come

We know many gods. Whatever we set our hearts on and cannot
do without *is* our god. But we Christians speak of one God, to whom
we ascribe all power and glory. We confess God as the ground of
all existence. We are to have no other gods. It is this God whom the
great religions of the world seek: Hinduism, in its search for mysti-
cal union with the world spirit; Buddhism, in its attempt to escape
from this unsatisfying, changing world; and Islam, in its intense
discipline and concentration on the unity of Allah. Together with
these religions we recognize the human longing for fulfillment. But
we are more closely bound to the Jewish faith—to the confession of
Yahweh, who reveals himself as the only God. Christians and Jews
are a minority in a world which worships progress and regards God
as a foolish dream. But when God does not speak we live in deathly
loneliness, without firm ground on which to stand. The deepest
things of life are sealed from us, and we remain locked into our own
observations, thoughts, and actions. When God is silent we do not
perceive that there is a bridge between the mystery of our existence
and the power which surmounts that mystery, confirming it today
and tomorrow.

3. God Speaks and Acts

How does God speak to us?

We have seen that Christian faith in God is not to be understood
as one religion among many religious options. A Christian's religious
experience is first of all rather the confession that "God has spoken
to me." It is second the conviction that "I can and should respond
to this word of God with my whole being." And we know that God
himself calls forth this answer in us. We can do nothing else, for
God constrains us from within to love and obey him. This is the
mystery and work of the word which God speaks. And this is just
what Christians mean by the word *faith*.

But how does God's word come to us? It comes neither as a voice from heaven nor as an emotion from within ourselves, but rather through the *gospel*. It is the good news, which we experience in the Bible and through the church's preaching from Scripture, which carries God's word and will to us. In the church and through the church—the community of believers in the fullness of time—the Bible is interpreted. The church lifts the word of God out from the Scriptures and proclaims Jesus Christ to be that very Word. It preaches him as the measure and center of the Bible. At the same time this Word of God is experienced by the community of believers as its hope and claim in living history. Therefore it is through those who have been empowered and blessed by God that this Word is mediated to us.

What does God say to us?

We must not equate the word of God with our words. Our words are mostly sound and fury; they are, as we say, "only words." But according to the biblical witness the word of God is the opposite: it is an event, history, action, and deed. When God commands, his will is done. And so for those who believe in God, history itself is his word to us. And the center of this word is Jesus Christ, who is himself named by Christian faith as the Word of God. God speaks to us personally in what Christ is and proclaims, in what he does, and in what is done to him.

Whoever brings love, compassion, trust, liberation, and redemption certainly cannot be wrong. Nonetheless it is important for us as Christians to bind all these gifts to one person: Jesus of Nazareth. Many good persons in other religions also know that love is required of us. As Christians we make it clear that Christ is the form of God's love, both its source and substance—its guarantee and the promise of its fulfillment. Many people tell us we must love. But in Christ we are *able* to love. This is the content of the word of God to us.

What does the Old Testament say?

The fact that God's word becomes history and living experience in us through personal faith can be seen in the history of past faith culminating in Jesus of Nazareth. The Old Testament recounts these events in many stories, prayers, songs, parables, legends, and chronicles. Believing Christians are participants in these events, which lead from the creation of the world to Christ's cross on Golgotha.

The Old Testament tells of God's acts in the history of the people of Israel, which bore the burden and grace of his choice. Israel was chosen to have a continuing encounter with God—the one who speaks his word into human hearts as the eternally just and gracious Creator, Lord, and Redeemer. At first Israel was hardly a nation: just a small cluster of nomadic families and tribes. It evolved into a nation only after fleeing from the anger of Egyptian overlords and wandering through the wilderness of Sinai. Israel occupied Palestine, though never driving out the original inhabitants. After many difficulties it created a kingdom under Saul, David, and Solomon. But almost immediately after Solomon's death that kingdom split apart into two powerless, rival states—playthings of the great powers of the ancient Near East. Eventually slavery and exile came, and Israel sacrificed its independence first to Persia, then to Greece, and finally to Rome.

But this history, which lasted almost a thousand years and produced the Old Testament, was experienced by the people as the coming of God. Israel could understand its history only in terms of God's will: as obedience and disobedience, deliverance and punishment, redemption and suffering, promise and anticipation of God's glorious future, and as a witness to and praise of God's never-ending power. God was the one who held back the waters of the sea so that Israel could pass over, and who then let the floods pour back again to engulf the armies of Pharaoh; who sent food and provided water in the barren wilderness; who led Israel through its wanderings and into the rich land of Canaan; who helped his people conquer so many enemies; and who raised up the man of his choice to be king. But God was also the one who punished the disobedient nation. In anger he took back his kings' lordship and his people's home. Israel's history was one in which fulfillment and longing remained in tension.

The faithful in Israel continually remembered with thanksgiving God's early saving acts. They were certain that God still loved his people and would continue to love them in the future, because he had proved his love in the past. Yet the fulfillment of this love had not yet come. Rest, peace, and freedom were already present with God, but had not yet been realized on earth. Yet on the evidence of

God's past goodness believers could go on to the very end, convinced that there would be redemption of the world, a return of God's people to him, and the revelation of God's righteousness. When that time came, the promised inheritance—the promised land—would become the home of God's people and his own dwelling place among them. This is the picture the Old Testament paints.

Can God be recognized in his law?

The promise of land, which was the object of Israel's restless longing and the sign of God's presence and peace, was the first bequest of the covenant God concluded with his people. The second bequest was the law. This was the statute of the covenant which continually accompanied the people. By the mouth of Moses God said to Israel, " 'See, I have set before you this day life and good, death and evil' " (Deut. 30:15).

The law of the covenant was carefully spelled out in the first five books of the Bible, which in Hebrew are called the *Torah,* or Law. These books describe in great detail what is good and what is evil. The content of this law is quite different from what we find in modern laws. The laws of nations today, with their rules and regulations, order our lives together so that the same justice can be enjoyed by all citizens. But in the law of the covenant God concluded with Israel what was offered above all was knowledge of *God's will.* This law went beyond the claims of states and citizens and taught how to discern God's nature and purposes. Therefore it was said of the godly person that "his delight is in the law of the Lord, and on his law he meditates day and night" (Ps. 1:2). This law, which was first proclaimed by Moses on Mount Sinai and later written down over the course of Israel's history, was for faithful persons God's first word.

Many of the details of this law were addressed specifically to the covenant community of Israel, and are not binding on Christians. But the basic outlines of the law's demands are the same as commandments taught by Jesus. For example, the commandment "You shall love your neighbor as yourself" is found in both the Old and New Testaments (Lev. 19:18 and Matt. 19:19). God's law both divides and unites people and nations. It creates divisions when it sets good and evil unequivocally before us. But the law also shows the compassion of God, who wants to lead us along the right path, and who never leaves us without guidance. God's law is an expression of his word. The Ten Commandments are a summary expression of God's law. By means of them God has openly declared his will in the midst of human history.

Does God speak through the prophets?

The third bequest of God's ancient covenant with Israel was the prophetic word. You may think of a prophet as one who foretells the future. A prophet may do that, but that is not what makes a prophet. The Bible calls anyone who bears witness to God's dealings with people a prophet. In this sense there is no living faith without prophets—those who are empowered by God's Spirit to tell of his will. It is not only in the twelve minor and four major prophetic books of the Old Testament that we read of prophets. The whole Bible is filled with the prophetic word: the warning, encouraging, directing, challenging, and reconciling voice of God.

For a long time prophecy was an office in Israel, just as it was in the early Christian church. Those who bore this office were gifted preachers who heard more clearly than others the will of God for particular moments in history, and who did not hesitate to speak what they heard. Old Testament prophets often stood under the direct command of God, so that they expressed themselves contrary to their own wills (as did Isaiah and Jeremiah). It was the prophet Nathan who had promised King David that his throne would continue and his son Solomon would build a temple for the Lord. But it was also Nathan who declared God's punishment because of David's acts of adultery and murder (2 Samuel 7 and 12). In the sixth century B.C. Jeremiah prophesied the fall of the state of Judah as God's judgment for the people's infidelity and disobedience. He even called for pacifism because the armies that threatened the nation were executing God's will.

The prophets of the Old Testament looked at issues of their day, but they also looked into the future when God's good will would be exercised in power. In times of hopelessness they made it quite clear that the day of God would come and deliverance would break through. Through his prophets God said he would establish a new covenant with his people, in place of the old one they had broken

(Jeremiah 31). God would give his people new spirits of free obedience to replace their slavish resistance, hearts of flesh instead of stone (Ezek. 36:26). The prophets spoke solemnly and with the goodness of God, saying to all that God is not only enthroned "above the clouds," but appeals to us every day and in every situation. In our sorrows and joys God calls us to knowledge, decision, and obedience.

Why is Christ God's Word for us?

The New Testament frequently calls Jesus a prophet to whom all the prophets of the old covenant have pointed. For Christians Jesus is the ultimate prophet of God, the only one in whose name and power future prophets and preachers can speak. He is the unfettered voice of God among us. God will not speak to us through some other spirit apart from that which is in Jesus. The old covenant has been fulfilled, and a new covenant has been established with us in Christ. That is the assumption of our faith.

If Jesus is to be called a prophet or a proclaimer, then we must think about what the Jews understood by the prophetic spirit which comes from God. Prophets speak under the command and authority of God. Their word receives and communicates the incredible creative power of God: the breath of renewal, the fire and storm which wipe out the old and awaken the new from the earth. And just as speaking and acting are a unity with God, so they are also in Christ. Thus it is in Jesus' appearance among us—in his life, suffering, death, and resurrection—that God enters into our midst. In Christ God both addresses us and acts on our behalf.

Where we have come

The living God is our contemporary. We do not say that because science has discovered it or philosophers have proved it. To be a Christian means to accept this good news because God himself has said it. According to the Bible the God whom the Jewish patriarchs Abraham, Isaac, and Jacob experienced is the life of our lives and our continuing companion. The prophets of Israel and ultimately Jesus of Nazareth testify to God as our Father, the one who loves us without end, whom we have to thank for our lives and futures.

God speaks to us by becoming involved in our lives, just as he did with our predecessors in the faith—the people of Israel and the Christian church in which Christ lives century after century. God speaks to us in Jesus Christ—the Word of God himself, in whom God makes his will known. God established a covenant with Israel which he has renewed in Christ. He promised his people a homeland that would fulfill all their longings. He gave them the law, by whose guidance they could find him. Israel remains the model for us. Here we can see how God acts on behalf of his people. The Christian church understands itself as the new Israel; in Jesus Christ God has at last spoken not only to this one people but ultimately to everyone, involving himself in the lives of all human beings until the end of the world.

4. God Created the World

Do we know the Creator?

Where do we come from? It was not out of curiosity or scientific interest that the biblical writers asked this question. Their starting point was rather God's involvement in the history of his people. In great saving acts God brought Israel through the sea and the wilderness; in fierce anger God pursued his people in their disobedience. The people of Israel experienced God's will through his holy law and the prophets he sent to comfort and warn them. God never left his people alone, but accompanied them at all times.

It was out of this experience that the biblical writers began to ask, "How did this all happen? How did the sun and moon, oceans and mountains, trees, animals, and races of peoples have their beginning?" They were not posing scientific questions, for they scarcely knew what science was. They asked out of faith. How did the God who had done such great things for his people make the world? Why is there a sea that keeps its bounds and does not sweep over the land with its fury? Why are there stars to light up the heavens, moving back and forth but never falling down? Why does spring return again and again? How do eagles get their flight, lions their strength, and gazelles their speed?

The writers of the Bible found answers to these questions in their faith, the same faith which we also share. As they experienced God in their lives, willing goodness and life for them, they realized that God wills *all* life. The same God who had worked wonders in their lives, who day by day had rescued them from sorrow and death, also created the world in freedom and in joy. He created all things simply out of the fullness and power of his own being. This faith is unforgettably expressed in the earliest chapters of the Bible, but is also testified to in many other biblical texts. For example, Psalm 104 sees the glorious works of the divine hand in bringing light from darkness, morning from night, firm land from the ocean, seed from the ground, a garden from the desert, and life from death. Faith never ceases to praise God for his amazing works, like the beauty and complexity of a single flower petal.

What does creation mean for us?

Nothing in the world, no person or thing, can stand by itself. Young people often think they can. Strong individuals sometimes believe they can build on their own. Artists may think their work is their own. But they are wrong. No person, power, or thing—not even the most brilliantly blazing star in the universe—comes from itself and rests in itself. Every created thing depends on God. This fact has a very important consequence for us. Since everything has been created by God, all things were therefore created *good*. We should pay no attention to those who degrade God's creation. For God himself is good, and can create only good things.

The Bible teaches that God created the world by his word. Other religions teach that the world was formed from a divine material, or that its temporal existence is part of the eternal being from which it arose. But creation by God's word means something different than this. When people speak together, they are joined by the words they exchange but remain distinct individuals. This is the dignity and pain of human relationships. It is the same with God's creation of the world. The Bible says that God spoke, "and it was so." This means God participated in the world, but nevertheless remained himself. Therefore a second important consequence of creation is that God remains God and the world remains the world. They are not mixed. Through his word which is itself action God has bridged the separation, but not abolished it. Otherwise it would be possible to raise part of creation or all of creation to the level of God—to make an idol out of it. But the biblical teaching of creation forbids that.

What is the deepest secret of creation?

When Christians speak of creation, they do not think of it as an event which has taken place once and for all, but as a *relationship*. Creation continues every day, new and growing in strength. Creation comes from God and is therefore good; it belongs to God and is therefore subject to his demands. Therefore creation cannot itself be God. What this means becomes clear when we apply it to ourselves. We are part of God's creation. Just as we experience the miracle of creation anew with the birth of every child, so we must become conscious of being recreated every morning. This miracle lies in our continuing relationship with the God who created us and all that exists. *All creation belongs together, because all creation comes from God.*

Is this why we are never at rest? Is it because we come from God that our spirits press forward, further than our eyes can see? Is it because God has created us as well as all living creatures that we get the irrepressible urge to know more about ourselves, to overstep the limits of this world and our own consciousness? Is it because God created us by his word that words strike so deeply into our own lives, that we ourselves use language, and that our lives answer to it? Haven't the demands of others, expressed in words, been in our ears since the day we first became aware of anything? Are we ourselves ultimately a word that God has spoken? Christian faith declares that there is someone who in fact embodies God's word—Jesus of Nazareth, the Christ. He is the Word who mediates between God and human beings—the Word by whom God created us and continues a daily relationship with us.

What does it mean that the world has been created in Christ?

In moments of serious consideration you may well ask, "What is the reason for all this? What is the reason for the world around me, which is so different and yet so closely related to me?" Christians answer these questions by saying, "Because God loves." They see this unending love in Christ. God's love is the reason for the world, the root of things, the motive and continuing secret of creation. Out of this love creation lives and we live. The love of God carries the name of *Christ*. The New Testament says, "He is the image of the invisible God, the first-born of all creation; for in him all things were created, in heaven and on earth, visible and invisible . . . all things were created through him and for him" (Col. 1:15-16). The Old Testament calls the first human being "Adam." But *Adam* is not a name. It simply means "man," just as *Eve* means "life." These are not names of historical individuals, but of figures in a story about the world's prehistory. Adam and Eve are the yet unwritten pages of humanity. In Christ the human race comes to fulfillment. Jesus of Nazareth—the man of God, the Son of God, the representative of God—is a human being as God originally intended human beings to be. Christ bears the word of God's will. Through Christ God communicates himself to us, and even this mediation is God's creation. The world has been created in Christ.

What isn't the Bible interested in?

The Bible is not interested in detailed scientific questions about the origin of the world. It does not tell us what to think about modern theories of evolution, leaving us the freedom to evaluate them on their own merits. In fact the Bible offers several different explanations of the world's beginnings without embarrassment. The first chapter of the book of Genesis takes water to be the basic substance of creation, while the second chapter takes it to be earth. The first chapter sees human beings as the aim of creation while the second sees them as the beginning. The second creation story in Genesis is five hundred years older than the first. The Old Testament also speaks of creation in many other places. It always does so with images and metaphors, which cannot be tied to one precise interpretation.

It is not *how* the world became as it is that is of final importance for believers, but rather the fact that it is *God's* creation and remains so throughout all eternity. It is a mistake to read a biblical story of creation as though it were a modern scientific account. When the Bible says God created the world in six days, it means creation took place in and through time. When it says God rested on the seventh day, it means the day of rest belongs to creation. Rest is possible, and given to us because God has completed creation and judged it "very good" (Gen. 1:31). When the biblical witnesses speak of creation they always have one and the same aim: to praise God as the Lord who brought forth an indescribably rich and good world simply through his will and word. And because this is God's world, it also has permanence. Nothing need trouble us or threaten us to the point where we lose our footing. And no astonishment over the unexplained mysteries of nature can threaten the confession of God as the Creator.

Do science and the Bible say the same thing?

Biblical faith in creation expresses something which science cannot, and says it in a way that can be neither confirmed nor disproven by science. Science considers the details of nature; faith affirms creation as a whole. Science tries to understand observable, repeatable, and measurable phenomena within a framework of natural laws; faith recognizes the most basic law of creation to be God's word and will.

Yet science and faith are not concerned with two different things. They are not two competing ways of considering the same reality. We know today that they complement each other. Through its study of nature—particularly in areas of physics that deal with the smallest realities that can be observed—modern science has become convinced that what is *true* is not to be confused with what can be *measured*. Science is gradually giving up its former position that nature can be understood as an unbroken chain of causes and effects. Many scientists no longer attempt to explain life in material terms. They recognize that there is no such thing as total objectivity in scientific experiments—because every observer is subjective, and even the *act of observing* can have an effect. And scientists now accept the fact that reality cannot be fitted into a system of concepts; our concepts themselves must continually change as we catch more adequate and precise glimpses of reality.

Modern science has no unified, complete picture of the world— and given its methods of measurement and deduction it is doubtful that it can ever achieve one. We must therefore free ourselves from the still widely held view that science knows the whole of reality and can completely investigate it. Science itself has come to the conclusion that it cannot by itself understand all of nature. Therefore it is no longer possible to assume that scientific and biblical ways of considering the world are in opposition. What serious scientist today would state that it is scientifically "wrong" for the Bible to say that the world had a beginning and will come to an end?

We must remember that 20th-century science and biblical stories of creation are not comparable. Scientists offer ever-new hypotheses based on ever-new measurements; the Bible offers a bold and poetic picture of the origin and meaning of the world which has lost none of its freshness and power after 3000 years. Both can stand together as complementary attempts to understand reality on different levels. A physicist or biologist can be a believer in the biblical doctrine of creation because it does not attempt to list natural laws, but rather states the relationship between God and the world. Christians can without difficulty follow the modern and ever-more-exact theories of the evolution of life on earth over many millions of years. There is no contradiction here. Those who see opposition are still stuck in the positions of yesterday, which have been abandoned by both scientists and theologians. Both have now learned to see more clearly the limitations and mandates of their different fields.

Where we have come

God is the source of all life, the Creator of all things and our Creator. This is not preached to us as a theory, but as a fact and an experience. As the people of Israel experienced God in their history —the one who rescued them from trouble and promised them new life—so we can experience God in our lives as our Creator. The God who rescues us has made a good world. He has made it by his word. This means that the deepest secret of the world is its relationship with God. Everything has come into existence simply through his will. We have been placed in an indissoluble relationship with God through his word, which became human in Jesus and was with God before all creation. God is not the world, but remains for all eternity in a loving relationship with that which he has made. This is what creation means. Faith does not debate the details of how creation happened; for the biblical view of creation does not stand in competition with a science that searches out the laws by which the world exists. We are free to choose the theories that seem most reasonable from among the many views of the world that thinkers and researchers have presented. Faith simply says that all development in time is and will remain encompassed within God's creative will. Everything belongs to God and has its meaning in him. Together with the world and all its powers and energies, its material and living things, God has also created time itself.

5. God and Human Beings

How are people created?

All that we have said about the world is true in a special way of human beings. We do not come from ourselves or rest in ourselves. We are dependent on God. God has made us with his hand and by his word. "Then the Lord God formed man of dust from the ground, and breathed into his nostrils the breath of life; and man became a living being" (Gen. 2:7). We are not God, even though at high points in our lives we sometimes think we are. But we are bound to God by his word. We are related to God and he to us. Like all that has been created, we are threatened at each step by the fear of nonexistence. And it is not only death which threatens us, but the same disorder and chaos within us that existed when God created the world. God's will must sustain and hold us as creation continues every day.

What is a person?

As long as we exist we ask who we are. We are an enigma to ourselves. We have already seen that as human beings we are eternally open questions. Yet the Bible gives us an answer. With clear, indelible lines it draws a picture of human beings. It gives us a standard by which to measure ourselves. The Bible says we are important enough that we cannot be measured against ourselves, but only against God, our Creator. People are dust, earth, and clay. Like the rest of creation, we are a mixture of all the chemical elements of the earth. We are alive, like plants and animals. But we are something more than other living things. We have been created in the image of God. This means we can be compared to God. Of course we are not God—but we do have a share in God's thoughts. God chooses to address us and communicate with us. We are not only created by God's word, but *for* his word and *in* his word. We become the people we are intended to be only when we say yes to God. We have been made to take part in what God does: creating, acting, hearing, and speaking to creation. "So God created man in his own image, in the image of God he created him; male and female he created them" (Gen. 1:27).

What about our spirits?

As creatures, we have a certain path to tread. We grow, mature, decline, and die like other animals. But at the same time we must tread an inner path. We are more than simply animals. We are persons, with personalities. Our spirits within us call us to something more than our animal needs and wants. At the same time we know that we are not divided, but whole. The Bible says human beings were created as a unity. We do not have "bodies" on the one hand and "souls" on the other. We are unified persons. Can we really say that only our bodies suffer pain when we are wounded? Is it only our ears that hear music, or the retinas of our eyes that see mountain landscapes? It is becoming ever more clear to modern medicine that illness touches the whole person. It is idle to ask if our bodies are extensions of our spirits or if our spirits are products of our bodies. We were created unified persons and we will die unified persons.

What is the significance of the body?

We are not to despise the body. It is not our enemy. Its needs are not contemptible. Our five (perhaps six) senses provide us with precious images of the world. The Bible would be quite misunderstood if it were interpreted as saying that evil resides in the body and good in the spirit. Our desires are evil and our thoughts meditate on wrongdoing, but the body is only their instrument. It is through the body that all we wish, think, and will is accomplished.

Creation means that God gives form to his thoughts and will. At our human level we do what he does. We complete projects, painters give form to paintings, and poets write works. Creation is *incarna-*

tion. Incarnation is the object of all creation. The Christian church confesses, "The Word became flesh" (John 1:14). This means God sent Jesus, his Word, into the world to become a man among us, flesh as we are flesh.

For the Bible there is no human existence without and apart from human flesh. But we must not limit flesh to our present human body. It is true that between birth and death our lives are in the form of flesh, and when we die all that remains is a corpse. But the Bible bears witness to the fact that in the resurrection we will become new, and therefore have new flesh. It speaks of the "spiritual" body of the resurrection. Our body—that means all that we are—with soul and spirit, will be changed into a new body, a "glorious body" (1 Cor. 15:35ff.; Phil. 3:21). God has created the world good, and one expression of this goodness is human existence as flesh.

How are we to live in relation to the Creator?

Because God has made us, to that extent he is related to us and remains linked with us. It is not only that he allows seeds to germinate and enables us to be born from our mothers' bodies. Every hour of our lives he also makes it possible for us to live, giving us the strength to continue and the desire to do what is good. God's love, which has allowed the world and all people to emerge from nothing, lays claim to us all our lives long. We should live in relation to the one who has enabled us to be and whose faithfulness sustains us. A thankful attitude expresses itself in praise of this Creator. To praise God and to love his good creation is the office of righteous persons, the fruit of their faith.

Those who can praise are not only righteous, but free. To many of our contemporaries, praise and thanks appear useless. What is the point of saying things to God which he must already know? But those who pray and sing in the Bible—in the Psalms, prophets, the Book of Job, on almost every page of the Holy Scriptures—serve not only God but also themselves. When we praise the Creator and his creation we establish and recognize that we are God's beloved through all eternity, and we renew the relationship in which we stand. We honor the work of which we are a part, assure ourselves of who we are, and gain freedom and pleasure.

How are we to live in relation to creation?

Because we are God's beloved creatures, we are not to encounter other creatures with hate, contempt, or destructive intentions. Because God made all creatures good (like us) and loves them (like us), we are to show them recognition, thanks, and love. We belong together with all that has been created because everything has been made by the same God. The Bible tells the story of how God commissioned people to subdue the earth. Our western technological spirit has accepted this mandate and actively sought to subdue the whole world. But according to the Bible we must also be careful not to forget that we constitute only one part of creation, and there are many other creatures which God created good and wants to keep good.

We carry *responsibility* for God's creation. We are wrong to exterminate other creatures—each a miracle in itself—simply through blind carelessness or in order to make possible a more comfortable life for ourselves. We must not use our powers without limit. For the sake of God's creation we must use our knowledge, abilities, and competence only with great care, as in our use of atomic energy. We are together stewards of the world and individually caretakers of those things entrusted to us in our homes and places of work. On the other hand we are only one species among many. That means we must recognize how small, weak, and dependent we are when measured by the greatness and glory of all created things.

Where we have come

As persons we are living beings on this earth. That does not say very much. Scientists can find out how our bodies developed and are put together and how our organs function; doctors can discover and perhaps heal our illnesses; psychologists can go deep into our repressions and try to understand our inner selves. But all of them look only at our appearance and manifestation in time. Who we really are they cannot say. But the Bible does. It says that we are God's creation. Like all creatures we are *dependent on him and related to him.* We live because he brings us out of nothing and sustains us. We are fashioned to experience God's thoughts and to be measured against God. We are his image in the world. We should therefore make a measure of his love visible among other creatures. The Bible speaks of us as whole persons. We come from God, belong to God, and go to God. We are to honor the flesh that God has given us. The world has been made our responsibility. We should live in relation to God, our eternal Lord, and establish his love among his creatures. Our existence is in God. It rests inviolable in his good hand and goes together with all the world to meet his glorious future. That is what our creation means.

6. God Accompanies His Creatures

What are we to do?

Because God has created us and the world, and every morning creates us anew in his love, he comes to us. This gives our lives direction. He from whom we come will always come to us. Who are we? What should we do? We are God's creatures, set in his good world. We should subdue the earth and yet love other creatures. We should fulfill our nature as persons and praise God by our lives and words, thoughts and deeds. What this means in detail, and what difficulties we meet on the way (especially how we often stand in our own way), we will see later. For the moment the first and simplest answer is that God accompanies his creatures. He does not leave our questions unanswered. As God has imposed laws to order his creation, so he has given *us* laws and commandments. God guaranteed the order of his creation when he promised the patriarch Noah that the seasons would always follow one another—there would be seedtime and harvest, rain and sunshine so long as the earth remains. In his law God tells us we are not to work *against* but *with* his creation, because we are his creatures and should live as such. We should love because God loves us. That is what we are to do.

Is death part of God's creation?

God has given his creation order. This order is both a blessing and a restraint. We are blessed because there is summer and winter, the seas do not flood over the continents, light remains separated from darkness, and heaven from earth. We are blessed by waking and sleeping, work and rest. We are blessed by the functioning of our bodies, those wonderful instruments. Yet we are restrained because life on this earth is limited, and like all of God's creatures we must one day die. Death occurs even in the midst of life in the form of weariness, illness, old age, and sorrow. When we look at the decay of all things and the disappearance of that which was so beautifully made, we may well become sad, like the writer of Ecclesiastes who observed "All is vanity" (1:2). This sorrow reminds us that mortality is the natural negative side of creation. Yet faith knows that God prepares the eternal destiny of all people. My eternal existence is promised to me, and in some ways accompanies me now. Because we are creatures, we must live *with* death, *for* death, and *against* death. But creation also means that the mortal and the immortal, human beings and the Creator, do not stand in contradiction. I did not originate from the action of some impersonal first cause. Rather, the eternal God has called me into life.

Does God direct our destiny?

We must say more about creation. We spoke first of the event: God created the world and called us into life. Then we spoke of the present: creation continues every day as God sustains us and the world. Now we must speak of the future: the Creator goes ahead of us. He directs our destiny. He guides our history. He allows us to die because we belong to him in eternity.

We have seen that belief in creation arose out of the people of Israel's experience with God. God led them out of slavery in Egypt and directed them through the wilderness. He protected them in their wanderings and gave them land. The story of God's covenant with his people Israel is the pattern for his dealing with human beings. God will deal with us in the same way, accompanying us and going before us on our way, even as he went before Israel in the forms of a cloud by day and a pillar of fire by night (Exod. 40:36ff.). It is the conviction of the Bible and the experience of Israel that God is revealed not primarily in nature but through his dealings with his people and with individuals.

God's creation is not static, but a process of becoming. Sometimes God shows us after the fact how wonderful the things he has done for us are. Sometimes God comes to us from within and we feel we are on a mountaintop of joy that will never end. But usually God comes to us as the insurpassable Lord of our life histories. He is our guarantee of eternity, the one we can unreservedly trust with the purpose of our lives. Thus God becomes the Creator of our future, and by his guiding power the history of our salvation is accomplished.

Does God act in world history?

With the creation of the world begins the history of God with human beings. The Christian faith sees the unfolding drama of human history, from start to finish, as the action of God. God accompanies his creatures with his furthering, directing, caring, and healing word. As God has worked a good work through evolution, so he works in our day and will continue to work in the future. The history of God's salvation is fulfilled within world history.

One of the restraints of creation is that we can read God's handwriting only with difficulty, and usually after the fact. Some Old Testament prophets thought God revealed himself most clearly as the creative Lord through the negative side of reality. When we are sick unto death, when all our friends leave us, when we are burdened with guilt—then God is there. Christian faith sees this image of the hidden God in the man who hung on a cross and yet is our Savior. As the world was created "in Christ" by the word of love, so creation continues in Christ in human history—in the presence of his suffering and the certainty of his victory. If we dare to believe that, then we will see it to be true. We can believe, though not prove, that present and future world history is fashioned by God, and that the evolution of the world is God's creation. We can believe that by his word God was, is, and will be our Creator.

There are innumerable theories that try to understand human history. Is history a turning wheel of becoming and decay, in which every event comes round again? Is it a continuous decline? Is it the progress of the spirit? Will one economic class gain victory and usher in a classless society? Or is there no development at all, but just a series of moments pregnant with possibility? In each of these theories human beings are either left to their own devices or are victims of impersonal forces. But the Bible reveals that the Lord and Creator of the world does not abandon his creation. In darkness and in light he accompanies us in our path through time.

Where have we come from? Where are we going?

To many of our contemporaries the state of the world today appears very dark. They look around and do not see a way out. What was the sense of two world wars and a hundred smaller ones in this century alone? Aren't there already too many people for the earth to support? What will happen when we double or even treble the population? Sources of energy and raw materials are running out. How will we survive? No one appears to think about the day after tomorrow, and even tomorrow seems far away. Education increases, but we don't seem to be getting any wiser. Will our end be poverty and hunger, ennui and hate? Was that the purpose for which God created us? Are we just an object of exploitation by a planner who makes good with his right hand and evil with his left? In the midst of our high standard of living in the West we are frightened. Only darkness seems to lie ahead. Many people are afraid to bring children—those signs of new hope in God's creation—into the world. And yet people have always been afraid of the future. That future must appear dark to those who do not know God is the Lord of creation and accompanies us in all we do, leading us day by day and by night. It must appear doubly dark to them when the signs of the times indicate we are at the turning point of world history. Where do we come from? Where are we going?

What is the goal of creation?

Christian faith says that we come from God's hand—the fruit of God's long history with his creatures. And we continue to rest in the hand of God. The fourth century, with its massive migrations of peoples into the Roman Empire, was a time of great confusion. The church father Augustine explained the past and the present in terms of the future. With prophetic spirit he looked beyond the great upheavals of his time and said that the purpose of creation is the Creator himself. God called the world into life by his word in order that he might be united with it. The Bible says that we not only come *out* of the eternity of God, but are also created *for* the eternity of God.

The drama of creation played out between its beginning and completion troubles us. We are involved in our part of this drama, and the floods may go over our heads—plunging us into despair. Christian faith says that the drama of world history and our little personal histories cast long shadows over God's good world. We have fallen out of our intended relationship with God; rather than receiving God's creation as a gift, we have snatched it away from him and appropriated it for ourselves. John the evangelist wrote that the world has not known God (John 17:25). That is the reason for our confusion and the drama of history. But God will unite his creation to himself when he has defeated all attempts to wrest it from his hand.

We may think that the world has never been as dark as today. But all of recorded human history reveals the same darkness, as human beings have taken their destinies into their own hands. Faith in God the Creator says that he who began a good work in us will carry it through to completion. This completion, to which all creation is called, will be more glorious than its beginning or any of its history through time.

Where we have come

The creation of the world does not lie behind us. It is no fairy tale that begins, "Once upon a time. . . ." The Creator is with us all the time. He accompanies us. We need to recognize him in the blessings and restraints of his creation. The Bible never ceases to say how wisely God has made the world and how carefully he has constructed us. His hand lies in blessing upon the progress of natural events, which science sees as ever more amazing. Christian faith says that God has set all things in order. In the biblical story of the great flood, the rainbow in the sky was said to have been an everlasting sign that God would maintain order in creation. God includes us in this order as well. We are under the laws of his creation. And he shows us our boundary—the blessing of mortality. Death is not the end of us, but is the expression of our creatureliness. As creatures of God we are mortal beings in time. We would like to do many things, but we cannot do everything. God directs our destinies, and we experience him in both good and evil days. God also deals with the larger history of nations. The darkness of our time should not plunge us into despair, because we know that all life stands under the control of the one who made it. Everything that lives does so for the God who comes to bring his world to fulfillment.

Summary

I experience

Everyone talks about God. Few take him seriously. They speak in hints and guesses. One person doesn't know. Another has "a feeling." Others have known God but forgotten him. Still others speak of God as though they knew him, even though they don't. Even those who want to forget God have kept his name in their language. In one way or another they are beset by that name. Some people are hostile. They say God is dead. But it appears to me that the more they talk about the death of God the more they talk about God himself. People want to be godless, but they cannot.

It is much the same with me. Regardless of what I have learned or forgotten, in practice I live again and again as though there were no God. I experience my life as though it can be understood without God. Each day has its duties, each week its day of rest, each year its calendar of events. My children grow up and I pay my rent. A new war erupts in Africa and I have no idea who is fighting who or why. God seems silent.

I question

Is God silent because he cannot speak, because he will not speak, or because I cannot understand his language?

Who is God anyway? The God of all the gods? The highest thing we can recognize? The first cause of all causes? That which alone is good, true, and beautiful? The last refuge of our dilemmas? The fulfillment of our needs? The wishful thinking of our unsatisfied souls?

Which god is the true one? The religions of the world offer many gods, old and new. The choice is great and confusing. Shall I follow the gods of India, who promise me salvation in world-denying oblivion? How about the god of the Marxists, promising a future day of total equality for all, without envy? Or shall I choose the little gods in my own home, where it is warm by the fireside and my window to the world remains closed?

I believe

I believe there is only one God: not the god of the philosophers, but the God of Abraham, Isaac, and Jacob. No one can escape from him. He comes to meet us all. No one can name him. He himself has given us his name: *Yahweh,* who was and is and will be. He has no place or time, for he himself has made space and time. He is not in the world, under the world, or over the world. No distance contains him. He is the Lord of the world.

I believe God has freely brought forth the world according to his decree, by his love. God protects the world in his love. It is his good world, which pleases him. God has created me, together with all creatures, by his word. He creates me daily anew, remaining near to me by his word and allowing me to come near to him, like a child to a father. God gives me responsibility for his creation. I am to use it but not misuse it or harm it. I am to love other people and all of God's creatures. God directs my life, as he does the destiny of peoples and nations, even when I do not recognize his will and cannot understand it. God makes possible a good fortune for his creation and leads it to the day when he will be all in all. At that time everyone will see him as the Creator, the Lord and Father of his children. God will call us and all creation to himself, to salvation, and to consummation.

I believe God is not the product of our thoughts or the fruit of our wishes. He is the living one who comes near to us in his word. Even if we were to master the whole world and fly to the stars, we would still need him. For without God we cannot exist. We are created in God's image, and have a part in his immortality. God's nearness to us burns us, but when we are far from him we perish. To talk of his death is nonsense. How could death come to the one who is himself the life and ground of our existence? Only our images of God decay. To call God a projection of ourselves cannot harm him, but only us. For if we could describe God he would be an object with limits, a part of the world, simply one of us. But God is both my

Lord and the heart of the world. He is the world's innermost life, focus, and never-ending beginning, just as he is the one who holds me lovingly in his hand.

Therefore this is the first article of our faith: we are called to put our trust in the Creator who surrounds us at all times with his love and good creation. The same God who is called Father in the Bible has created the world. Our lives are sustained by his love. With God's love we have something in us which cannot perish, because his love will not let us go. The Bible says we are the image of God's love. And it is this same love which has appeared among us in Christ. When we look to Christ we can realize what depth, peace, and riches are present in a person who is at one with the living God, the Creator and Perfecter of all things.

3

WHAT
DISTRESSES US

**We Rebel
Against God:**

Sin

1. Knowing Good and Evil

What is our first question?

Where do we stand in God's creation? Creation has its boundaries: weariness and sorrow, old age and sickness, decay and death. Doom is laid upon us, and we are inextricably bound up with the history of the world. We would like to trust creation, but we cannot. Too much of it troubles us. What are we? We are God's creatures. But we are special creatures, placed in a relationship with the Creator and his creation. Yet we also alienate ourselves from creation by our strange desire to destroy.

In the ancient story of creation in the first few pages of the Bible, God is said to have planted two trees in the middle of the garden which he had prepared as a home for human beings. He planted the "tree of life" and the "tree of the knowledge of good and evil" (Gen. 2:9). God commanded Adam and Eve not to eat the fruit of that second tree. But they ate it anyway. In so doing they first acquired the ability to distinguish between good and evil. Like the whole of humanity that they represent, they were given the burden of distinguishing between them. Wherever we stand, whatever we do, and whatever happens to us or to our neighbors, our first question is, "Is it right or wrong?" Is it good or evil?

What question makes us persons?

Animals also have a sense for what is good. But animals have scarcely a thought for the past and very little fear of the future. The most we can say is that the past of an animal species is stored up in its instincts. But value judgments can only come with consciousness. And consciousness has hardly appeared yet among even the higher animals. I make judgments when I experience the past as good or bad and when I hope that the future will be good or fear that it will be bad. Certainly animals can learn, because they see what is good for them and what harms them. But these are not value judgments about good and evil. In this sense it is the question of *what is good and evil* that makes us persons. It is certainly no accident that the biblical story of the first human beings places this question at its center.

Does what is good give meaning to the whole?

The question of good and evil is identical with the question of meaning. If we possess a measure by which to judge what is good—not just for us and our own pleasure, but good for others as well and even for all of creation—then we also know what is meaningful to do. Whether we can carry through with it is another question. What we know to be good must find its expression in our actions. Here lies our greatest difficulty. Jesus refused to accept the title "Good Teacher." Only God, he said, is good (Mark 10:17ff.). How can we grasp God's goodness? How can the meaning of his goodness enter our lives? God gives commandments which make it possible to judge what is good. The good which God calls for gives meaning to the whole of life. And if I were to become good, my life would acquire meaning.

How can we become good?

In the Bible we learn that God, who alone is good, shows us what is good in his law. He does not want to threaten us with punishment. With fatherly concern he wishes to instruct us. He wants to show us that it is good for us to love him with all our hearts and our neighbors as ourselves, that it is good for us to neither kill nor steal nor commit adultery. " 'But the word is very near you; it is in your mouth and in your heart, so that you can do it. See, I have set before you this day life and good, death and evil' " (Deut. 30:14-15). All that is in me cries out that I might become good. I want to gladly receive what God gives me. But again and again I fail in keeping his law. I should love. But I cannot love everyone. I should pursue peace. But so often those who seek peace stir up wars. Not only should I not steal, but I should not be greedy. I have to do so many things at once. I should give generously, but also save so that I have something to give. I should not judge, but I must not be cowardly. I should give way, but not always—I must avoid complacency. God shows me what is good with so few laws, but I must apply them in every new and different situation. I must approach each person imaginatively. That is my difficulty.

Are we free to do good?

What is good is therefore not simply a set of rules to be applied. We have to discover it anew every day of our lives—sometimes every hour of the day. And yet the direction that goodness takes is unambiguous. It follows the path of love. But are we free to love? Here we must distinguish between the answers given by science and by faith.

Science assumes that there is a cause for everything. It traces human beings to an animal ancestry and to a collection of inherited characteristics and instincts. It sees us as also dependent on our immediate and general environments. The philosopher Schopenhauer thought that human beings are nothing more than the sum total of these dependencies; he did not believe we are capable of any will other than the dependent will we have inherited. But in such a view there is no possibility of being free to love. We can only do what we have been programmed to do.

We must recognize the influences that are in us and surround us. Science points these out to us. And yet faith knows that each day we are responsible for everything we do. What have I really done today? Was it good or evil? Have I loved? These questions would be meaningless unless I had the possibility of doing something different from what I actually did.

What is the price of freedom?

In our hearts we carry an image of the perfect person. A person is perfect when he or she is free to do what is right, even when it is against his or her own interests. For Christians, Jesus provides the image of a perfect person. In order to do what was right and be in accord with God he took suffering and death upon himself. Many of his disciples also proved their freedom by refusing to compromise their faith or their preaching.

But even the highest human freedom is not absolute. Our freedom is limited by our neighbors' own claims to freedom. And we must come to terms with the limitations of the world in which we were born. We want to be absolutely free, but we cannot achieve such freedom. We cannot save ourselves from the painful consequences of exercising our freedom. Christ himself was not free in that sense. Human freedom stands under God's limitations and has its price.

And yet failing to do God's will brings a far greater loss. By subordinating himself to God's commands and becoming a servant, Christ gained freedom in relation to people and the world. He became a master in the freedom to do what is right. What troubles us is our weakness in really listening to God and seeking his will. We so often lose the freedom that Christ displayed through his obedience to God. And we are not alone in this. The history of the church reveals both courageous moments and times of great weakness.

Where we have come

We have not inherited freedom, but it has been promised to us. All things are influenced by their past and their environment, and even human beings stand in a chain of causes and effects. But if we were as limited as animals are, then we would not be human. We could find excuses for everything we do, just as Adam and Eve did when they disobeyed God's commandment. We carry responsibility for others and for creation itself, and we must answer to God. Responsibility sets the question of freedom aside. Responsibility asks, What is right? What is wrong? Moral standards vary with times and places. Nonetheless, the direction in which human values ought to move has been firmly established by God. The more we love, the more human we are. How love should be expressed and realized for the healing of others differs with different situations, depending on people's knowledge and customs. But these adaptations are not arbitrary. Our love must exert itself to find out where and how it can best express itself today. Christians are therefore servants of God's love for his creation. But they are also bound to the absoluteness of this love. What troubles us is not our lack of freedom, but the fact that we make so little of it. Since the human race has been promised freedom, why does it so seldom achieve it or use it? When we ask that question, we ask about the secret of humanity: about the basis of our freedom, the depth of our guilt, the burden of our affliction, and our irrepressible longing for salvation.

2. Sin and Guilt

What is sin?

Questions about good and evil lead to questions about guilt. Why do we make so little use of our freedom to do what is right? God tells us what is good. There is a voice within each of us that can be called our conscience. It knows what is good and wants to do it. Nonetheless we live for the most part without doing what is good. The apostle Paul wrote, "For I do not do the good I want, but the evil I do not want is what I do" (Rom. 7:19). We have set ourselves in opposition to our consciences. What is wrong with us?

In the same chapter of his letter to the Romans, Paul spoke from his own experience about the results of trying to live by one's own moral strength. Paul knew how God's law reveals the power of sin within us. Sin is not just what we do in defiance of the particular moral code of our time. Sin is less individual acts than the *attitude of our heart,* which expresses itself in our life. Paul shows how those who try to live by their own moral strength (according to "the flesh") are driven by their natural impulses into self-pride, becoming cut off from God. They no longer let themselves follow God but pursue their own appetites. They become gods to themselves.

We are created to have a relationship with God. When we lose that relationship we lose ourselves. The more we pursue our independence, the more we lose our true natures. When we make the terrible exchange of our relationship with God for the pursuit of our own desires, we lose our very selves. This is the meaning of Jesus' words, " 'Whoever seeks to gain his life will lose it' " (Luke 17:33).

Who is the devil?

The Bible often speaks of sin as though it were outside us. Paul called it a power which dwelled within him (Rom. 7:20, 23). Again and again the New Testament speaks of Satan and the devil as though evil had a personal form. Today we are accustomed to think of the devil as "merely a symbol" of radical evil—no longer as a personal being. And yet again and again we experience an irresistible evil force that comes into our lives, ruining us and leading us toward things that our consciences find questionable or even hateful. Isn't it the devil who resides in us when we sin? The horns and hooves artists have given him belong, of course, to an age that lacked a scientific view of the world. But we must recognize what truth there is in this talk of a devil. In him anonymous evil has been given form and acquired a name.

In the Bible we read less about evil than about evil people. What is meant is that within the created world the devil carries on a war against human beings. This is one side of sin and evil, which comes over us and takes possession of us like an outside force. It is not the product of who we are. We should arm ourselves against it as against a burglar. In this sense, and only in this sense, is evil a person. We do not mean that it has a form like a human being. That is why we cannot really say the devil "exists." He is the negative side of reality which should not be. He is death and destruction. He does not exist, but he seeks a home in us. He is our unthinkable possibilities that become real in sin, evil, and wrongdoing.

The devil is everything that God does not will. For God desires what is good. The contradiction which constantly troubles Christian faith is, How can evil (which the Bible calls the devil) exist if God is all in all? We cannot resolve this contradiction. We do not understand how evil can be a real force in the world and yet not come from God. This remains a mystery of creation, which is good and yet includes evil. Persons who are destined for freedom are thrown into the slavery of sin.

What is "original sin"?

The church's doctrine of "original sin" is an attempt to make intelligible another side of what troubles us. Forget once and for all what you have heard about original sin, particularly that old, erroneous, and unbiblical idea that sin is inherited by a child from its parent (or even that it is the act of reproduction itself). The expressions "original sin" and "personal sin" need to be carefully distinguished. How can we do this? The answer comes in three statements which reveal the tragic nature of sin.

1. Sin is always individual guilt, but individual guilt is almost always interwoven with the guilt of others. We live in societies, nations, groups, and families. We share their privileges and weak-

nesses, become guilty of their prejudices, and participate in their collective guilt.

2. Sin is always individual guilt, but we are born into it. It is our doing, and yet we cannot say when it began. Are children innocent? The law sets a late age for legal punishment. But children are human in the full sense. At quite early ages children ask about right and wrong, and they do not want to be found guilty. They come into a world marked by sin. Neither from experience nor revelation can it be established that human beings were first good or "natural" (as some gladly describe it) and then became evil.

3. The church's doctrine of original sin attempts to correct the tension between freedom and fate, responsibility and tragedy. There is an evil in the world which is often much stronger than we are. Misfortune pursues us and we know not why. Heavy burdens are laid upon us. Why? Our good will achieves nothing. Our freedom is broken by our fate. A force pushes us down which is stronger than us and was here before we were. There are factors in our lives— demonic powers—which we cannot subdue and which we nonetheless have a share in. Sin alienates us. It is part of us—and yet again it is not.

Can one's conscience be trusted?

So far we have not clearly distinguished between guilt and sin. Do Christians speak of sin and non-Christians of guilt? No. Everyone speaks of guilt. Guilt relates to offenses against others or against the laws of society. Sin relates to an attitude before God. It is only in faith that we can speak of sin. We must learn to distinguish between guilt and a sense of sin. We must test our feelings. People can develop anxious and depressive conditions where everything that happens throws them into a sense of guilt. When this happens it may be necessary to see a doctor. Religious people are particularly prone to overscrupulousness. But only a believer who is ill indulges in groundless self-accusation. Whether a psychotherapist can then help depends on his or her understanding of the particular person and of guilt. On the other hand, private confession and pastoral discussion or therapeutic counseling must discern between true guilt and mere self-seeking. When the voice of one's conscience is involved, then there is real guilt. We must learn to pay attention to such guilt, and overcome that which has no foundation. We are in the most danger, however, when there is good reason to feel guilty but that feeling is very weak. Then our conscience is sick.

How can we handle our guilt?

There is something peculiar about people. We could draw premature conclusions from what we have discovered about sin and guilt, freedom and fate. We could say there is no human life without guilt. Every day we remain guilty before God and other people. Therefore the offenses we commit today do not count for much. This sounds logical. But something within us rises up against it. We will not let ourselves solve the problem so cheaply. What are we, when after hurting another human being we are so easily absolved? We are destined to be guilty, but we nonetheless feel responsible. And we are. We cannot avoid it. The guilt I incur today is *my* guilt. Despite everything, I am responsible for it. What have I done about it?

Many psychotherapists hope they can set people free from guilt. The practice of psychotherapy attracts people who want to understand the roots of their guilt feelings. We are much more willing to put ourselves into the hands of a psychotherapist than to be questioned by a pastor. We expect a psychotherapist in a white coat to deal with us neutrally, without value judgments. He or she can help us see our guilt as the result of factors beyond our control. We understand our past better. But is our guilt thereby eliminated? Today even depth psychologists doubt whether this is possible. Rather, the more patients become aware of the meaning of guilt, the better they understand what responsibility they have for the offense their actions have caused to others. Depth psychology attempts to remove the reasons for the neuroses of sick persons obsessed by guilt. And the most frequent reason for their neuroses is their love of helplessness! Psychotherapy cannot free us from our guilt. But it can help us to recognize it and live with it without becoming sick.

To what does our guilt call us?

Pastors of the church or individual Christians render great service to their neighbors when they understand what guilt is and its relationship to God. Naturally doctors can also render this service if they are persons of faith. A Christian who understands guilt as sin, as separation from God, will not shut it out. But the Christian faith promises more than just the possibility of living with what oppresses us. It also calls us to freedom—to the day when all will be made new and we will be made whole. Not only will our feelings of guilt be resolved, but our guilt itself will be forgiven and removed from us. God gives to us guilty people eternal salvation in the discipleship of faith. The forgiveness of sins is the first and most important part of God's gift to his sinful people. The fifth petition in the Lord's Prayer asks God to forgive our sins. This is fulfilled in the church day by day, after the pattern of Jesus and in his power. That which oppresses us we must know no more. Christians are those who are freed from their sins, children who have returned home to their Father.

Where we have come

The New Testament holds a mirror before my eyes. Who I am can be seen in that which oppresses me. Called to freedom, I find myself in bondage. Why? I want to do what is right, but cannot. Why? It is because I have separated myself from God, the one who has given me life and sustains it day by day. This is what tears me apart. As the apostle Paul said, sickness and death have come into my life because I have set myself in God's place. Paul called this existence of mine *sin*. When we think about the meaning of sin, we must think big. Sin is not the sum total of our individual sins and failings, as most people think. It is rather a power from which we cannot escape by our own strength. Satan—the devil—has power not only in the world but also in my own inner self. The order which God intended has been destroyed, both in the world and in me. That which *is* should not be, and that which should not be *is*. I have to struggle against nothingness and the one who brings all things to nothingness. This power is at work within me, and at the same time it is universal. It is the common fate of all people. I am alienated from God and from myself. The phrase "original sin" or "inherited sin" expresses this tragedy. When I acknowledge this alienation as sin I have made confession before God. It is not just that I am guilty along with everyone else, or that I have failed to keep some rules, but I have become *separated from God*. For me to learn how to get rid of my guilt feelings or live with them may be helpful, but this is certainly not enough. My sin must be dealt with on a more basic level. I need to be restored to communion with God, and I need to be freed from the force which oppresses me.

3. Evil and Death

Why does God allow evil?

As all who have experienced forgiveness can testify, both sin and guilt bring suffering. But it is hard to explain everything that is wrong with the world by blaming it on human sin. We must ask not only about the wrong which is within us, but also about the source of the larger evil which continuously threatens God's creatures. What is the meaning of this evil, and why does it wreak such terrible destruction?

Bolts of lightning sometimes send hundreds of airline passengers to their deaths in fiery crashes. Thousands perish each year in earthquakes and floods. Who justifies these anonymous forces? Who has let loose this power, and why? Are the victims of natural disasters simply receiving their just punishment? Then why are only some overtaken by them, while others sleep peacefully in their homes? The tower of Siloam fell on the just and the unjust alike (Luke 13:4); the passengers on the Titanic drowned without distinction when that ocean liner struck an iceberg; and on one single day in 1755 the fair city of Lisbon was destroyed. Such disasters shake us out of our sense of security.

In the last section we spoke of the long shadow which sin casts over God's creation. We must now deal with this different question. Unbelievers ask: "How can there be a God when such things happen?" Believers ask: "How can we reconcile these things with the God who is just and good?" Both are troubled, but the question posed by believers is the more difficult. We hear it repeated by each generation, and none of the great confessors of the faith has been spared it. It reawakens one's earliest doubts about God. "Why does God allow that which I do not understand?" We know about human sin and injustice, but the world's sufferings are out of all proportion to them. Who sends plagues and lets deformed children be born,

while allowing a rich miser to live for a hundred years? Faith knows
of only one—and seemingly terrible—answer: Here, too, God must
be at work. Otherwise he would not be all in all—the Lord and
Creator of the world. But how can this be? No other question is so
troubling for faith.

Would God be untrue to his creation?

God has made the world as an image of his own goodness. Yet
as we have seen, the goodness of creation has been put into question by our own human unfaithfulness. We have turned aside from
God and allowed sin to become powerful. We have misused our
authority as God's representatives and idolized ourselves. We want
to find happiness in ourselves, not in God. But now another terrible
possibility emerges. Creation seems to be threatening its own
existence. Over and over again the worshipers in the Old Testament
asked, "Has God withdrawn from his own creation?" They dreaded
this thought, but they had to face the possibility that it could be
true. We asked why God could not prevent the crash of an airplane
or the occurrence of an earthquake. Natural disasters seem to
increase in strength every day. "Many are the afflictions of the
righteous" (Ps. 34:19). Could it be that not only the human race,
but God himself is unfaithful to creation? The Bible gives a central
place to this charge. For this complaint does not come from outside
a believer, but from deep within. "Lord, I believe," I say, "that
you have fashioned the world and guided it in love. But why doesn't
it look that way? I am deeply troubled by this contradiction between
your promise and my own experience."

Must God justify himself to us?

If I did not believe, then I could not be so disturbed. That is
unfortunately the way it is. To those who do not know God, the evil
in the world belongs to the world. There has always been injustice,
and we must work to destroy it and defend ourselves against catastrophes. We want to share in that task, for it belongs to the mission
the Creator has given us. But we cannot overcome the contradiction.
Does God contend *against* himself *because* of himself? He has promised to be near us, but now he is far away. He hides himself in fire

and water and tumbling mountains, and in the triumphant cry of the strong—who are liars, murderers, and oppressors.

No complaint against God remains unexpressed in the Bible. To worshipers in the Old Testament God sometimes appeared like an enemy, "like a bear lying in wait" (Lam. 3:10). This is most sharply taken up in the Book of Job, where that God-fearing man accuses God of visiting him with unjust punishment. In that book all our explanations and justifications of God are put aside. The well-meaning sentiments of Job's friends, who would defend God and resolve the contradiction, receive God's angry rebuke. God does not answer Job's complaints by defending himself, but in a quite different way.

The message of the Book of Job is that the doctrine of creation is not a matter for human speculation. Animals do not exist because they have a use, but because in his freedom, love, and grace God called them into the glory of life before him. The same is true of human beings. And if we ask God why his ways are so dark, no more than Job should we expect an answer directed toward our understanding. God is not required to give such an answer. Even if he chose to do so, wouldn't it be as incomprehensible as fate is to those who know nothing of God? Job knew that God would be faithful to his covenant with humanity. This is the only answer God chooses to give us.

Again and again this is the experience of faith. God does not speak to us in theoretical statements, but as a person to other persons. God revealed himself to Job. He admitted Job's right to complain to him. He blessed Job's faith, which endured the darkness of God's ways. By passing through God's testing Job's faith became more mature. And the more mature a person's faith is, the more it can complain to God and yet endure. No one who believes will be able to completely banish the awful questions of our time, which are indeed the questions of every time.

What answer did Job receive?

The Book of Job has been called the New Testament in the Old. The reason is that Job, whose uprightness was tested by God, still believed that a deliverer, advocate, and savior would set him right before God. He believed this in spite of all that afflicted him. The salvation which cannot be seen is nonetheless certain. The evils which oppress us will be conquered. Despite all appearances, God's promise is valid. Just at the point where I am threatened—where the innocent suffer and wrongdoing triumphs—there faith drives me to acknowledge God's greatness. God's motives cannot be investigated. Today that may seem terrible, but tomorrow he will reconcile his goodness with what we see around us.

Jesus took up the problem of Job, and taught us to set aside our questions so that we might see the larger question of faith. Eighteen men had been killed when the tower of Siloam fell on them. Jesus said, "Do you think that they were worse offenders than all the others who dwelt in Jerusalem? I tell you, No; but unless you repent you will all likewise perish" (Luke 13:4-5). *Repentance* is the recognition of God as my Lord. In his majesty he questions me, so that my own questions are stilled.

Will we remain dead?

Our ultimate problem is death. Behind our questions about evil in the world, injustice among people, and wrong within God's good creation stands our concern about the end. Our lives are shaped by this end. There is a sense of immortality within us, but we shall die. We are not prepared for that. Yet we see how many die around us each year. We see the vast numbers across the globe who perish. Our life expectancy has been greatly increased, but immortality is not possible. We are afraid of death and we do not speak about it. Yet it is death and not sin which is the real evil in the world. Today the thought of the death of all humanity is much nearer. Scientists tell us that it could be only a hundred years (or even fifty) before the amount of food produced on the earth will not suffice for all living creatures. The world population may become so great that humanity will face decimation from overcrowding.

However much we think these dire predictions apply to others, sooner or later we realize our days are numbered. It is part of the human condition that the details of one's own death are not known. The hand of death beckons every day. Nothing can remove this distress. And no hope of a resurrection can set aside the seriousness of death. In fact, we see the seriousness of death most clearly when we believe. Others can say, "Well, now everything is over!" That is sad, because life even in its worst form has value. But if we believe

God set us in this existence, then we also believe we will be delivered over to him when we die. As an encounter with God, death can trouble us. The Bible paints the seriousness of the situation in bright colors borrowed from the literature of the time. It presents our encounter with God as a judgment. What will happen to us when we appear before God? This is not just a question about the future. It accompanies us our whole life through.

Who will rescue us?

Yet if death were the final word, and if we had no expectation of meeting God, our Source, then the world would be one vast cemetery. But an encounter with God opens up new life. Without this encounter everything would end in the stillness of death. Then our fate would be the same as that of the planets, which carry life for a time and then are lost again. Faith fights against this faithless view of the world and of humanity. Against the ambiguities which I see, faith stretches out before me an unambiguous life in God. But if I stare into this present enigma I will find no deliverance.

The Bible urges us not to seek salvation in flight from the world. To run away is very appealing. People try it again and again. Christians have often succumbed to the temptation to let the world be the world—to give up on our disturbing questions, miserable insecurity, and disobedient existence and flee into otherworldly thoughts. "In another world," Christians sometimes say to themselves, "God will solve everything, quiet our longings, and accomplish what we believe in and yet do not see." They put all their energies into these thoughts, cut themselves off, shut themselves up in their seemingly safe strongholds. They want salvation for themselves. But God wants to give to all. To flee is to give up faith. Faith stands fast with us when questions trouble us, protecting us in the midst of them.

We must face up to the enigma of evil in the world. Perhaps, like Job, we will complain against God. But we must retain our places in the world and struggle on behalf of humanity. Then we will know that God does not give up on his creation, even when it appears he has deserted it. In his own good time he will give us his answers. They will be different from our answers, and will reveal his faithfulness. At various times in our lives we experience blessings in the midst of our darkness. At the end of the Book of Job it is said, "And the Lord restored the fortunes of Job . . . and the Lord gave Job twice as much as he had before" (Job 42:10). Here God's promised blessing becomes visible, and even death, that worst of all riddles, has another face: "And after this Job lived a hundred and forty years, and saw his sons and his sons' sons, four generations. And Job died, an old man, and full of days" (Job 42:16-17).

Where we have come

It is as though there were a rift in creation. In the Bible we read that God praised it as his good work. But we see awful, meaningless suffering, accidents and catastrophes. No sin could be great enough to justify such suffering. When they brought a man born blind to Jesus, he said such affliction was not punishment for the man's sin or the sin of his parents (John 9:3). God hides himself behind this terrible situation. As Martin Luther said, God wears a mask. If all that happens comes from him, then much of what happens simply cannot be understood. Faith is put to the test. But when Job complained to God and rejected all that our pious human logic would suggest in God's defense, God blessed him. God would have us accept him even in his enigmatic activity. He would have us praise him even in death. Thus faith does not live in security. Only if I remain hidden in God through suffering, enigma, and upheaval do I, like Job, experience his blessing.

4. Progress and Destruction

Do we know today's worst afflictions?

The afflictions of faith have from the beginning had the same twofold form: our weakness in the face of the *world* and *ourselves;* the wrong which is *outside* us and the wrong which is *inside* us; *physical* and *existential* evil. People have always sought after themselves and have always had death in view. Destined to be free, we find ourselves enslaved. And we are intertwined with the world. We cannot be independent. Perhaps we have all the relationships we need, enough money, some rest, and have even carved out a little freedom for ourselves. But this is not enough to make us free. There is a lack of freedom around us: early death, mental illness, social deprivation, brutality, and war. We are also involved in history. Just as the forms of our personal constraints, temptations, and afflictions change as we develop from youth to middle and old age, so the consequences of morality and the misuse of freedom are forever changing for the whole of humanity. We cannot extricate ourselves from this history. We must suffer with it and be shaped by it. Three great troubles afflict our generation. All three bring the uncomfortable, inexplicable, and threatening sense that the evil outside us is mixing with the evil within us. We are both powerless before overwhelming forces and at the same time guilty of the irresponsible spread of these forces. Each of the three troubles expresses a lack of faith. Each is deadly: progress, war, and intoxication.

What does it mean to subdue the earth?

God has entrusted the earth to human beings. We are to be God's representatives among the other creatures, multiplying and "subduing the earth." This command was formulated in times when people had to struggle for a place on the earth against great dangers, against want and hunger. It was a promise to creatures who felt powerless before the impressive and violent forces of an unpredictable and inexplicable world. Great floods swept over the land. People marvelled when the waters subsided and the earth became green and blossomed again. The Bible gives us a new, trustworthy promise of God: "While the earth remains, seedtime and harvest, cold and heat, summer and winter, day and night, shall not cease" (Gen. 8:22).

It is not for ourselves that we assume lordship over the inanimate objects, plants, and animals of the earth, but by God's will. More clearly distinguished from the animals by the Bible than by the descriptions of modern science, we are privileged to bear the image of God in creation. This means we should and must deal with the world as God deals with us: in faithfulness and love; with responsibility; carefully and patiently. We must not think only of ourselves. Our task is not based on a so-called law of nature ("all power to the strong"), but rather on the law of love. Lordship in God's name must be accompanied by care for everything that is governed. That the earth has been given over into the care of human beings means that it remains the place where all those curious and wonderful creatures of God are nourished and live together with people to his honor and glory.

Do we need a second creation?

Until the middle of this century nature maintained its dignity against all human attempts to conquer it. The process of taking nature into our service has been a slow one, beset with many disappointments. Only in the past few generations have we humans felt safe outside our own dwellings. But overnight the picture has changed. It is now not so much that nature threatens the human race, but rather that human beings threaten *it*. The superficial aim of human lordship has been achieved. We no longer tend nature; we use it and use it up. We no longer pursue a vigorous hunt in order to live; we plunder fruit and animals. What is worse, God's creation no longer appears to us to be good enough. We dream of demolishing the first creation and building up a new one.

Naturally we could not build a totally new creation. We can only rearrange the elements. But this is no less a new creation. Every day we are confronted with new acts of creation, and they imitate the old creation. Materials are artificially created, we launch our own heavenly bodies, we create new plants, animals, and robots. We even create gifted new people, thanks to favorable genetic engineering. Human beings are scarcely still just one group among God's creatures, but are *the* group which threatens all that is not directly useful to it with extinction. We threaten the very nature of this planet. Species after species of God's creatures—who play before him, praising his greatness—are disappearing without a trace, never to return, as though the millions of years that went into making them were as nothing. It is not sentimental to imagine God weeping over the desolation of the earth. We pollute his beaches with our oil, and his forests, plants, and animals all fall victim, giving way to roads, chimneys, and desert.

Is the Christian faith responsible?

Science and technology have made possible enormous human growth. Now they try to squeeze an immeasurable amount of raw materials and energy out of the earth, to produce flour so fine and sterile that even a maggot can't eat it, and to press God's leviathan and behemoth, the last blue and sperm whales, into the oil mill. Some say this is all the fruit of Judeo-Christian thinking. It is the destruction of the natural balance, the inevitable consequence of God's damaging command to subdue the earth. For only a race which puts its trust in the Bible could acquire the independence which today presents us with this catastrophe.

How does faith respond?

Only a misunderstanding of God's command could be at the root of our present predicament. And if there is to be any deliverance at all, everything must be done to eliminate this misunderstanding. For what is happening everywhere today is the plunder of the earth's resources without thought for the future. The goal is merely to make life more comfortable now, and that goal is then called the task of humanity as ordained by God. This is not biblical thinking, but the attitude of the Enlightenment, which fatally dominates present-day science, technology, and planning.

The Enlightenment was opposed to biblical faith. Even if in the 18th century it spoke of God, it was not the God of Abraham, Isaac, and Jacob, and not the Father of Jesus Christ. It was rather the god that human understanding recognized as the highest form of reason, one who is acknowledged only in theory. Only in this way could the Enlightenment see humanity as unlimited and autonomous, placed in the center of all thinking and action. But the Bible sees human beings as empowered by God to fulfill a *limited* task in his name. With humility and praise we are to care for the works of God's creation on earth. Only in obedience to God do we remain his representatives and properly manage his creation. Our progress today destroys nature, because we still stand under the delusions of the Enlightenment, which exchanged nature for the mechanism of a clock! It may be that many Christians follow this error, but the Christian faith cannot be made responsible for that.

What if we are approaching the last days?

Many Christians think the catastrophe which threatens us is simply to be accepted, because the end of the world and of the human race is clearly enough foretold in the Bible. Many generations of Christians have lived with an awareness of the nearness of the last days. To know that our world is passing away can deepen our faith. It can give us confidence and spur us on to more faithful service in times of trouble. Martin Luther spoke of the "beloved last day" and suggested planting an apple tree the day before. He meant that God alone knows the hour, and that God will carry his world even through the final catastrophe. Just because things look hopeless is no reason for us to put our hands in our pockets. Rather, when the days of growing affliction come we should continue to act out of faith.

A growing number of scientists are saying we must radically change our way of thinking if we are to avert disaster for our grandchildren. The statistics speak unequivocally about our present population growth rates, the destruction of our air and water, the plundering of the earth's raw materials, and the growing poverty of two-thirds of the world's population. All these indicate that the human race no longer has any chance of survival. We will die out like the dinosaurs. The only question is how long it will take. Fifty years, or a hundred and fifty? No serious futurist gives us more than two hundred years.

God's commandment to us contains important elements for the change in thinking which is required. To "subdue the earth" means first that we should use our opportunities. Progress is necessary and desirable. When we are treated for illnesses in hospitals we can be thankful for these blessings. But we cannot and must not do everything. When we split the nucleus of an atom a halt is clearly demanded of us. We must respect the household of nature and therefore impose a drastic discipline upon ourselves. We must not artificially change human beings and prolong life at any price. We must break off our overall progress where it achieves lordship over our souls and drives us into pride. We must restrain our consumption and self-gratification, and learn once again to depend on the one who makes all things. This change will not be reached by appeals. Christians know that the law alone will not help. To become masters of our affliction and to help others overcome it we must rather come to a new understanding of our faith. God has offered us unity with his creation. He has made other creatures to be partners with us—not our enemies. He has commanded us not to treat our fellow human beings with indifference. He has forbidden us to kill. God will be faithful to us, and does not desire our destruction. The unity of his creatures on earth depends on their unity with him.

Where we have come

Today three great troubles threaten our faith. The most comprehensive is the imminent approach of a final catastrophe. Is this the result of fate, destiny, or guilt? A fatal chain of events has occurred. We have become caught up in a kind of progress which only serves ourselves. As a result, Christian thought has been fatally separated from Christian faith. We sinfully participate in this error because we profit from it, and we don't want to give up that profit. We assume that God has given creation over to us for our unbridled use, arbitrary alteration, and merciless plunder. We think God's plants and animals do not possess, as we do, a right to their own existence. We do not believe they have value in their own right. But they have an explicit and permanent value and right to existence, because God made them and loves them. We assume we can live as if there are no other people in the entire world, either now or in the future—as though we can have creation all for ourselves. But we must bear witness anew to the truth about God's creation in this atomic age, which began so confidently and now presents us with the probability of human extinction. I believe God's good hand is in all things, but I also know that only a different way of thinking and a different kind of behavior—renunciation, solidarity with creation, and love for it—can turn aside this approaching disaster.

5. War and Peace

Hasn't God forbidden war?

Human history has been accompanied by wars. We know of no age in which there has not been collective aggression. And yet just as war has been the grim reality, peace has always been the deepest human longing. If we have peace at home we call such times happy. There are many people living among us who bear the marks of war on their bodies. Every day in the newspapers we read of threats, invasions, resistance, commando operations, skirmishes, and war. In wartime soldiers are given the right, even the duty, to kill. Of course there are always "good reasons." But what reasons suffice when God has forbidden killing?

Can nuclear war still be called war?

War, which has been waged throughout history, has become especially threatening in our time. In our false sense of progress, thinking we must do everything that we are capable of doing, we have developed weapons which can destroy not only individual lives, or even many lives, but *all* life. Even as we strain the earth's resources for sustaining life, we stock our arsenals with the means for war on a scale never before seen. The destructive power hoarded in the United States is one million times that of the bomb dropped on Hiroshima. Only slightly smaller is the destructive power of the Soviet Union. Six other nations possess nuclear weapons, and many others are within reach of them. Almost half the scientists and technicians in the world work on weapons research and development. The military budgets of the developing countries double every six years. More than once the grim threat of a nuclear holocaust has seemed far too close. Plans for biological warfare are directed against all life, including vegetation. There are already bombs which can turn whole stretches of land into desert. Any potential change in the "balance of terror" creates alarm and anxiety. What does faith say to the lunacy of this situation?

What does the Bible say?

In this matter Christians should turn first to the Bible and then look at their own history. In the first few pages of the Bible we read that human life was inviolate in Israel. Blood was holy. From the beginning there was murder in the world, but murder would be punished. The Fifth Commandment reads clearly and without exception, "You shall not kill" (Exod. 20:13). Israel's history is admittedly one of wars, and Israel's God can be called "The Lord of hosts." Yahweh led the people of Israel into battle to protect them and to secure the land he had given them.

There is nothing in the Old Testament which contradicts this theme. Ancient Israel understood itself as God's people, even God's nation. It was God himself who triumphed, and secular and sacred actions were therefore identical. We need to realize that the notorious formula "an eye for an eye and a tooth for a tooth" was historically not a command for revenge but a limitation of it. The legal punishments of other ancient near eastern peoples were much more severe and arbitrary. We also read the message of peace from Israel's prophets, who announced the end of their nation's conquests. They called for surrender and faithful trust in God the deliverer, even in the face of the enemy. In Isaiah you can read a great vision of peace at the end of time (2:4) and find longing for a Savior who will be called prince of peace (9:6). Salvation itself is peace, and "*Shalom, shalom*" ("Peace, peace") has been the Hebrew greeting from earliest times. Israel needed a long time to be freed from the warlike characteristics of its age and environment. But eventually it happened.

Christian faith believes that Christ brings peace with God (Rom. 5:1) and peace on earth (Luke 2:14). He himself is our peace (Eph. 2:14), and he says, "Blessed are the peacemakers, for they shall be called sons of God" (Matt. 5:9). Jesus radically reinterpreted the ancient commandment against killing. Not only are we not to kill, but we are to support and defend life with all our strength! Even to utter a hard word without love to a fellow human being is to kill (Matt. 5:21-26, 38-48). In the Bible we find a sharp and inescapable condemnation of killing. And at the same time we find the promise that through a savior God will bring peace to all people.

Why is the church's history so disappointing?

It is disturbing that through most of its history the church of Christ has not furthered peace. A certain peace was realized among early communities of Christians, but Paul said the cause of peace is furthered by the state as it maintains order (Romans 13). The majority of Christians to this day grant the state the right to call citizens into military service. The Reformers wrestled with the issue and reality of war. They tempered Jesus' radical statement about peace by speaking of the state's "office of the sword" (Rom. 13:4). Luther maintained that a prince may engage in war, but only in self-defense for the protection of his subjects. He said Christian princes must examine whether a particular war is necessary and justified. War is never a God-given state. It belongs to our fallen human condition. In order to set limits to war, theologians later developed the doctrine of the "just war." Far too often the church has given its blessing to arms and to war both in principle and in actuality. The problem reoccurs century after century. It is important, however, to see that the Reformers' attitude came at the end of the medieval era, a time when everyone believed rulers represented God and held the fate of their subjects in their hands.

Is there such a thing as a "just war"?

In the last world war, many Christians again asked whether the doctrine of the "just war" was helpful. How can justice come from the methods of modern warfare? Who is an aggressor and who is a victim? Who is a soldier and who is a civilian? Are we still talking about "war" at all? Can full-scale conflict in our time have any other result than the total destruction of the opposing nations? We are again hearing the Bible's radical command against killing, from both traditionally pacifist churches and members of major denominations. Many Christians are increasingly dissatisfied with capital punishment for either criminals or enemies. We no longer concede sacredness to the state, but only expediency. War sometimes seems an expedient means of doing politics. But we must realize the consequences. Our world is filled to the brim with highly destructive weapons. The superpowers have now declared war "obsolete." But wise observers realize that "the next world war will be waged when it can be won" (C. F. von Wiezsäcker). Christians should therefore remind their governments that they cannot "win" a war. The only possible result is our extermination.

Accepting and refusing military service

Can Christians reconcile their commitment to peace with service to the state as soldiers? We can find no direct answer to this in the Bible. Ancient states did not have universal military service, and in the Middle Ages it was an assumed commitment that each man would fight for his lord. Today one's motives for serving the state as

a soldier or refusing military service must be more deeply grounded. Christians must face this question with deadly earnest. We cannot sit on the fence. Neither can we think only of our own personal
comforts. We must also consider the societies in which we live. We
may choose to suffer the consequences if an aggressor attacks our
land and we do not defend it. But to most people, and to the leaders
we depend on to protect us, the question looks quite different. Politicians carry responsibility for preserving their nation's freedom and
protecting the lives of its citizens. Many see no other alternative for
the preservation of world peace than the alarming balance of terror.
Our consciences may lead us in the opposite direction—we may say
such views conflict with the Bible's clear commands. But aren't the
consequences of unilateral disarmament as terrible as those of outright nuclear war? The truth is that only a real conversion to peace
on the part of all people can protect us from catastrophe. As we
work and pray for such a conversion, we must make a decision. We
can be responsible Christians whether we accept or refuse military
service. But we must know exactly what we are doing and why.

Where we have come

The second great trouble for faith is war. God does not desire
war. He nourishes his creation. The Old Testament shows how
Israel gradually moved beyond contemporary categories of national
pride, revenge, and retribution. It was led, step by step, to a longing for universal peace. The New Testament forbids the harming
of strangers, all hatred, all offense, and every hostile thought. The
Christ who brought peace with his life is the one who commands
this. The earliest Christians lived in an empire which knew war
only on its far-flung borders. War and rumors of war were for them
the terrible signs of the final catastrophe that God would visit on a
lost humanity. The medieval views of war seem strange to us. Today
we must place the commands of Jesus before us and seek advice in
our present situation. Nuclear war appears to be avoidable. But at
what price? Only through a continual balance of terror. Should we
participate in this dangerous game by performing military service,
or should we refuse? The Bible does not make our decision for us.
We must decide for ourselves. But Christ does not leave us alone
in this decision. •After we have seriously thought through the mat-

ter, examined our motives, and chosen our path, he goes with us. Our decision may be the wrong one. We must risk that, because we cannot know all things or predict the future. But we can share even our anxiety with God. Jesus said, "Lo, I am with you always, to the close of the age" (Matt. 28:20).

6. Intoxication and Despair

Who knows the cost?

Alcoholism begins as a very amiable, private pleasure. But in the end so many people are destroyed, and we are at our wits' end as to how we can help them. Are drunken people "happy"? They aren't satisfied with what they see and experience. They long for something different. There is something in their search which shows that we humans have been made for eternity. We want to reach out of ourselves. We are attracted to almost any means of escaping the present. Drug addiction has become one of the greatest and most dangerous adventures of this century. Young people have observed their parents: in the last decade the number of alcoholics has greatly multiplied. And despite all the evidence and warnings about the dangers of smoking, the consumption of tobacco has not significantly decreased. The grim figures of drug addiction in our day must be taken very seriously. We need to study the causes and consequences of drug abuse.

Is the use of drugs an expression of sin?

Every state of intoxication poisons the body and restricts the brain. But our bodies and brains, with their wonderful gifts and possibilities, were not created for such abuse. The pleasures and delights of a "high" are as brief as the work of an LSD tablet. The only difference between drugs and alcohol is that drugs can get you there faster. What remains behind is a person poorer than before. We may think this is a cheap price to pay for a ticket to the beyond. But we remain in the world. In every photograph we encounter the self that we want to avoid. This kind of adventure separates us from ourselves, and in seeking that separation we flee from God. When we run away from ourselves and from God, we sin.

Why do drugs tempt us?

Perhaps I do not take drugs, do not drink, and am not a chain smoker. But I sense the lurking danger that I might become addicted. Today there are special reasons for temptation. Our society's false sense of progress, the constant threat of war, our many unanswered questions, our search for meaning in our daily work— suddenly all these cry out for us to give up. Young people in particular are challenged by such self-doubt. Intoxication is a modern form of despair. Addicts are lonely. They despair of a sense of community and social order. They give up. Despair of this kind is widespread today. Alcoholics are looking for freedom, but drinking produces only the worst kind of slavery. The poison can take hold very quickly, and it can take years to get free of it again. The number of those who are rehabilitated is terribly small. What do we gain by drunkenness? We solve none of our problems and are relieved of none of our miserable dependence. We only find a much worse dependence. Even those who are rehabilitated usually retain the marks of drinking on their bodies and minds for the rest of their lives.

What do drugs have to do with religion?

There are very ancient links between drugs and religion. Many tribal religions have drunkenness as their aim. The use of drugs among young people today is very often a substitute for deep religious experience. Drugs are offered as a kind of religion for people who suffer from the coldness and rationality of our age, from the irritations, emptiness, and singleness of purpose of our technical way of life. Drugs fill a religious gap. There is no reason to defend the world that drug users are running from. But in our culture a person can only be destroyed by drug addiction. By using mescaline or hashish we can go beyond ourselves in a fantasy of colors. But if anything close to a real religious experience comes, it soon disappears again. Modern drug addiction is religious in nature. But in this religion a person must be self-redeemed. No god is to be found—only our own longing.

Intoxication or inspiration?

Alcohol, drugs, and nicotine are not the only deadly addictions of our time. We are troubled that we have such low resistance to the various temptations to addiction. It seems to be the same with bodily illness. When medical science has rooted out one problem, another raises its even more terrible head. Is this simply part of being human? Are we condemned to hand ourselves over to the idols of our own longing? Why is it that when we become used to an evil, we cannot leave it behind even when it is destroying us? We press forward with "progress" even when it brings disaster. We pile up our bombs even as they fill us with terror.

After Jesus' humiliating death, his disciples were left comfortless, weak, and empty. But on the Day of Pentecost "they were all filled with the Holy Spirit" (Acts 2:4). Suddenly they were empowered to transcend their own weaknesses and proclaim the gospel to the crowd in many different languages. Some of the onlookers assumed they were intoxicated: " 'They are filled with new wine' " (Acts 2:13). They were indeed inspired, but not drunk. The apostle Paul was himself acquainted with ecstatic experiences. Once he was "caught up into Paradise" (2 Cor. 12:1-4). But when he returned he found the holy soberness to proclaim his faith and to live it. He had not brought back drunken fantasies. He did not experience simply his own elation, but rather the very voice of God in Jesus Christ. That is the inspiration which contradicts all unspiritual intoxication.

How can we help?

Every addiction is a search for something better. It is helpful to stand by addicted persons in their difficulties, showing them that despite everything there is much good in this world which God has made. We need to offer loving, constructive opposition to their habits—not condemnation. Those who seek alcohol or drugs are suffering from a deficiency. We cannot talk them out of what they are doing. They need our love, in which they can see that life is meaningful for us and awakens thankfulness. Alcoholics who flee from the coldness of our time challenge Christians to show their faith. We should pray that our faith will be less ascetic than sober, less frivolous than joyful, less rash than lively. We must respect the work of doctors, psychologists, and social workers. But troubled persons also need the love of those who have a living faith.

Where we have come

The third great trouble for faith in our day is drugs, which can enslave us. God does not want us to become dependent on habits that do not serve life but rather destroy it. We cannot find freedom in easily-acquired drink and intoxication, but only when we are bound together with God. We are troubled that it is so difficult for us to reconcile the Spirit of God and our own spirits. The growing number of those addicted to alcohol, drugs, and nicotine shocks us. We ask ourselves what our continuing responsibilities as Christians are for these people. They steer themselves away from a shattered world to an imagined wholeness. With our feeble strength we should work so that this world of ours remains whole. Only then will there be no need to flee from it into madness. The advice of Christian faith is, "Be sober, set your hope fully upon the grace that is coming to you" (1 Peter 1:13).

Summary

I experience

God has made me like other creatures, accompanies me through my life, and keeps me in his love. All the questions which I have and the open question that I am are renewed and sharpened.

At the center of all my questions is the question of good and evil. It pierces remorsefully into me. What is good? What is evil? What happens to me? Was what I did right or wrong?

Every day teaches me afresh that I am not good, that people are not good, even though we want to be. But we are not able. Even with the best of intentions and efforts we can never be. Only complete goodness is really satisfying. I feel guilty, and it troubles me.

I betray God's good creation in my dealings with people, with animals, and with things.

I do not understand the way in which the world operates. Illnesses, accidents, storms, epidemics, deprivation, and catastrophes break in upon us. Their menace and the ultimate threat of death remind me every day of my limitations and the limitations of God's good creation.

I question

Why must I become guilty?
How much freedom do I have to do what is right?
How did sin and evil come into God's creation?
Has God deserted his creation?
What are the great troubles of our time?
How does our dealing with troubles reveal our human identity?

I believe

God has given me knowledge of good and evil. He wants me to be free to do what is right. He accepts the risk that I may fail.

That which people call *guilt* is often the result of sin against God. Because I know God, I cannot separate myself from God's goodness. Nonetheless, I do. I want to be my own God, to win my own salvation, to build my future without him. That is my sin. Betrayal, guilt, and failure are its consequences. Christians often see evil more clearly than those who do not know Christ. For society values the norms which make it possible to live together, while God looks into our hearts.

I experience a power within me which provokes me to evil. And yet this power is neither me nor something that I will. Many generations have called this power "the devil" because it feels like a person struggling within our inner selves. In the face of the anonymous evil which shatters the earth and brings undeserved and meaningless suffering, I receive the same answer as Job: God is hidden in these inexplicable things. He does not reveal the reason why he does them. We need to be humble and repent. This is not the sort of answer that I can give to others. I must accept it for myself in faith.

In the three main troubles of our time I see fate and guilt inextricably interwoven. Our scientific and technical advances have brought us many blessings, but they are also proving fatal to us. The peace which nations seek evades us. And many people suffer from addiction because they lack both love and meaning in their lives.

I believe God has made his creation good. I believe he calls me to freedom. I believe he will lead his creation to fulfillment and assure all creatures freedom and joy. But I see that our sin is mixed in with all that we do and experience. God's work has been corrupted. We cannot help it. We cannot rescue ourselves. We must rely on God.

4

WHO RESCUES US

**God Acts
Through Christ:**

Salvation

1. How Do We Speak of Jesus?

Do we need Jesus?

So far we have discussed questions of life and the difficulties of conscience. We have spoken of God, who is the life of our lives. God speaks to us if we will only listen, cares for us if we could only see it, and accompanies us just as he accompanied the people of Israel and all believers through the centuries. In short, we have spoken of the God whom we call *Creator*. Christians believe themselves to be God's children, creatures who have come from God and go to God, together with the whole creation. But we have also spoken of Jesus. The New Testament and the church call this person "the Christ." The Greek word *Christ* literally means "the anointed one." The Hebrew word *Messiah* means the same thing. By this title Jesus is proclaimed a king, for in the ancient world kings were dedicated to their offices by being anointed with oil. Believers take the title *Christ* to mean that Jesus is the King who rescues all people. He is the King of our lives. Christians are named after this King, for they come to God through Christ. This is actually far too weak a way of expressing it. Christians do not first believe in God and then in Christ. Christ is not an addition to all that Christians believe about God. Rather we know God first through Christ and therefore can speak of God only as we learn of him through Christ. In this sense Jesus Christ has been present in everything we have said about God so far, even though we have not used his name very much. Without Christ we know nothing about the Christian faith.

Who was Jesus?

No figure in world history has caused so many problems for so many people as the Jew Jesus. Only a very few people have still heard nothing of him, and all who know something of him have some kind of positive or negative attitude toward him. A person with such pervasive influence can be truly said to be alive today. But if we ask who Jesus *is*, we must first of all ask who he *was*.

Jesus was a Jew who grew up in the first century of our era. He was the son of a carpenter in Nazareth, which was a small town in the Roman province of Galilee. Educated at home within a strong Jewish tradition, he went about proclaiming that the kingdom of God was at hand. When he was a little over 30 years old he was arrested, tried, and executed by the Roman authorities.

Although the basic historical facts about Jesus are few, nations now date their years and centuries from his birth. Jesus' friends were small artisans and fishermen, but we name our children after them. Jesus himself did not write a single word for posterity, but the libraries of the world are full of books about him, and new titles appear every year. Many people either cannot or will not understand him. But neither the hostile nor the indifferent deny his personal influence. Even Jesus' enemies always come away from him with something.

There is a mystery about Jesus, and he himself did little to dispel it. Sometimes people repeat the charge of a century ago that Jesus in fact never lived, but was invented by the disciples. If this is true, then the disciples invented a person who will not let people go. But no serious scholar today maintains that Jesus never lived. After generations of intensive study and discussion it is generally agreed that the writers of the Gospels adapted and retold earlier stories about Jesus. They did this in order to present the meaning of his life and death for their own communities. The Gospels reveal the faith of the first followers of Jesus as they confessed it before the world. But the substance of that faith was not their own invention. Jesus himself, the historical person, awakened that faith. And he remains tangible in a way scarcely any other person in history is.

Most of the books of the Old Testament also recount in story form people's experiences with God. In their lives and in the history of their nation the people of Israel perceived God's activity and word. When we compared scientific investigations of the world's origins with the biblical stories of creation we saw that both have their own particular tasks and purposes. Whether the biblical message of creation—that the world comes from God and is good—is true or false can only be decided by faith. This question is foreign to science. In the same way, a researcher who wants merely to establish historical facts about Jesus does not become concerned about whether God was speaking through him or whether he was deceiving himself.

The question of who Jesus was as a human being does not yet deal with the meaning of his life and death for us. Many people admit that Jesus was a person of high moral stature. Some even say that only one such person has appeared in human history. A few go so far as to say they would like to love their contemporaries as Jesus did. None of these people can deny the basic facts about who Jesus was. Neither can they disprove what Christians believe about this Jew: that he has brought salvation and given new life to the entire world.

Why are there differences in the sources?

We read about Jesus of Nazareth in the Gospels. Together with the so-called Epistles (letters attributed to the first Christian apostles, or teachers) they constitute the New Testament. The term *gospel* means "good news." The simple fact that this news is communicated through four different books shows that it is not like a news release from an information office. In the New Testament, events are not reported from a supposedly "objective" viewpoint. They are rather retold by people who are personally involved in them. Each story is told with specific purposes in mind. Matthew, Mark, Luke, and John tell of Jesus of Nazareth in quite different ways. The gospel of John, with its highly explanatory style, stands out particularly from the other three. If we are disturbed that the four Gospels are so different from each other, we need to remind ourselves of Luke's introduction (Luke 1:1-4). Each evangelist set out to compile an orderly account of the events that had taken place. In doing this they collected and reshaped familiar stories about Jesus. Each writer was familiar with different traditions and came from a different congregation of the widely-scattered early Christian church. The diversity between their accounts tells us that the identity of Jesus cannot be explained in a mathematical fashion. Jesus rather becomes real as he is accepted or rejected by living people.

How do the Gospels describe Jesus?

The Gospels show how Jesus was by stories and accounts of what he said and did. The stories are short, and what Jesus says is straight to the point. Nowhere do we find what Jesus looked like, what kind of a body he had, what his voice sounded like, or how he dressed. Quite different things are recounted than in a modern novel. What went on inside Jesus is seldom revealed to us. The Gospels do not look back to a personality of the past, but forward to the risen Lord. It is in the light of Jesus' resurrection that they tell of his childhood, miracles, healings, and also his suffering.

It is clear that each of the four evangelists took Jesus' suffering and death as their starting point. These events formed the core of early Christian proclamation, and the evangelists reserve the most space for them. The one who loved all people was persecuted and betrayed, accused and condemned, derided and crucified. All this took place in Jerusalem, the city of God which he loved. All of the Gospels can be called extended accounts of Jesus' suffering. They were thus written from a particular point of view.

The evangelists portray Jesus in the light of the Old Testament history of Israel. God announced his salvation for all people when he concluded an eternal covenant with his people. He brought them out of Egypt, giving them his law and a land of rest. Israel's prophets proclaimed the coming "day of the Lord," when the Messiah would come and the people who had fallen away from God would be reunited by that servant's love and suffering. The Gospels maintain that the very thing which God promised by his prophets, from Moses on down, had come to pass in Jesus. God now showed his love for all people by fulfilling the law and establishing a new and everlasting covenant. A new people came into being through Jesus. This is how the Gospels describe him.

How does Jesus live on?

It is not only the first eyewitnesses and evangelists who tell us about Jesus. There is also the so-called Acts of the Apostles, which was probably written by the author of the gospel of Luke. The book of Acts describes how the church of Jesus passed beyond the bounds of Jerusalem, focusing especially on the experiences of two of the apostles, Simon Peter and Saul of Tarsus. Acts traces their missionary journeys to Asia Minor and Greece, the founding and life of the new churches, and the persecution of the apostles. In Acts we are told how Jesus continued to work in the church after his death. We learn still more of Jesus' continued activity in the 21 letters of the New Testament, which were written to the various Christian churches by the apostles and their disciples. The final (and probably one of the latest-composed) books of the New Testament is the Revelation to John, which gives a quite different witness to Jesus as the coming Lord.

Biblical scholars have carefully investigated all the books of the New Testament, attempting to discover their interrelationships, underlying influences, dates and places of origin, and original intentions. This work is very important for understanding these books. Many Christians have been disturbed by such detailed analysis of the Bible. But faith knows that Jesus lives on in his church. He did not cease to instruct his people when he died. Jesus lives in their midst and teaches them. We can see this already in the New Testament, the greater part of which is given to the early Christians' experiences of Christ living in their midst. It is therefore not true that we know all there is to know about Jesus when we have read the accounts of his life. We can understand Jesus as Savior only if we include the history of those who have believed in him.

Does Christ come to us apart from Christians?

That which people openly declare to be true is called their *witness*. In the New Testament we find the witness of those who were the first to know Jesus. But they did not bear witness to a dead figure from the past. They were related to Jesus rather as to one who continued to live in their midst. The same Jesus who was dead now worked among them. Every generation of Christians has borne witness to Jesus in much the same way. Jesus is alive and new each day for us, and yet he always remains the same.

Therefore that which Christians confess today rests on what past Christians have confessed. In my present time and circumstances I must seek to find my way as a Christian. I must take the trouble to think through my faith and formulate it anew. But I will only be successful in this if I learn and test what has already been said by others. I may have to set aside that which is irrelevant to me. In the church's traditions I will find answers to many questions which I have never asked. Different questions may trouble me now. Because Jesus is alive and present every day, we are able to see that not every tradition is helpful in every time. But if we discard a tradition, we need to know why we are doing it.

The Christian faith maintains that the test of all further confessions of Christ is "the witness of the first witnesses." After several generations of Christians had died, the church began to agree on certain early Christian writings as authoritative. These contained the witness and confession of some of the apostles and early disciples, and they were eventually collected together to form our New Testament. Whatever we experience of Jesus and whatever we confess about him must be tested by what is said in these writings. This does not mean that the witness of Christ ceased long ago. Throughout its history the church has developed new confessions of Christ out of its continuing life with him. The reason Christians examine the New Testament so carefully is not so much because they want to discover who Jesus was, but because they want to understand and explain who he is today. A few of the ancient Christian texts found in the New Testament have been printed at the end of this book. They are priceless treasures, because as we read and interpret them Jesus comes to us. He is new every day, and yet makes himself known through past tradition. We are only Christians in company with those who have lived before us.

Where we have come

Our access to God is through Jesus of Nazareth, the Christ of faith, the Savior of the world. Access to Jesus is through the witness of his disciples. The Gospels do not give us a historian's report about him, but rather recast various traditions of the early church. Nonetheless, through the New Testament and the work of his Spirit throughout the centuries, the person of Jesus is more easily comprehended than anyone else in history. There is no such thing as a purely historical Jesus. We must find him in the confessions of the church. We cannot get behind these to a so-called Jesus of history. We cannot describe him historically in more than probable terms. His life is his reality. The confession of Christ, the Savior, must therefore always be formulated anew in the church. It must constantly be related again to contemporary questions, without losing the connection with past Christian tradition. But it is the canonical writings of the New Testament, as the confessions of the earliest Christian witnesses, that remain the basis for all the church's later confessions. If we ignore the revelation of the New Testament or disagree with it, we will find no other access to Jesus. We must test what Christ says to us in our hearts against what the first disciples experienced of him. It is for that reason that Christians turn again and again to the Bible.

2. Four Stories About Jesus

Why was Jesus baptized?

We will listen to four stories about Jesus. Here is the first:

In those days Jesus came from Nazareth of Galilee and was baptized by John in the Jordan. And when he came up out of the water, immediately he saw the heavens opened and the Spirit descending upon him like a dove; and a voice came from heaven, "Thou art my beloved Son; with thee I am well pleased." The Spirit immediately drove him out into the wilderness (Mark 1:9-12).

What does it mean that Jesus was baptized by John? John the Baptist belonged to the long line of Israel's prophets. All of them had declared that God would come and establish his kingdom in Israel. God would reveal himself so that everyone could see and know him. He would establish righteousness and bring gracious blessing: " 'I will give them one heart, and put a new spirit within them; I will take the stony heart out of their flesh and give them a heart of flesh, that they may walk in my statutes and keep my ordinances and obey them; and they shall be my people, and I will be their God' " (Ezek. 11:19-20). Our story says that this future has now arrived. On the day Jesus was baptized by John the heavens opened and the Spirit of God came down and was poured out on him. The voice from heaven called Jesus God's Son. What does that mean? In the language of the Bible, it means the following:

1. Jesus is as closely related to God as one can possibly be.

2. Jesus entered into God's relationship with the people of Israel, for God chose that people to be his child, his inheritance, and his possession.

3. In Jesus, the intended relationship between God and human beings would be restored. This relationship is destroyed by our

turning away from God and our alienation from ourselves. Jesus restores it again. He stands therefore as the renewer of what God wants us to be, in opposition to who we have made ourselves to be. In Jesus, God fulfills and renews human beings. Jesus is God's new human being.

What did Jesus teach?

We listen to the second story:

And Jesus returned in the power of the Spirit into Galilee, and a report concerning him went out through all the surrounding country. And he taught in their synagogues, being glorified by all. And he came to Nazareth, where he had been brought up; and he went to the synagogue, as his custom was, on the sabbath day. And he stood up to read; and there was given to him the book of the prophet Isaiah. He opened the book and found the place where it was written, "The Spirit of the Lord is upon me, because he has anointed me to preach good news to the poor. He has sent me to proclaim release to the captives and recovering of sight to the blind, to set at liberty those who are oppressed, to proclaim the acceptable year of the Lord." And he closed the book, and gave it back to the attendant, and sat down; and the eyes of all in the synagogue were fixed on him. And he began to say to them, "Today this scripture has been fulfilled in your hearing" (Luke 4:14-21).

Jesus stood before his people as a Jewish teacher of the Scriptures, as a rabbi. He told them what God wills and provides. The "acceptable year of the Lord" was in Israel an ancient symbol for the lordship of God among all people—a symbol for the kingdom of God. Jesus appeared before them as a teacher and preacher with a tremendous claim. God had empowered him to announce the coming of his eternal kingdom. For centuries Israel had longed for God's kingdom. The prophets had said it would appear in the future, at the end, on the last day. Jesus announced that it had arrived. Even more audacious was his claim that *he himself* was the content of this message. In him God had come to human beings. God had established justice and grace through Jesus, the Anointed One of God, the Christ.

How did Jesus teach?

Jesus spoke in the manner of his time and people. He did not lecture like a professor. He did not seek reasons and proofs. He spoke rather as to children in short, clear sentences, in sayings, stories, and parables. But he also spoke to mature people who have nothing more to lose, who are making a desperate stand, who will not be satisfied with words that do not help them. He spoke inexorably, with authority. His words were gentle, but demanded a decision. They painted brilliant pictures which his hearers could never forget, but they also pierced into the very depths. Our hearts still shudder before them. Jesus taught the old law which Israel had preserved for centuries: "Hear, O Israel: The Lord our God, the Lord is one; and you shall love the Lord your God with all your heart, and with all your soul, and with all your mind, and with all your strength. . . . You shall love your neighbor as yourself" (Mark 12:29-31). But he taught with such authority that devout and idealistic persons went away shamed. And so in Jesus the old became new. When spoken by him, the voice which all had known from books became the very voice of God. Divisions between God and the human race, between religion and the world, disappeared. Jesus was the Teacher who knew no alienation. Because he was totally oriented toward God, he could be totally present for his fellow human beings. In him all things find their unity.

How did Jesus act?

We listen to the third story:

And behold, they brought to him a paralytic, lying on his bed; and when Jesus saw their faith he said to the paralytic, "Take heart, my son; your sins are forgiven." And behold, some of the scribes said to themselves, "This man is blaspheming." But Jesus, knowing their thoughts, said, "Why do you think evil in your hearts? For which is easier to say, 'Your sins are forgiven,' or to say, 'Rise and walk'? But that you may know that the Son of man has authority on earth to forgive sins"—he then said to the paralytic—"Rise, take up your bed and go home." And he rose and went home. When the crowds saw it, they were afraid, and they glorified God, who had given such authority to men (Matt. 9:2-8).

Words and actions are one with Jesus. The Gospels often tell us that he stooped down to help the poor in body and soul. Children, men, women, the sick, the guilty, sinners, and outcasts were all drawn to him. The friends of Jesus were those who needed him. God enabled Jesus to help and heal others. That is why he could perform great signs and wonders. Most of these were extraordinary healings. They were signs of the kingdom of God. God's kingdom begins in the heart. Therefore the heart must change. Past sins must be forgiven in order that the new may arise, the new in which plague and disease, human wrong and the world's evil will have no place. It is to this new life that Jesus called his disciples, by the power of God's forgiving love. We, too, are called to him, called into the new people of God, the new covenant which God has concluded in Jesus. When Jesus said to sick persons, "Your sins are forgiven," not only devout Jews were offended. Every Jew knew that only God can forgive sins. Jesus was acting like God, doing God's works in God's place. He was the very human "Son of man," a title coming out of Old Testament tradition and meaning the same thing as Savior, Messiah, or Christ. The Savior had come.

What end did Jesus suffer?

We listen to the fourth story:

That very day two of them were going to a village named Emmaus, about seven miles from Jerusalem, and talking with each other about all these things that had happened. While they were talking and discussing together, Jesus himself drew near and went with them. But their eyes were kept from recognizing him. And he said to them, "What is this conversation which you are holding with each other as you walk?" And they stood still, looking sad. Then one of them, named Cleopas, answered him, "Are you the only visitor to Jerusalem who does not know the things that have happened there in these days?" And he said to them, "What things?" And they said to him, "Concerning Jesus of Nazareth, who was a prophet mighty in deed and word before God and all the people, and how our chief priests and rulers delivered him up to be condemned to death, and crucified him. But we had hoped that he was the one to redeem Israel. Yes, and besides all this, it is now the third day since this happened. Moreover, some women of our company amazed us. They were at the tomb early in the morning and did not find his body; and they came back saying that they had even seen a vision of angels, who said that he was alive. Some of those who were with us went to the tomb, and found it just as the women had said; but him they did not see." And he said to them, "O foolish men, and slow of heart to believe all that the prophets have spoken! Was it not necessary that the Christ should suffer these things and enter into his glory?" And beginning with Moses and all the prophets, he interpreted to them in all the scriptures the things concerning himself.

So they drew near to the village to which they were going. He appeared to be going further, but they constrained him, saying, "Stay with us, for it is toward evening and the day is now far spent." So he went in to stay with them. When he was at table with them, he took the bread and blessed, and broke it, and gave it to them. And their eyes were opened and they recognized him; and he vanished out of their sight. They said to each other, "Did not our hearts burn within us while he talked to us on the road, while he opened to us the scriptures?" And they rose that same hour and returned to Jerusalem; and they found the eleven gathered together and those who were with them, who said, "The Lord has risen indeed, and has appeared to Simon!" Then they told what had happened on the road, and how he was known to them in the breaking of the bread (Luke 24:13-35).

The life and mission of Jesus of Nazareth led to this end and this beginning. However much the reports of the four Gospels differ from one another, they are at one in this, which was the heart of the earliest Christian proclamation: Jesus, the one who exhibited only goodness in dealing with people, had to suffer. He knew that this suffering would lead to his death. It was necessary that he suffer—innocent and powerless, defenseless and yet like a king, full of sorrows and yet a victor, shamefully persecuted, accused, and forsaken. He also had to be forsaken by God, as we learn from his cry from the cross, "My God, my God, why hast thou forsaken me?" (Matt. 27:46; see Ps. 22:1). But the godforsaken Savior would be rescued from the grave by God. That is the other side of the message. The Crucified One was raised so that he might remain with his own and break the bread of friendship with them. He would remain with them until the close of the age. All that is what the Christian faith says to the question, "Who is Jesus?"

Why four different ways?

In four ways, similar and yet quite different, the Gospels tell us of Jesus. Mark, the shortest of them all, appears in important ways to have been the oldest of the Gospels to have been circulated. It tells of Jesus as the hidden Messiah. Matthew portrays Jesus as coming from among the poor of Israel and bringing his people peace and goodness. And yet he is also portrayed as taking the office of King and Judge of the world. Luke, doubtless written somewhat later, portrays Jesus as the Savior of all peoples. The gospel of John gives us the fewest details about the life of Jesus, but does not lose sight of it. Here Jesus is described as the cosmic Redeemer who reveals the Father in heaven to us. He is the Word of God become flesh, the eternal Lord who brings the mysteries of God to the people. He hides his own worth and majesty and knowingly proceeds toward the powerlessness of his death on Golgotha. These differences show us the richness of Jesus' work. The Gospels are not to be read like biographical novels or chronicles. They don't try to be like that. And that is not what faith needs. Faith is not knowledge of facts or a collection of data for scientists to argue about. Faith does not depend on whether Jesus' life and history can be recounted without contradictions. Faith rather grows out of an encounter with Jesus himself, out of acceptance of his word and nature, love and suffering, death and resurrection. Faith grows out of the reality of Jesus in his life and acts. We believe when we confess Jesus as our Lord and Brother, whose actions and sufferings were for *us*.

Where we have come

God speaks to us through Jesus. The four Gospels, in quite different ways, inform us about what and how Jesus taught in relation to his people, and how he acted and suffered. In his preaching he announced a totally new relationship between God and all people. In this way God established a new situation. Peace was inaugurated, reconciliation dawned, human sin was forgiven, and sinners found God's grace through faith and conversion. Thus Jesus spoke and acted as the Christ, in the name of God—as God—and in him action and speech were one. He is the Word of God. He taught the will of God among people with great authority and power. Through wonderful acts he announced the beginning of the kingdom of God, the rule of the one he called Father. In these acts he appeared before all as a physician and Lord over all disease, as a person for others, as a victor over demons and powers, as God's representative in the struggle against sin. His work offended many. He was thrust out of society, betrayed, accused, and condemned to death. But even on the cross he remained God's suffering servant, the Son of the Father empowered by God to bear witness to his love among people. In spite of the shadow that fell over their lives at Jesus' death, his followers testified that the crucified one was alive. He made himself known to his disciples and sent them into the world. That is the gospel of Jesus of Nazareth. No figure in the ancient world comes to us with such certainty and detail as Jesus. Yet the New Testament does not give us a historical record. It gives us only what Jesus' disciples experienced.

3. Confession of Faith

How is the living Christ related to the church's confession?

In the New Testament we can trace growth and development of Christian confession. The consideration of who Jesus was began with experiences of faith and radical change, and then developed into confessions of Jesus and teachings about him. Different encounters with the living Christ raised different questions in the various Christian communities. Different churches in widely separated parts of the Roman Empire had different origins and different cultural backgrounds. Out of this variety came a search for a confession of Christ which could be valid for all. The writings of the New Testament reflect great variety. But together they also bear witness to the one and only Jesus Christ. For however different the churches of Jerusalem and Corinth, Ephesus and Rome might have been, both the pagan and Jewish worlds of the first century heard the same message of the redemptive death and resurrection of Jesus.

All that we know about Jesus comes from those who followed him. They were engaged in a revolution beside which all political revolutions are child's play. Jesus declared that humanity must turn from its path and change, that everything must relate together in a new way—for God was coming, and was in fact already close at hand. The first Christians asserted that Christ was wonderfully active among them in word and deed, that he worked in their midst and ordered their lives in love. The Christian confessions of faith were the confessions of this revolution and of the one who brought it about. Christians called their confessions *doxa*, which means "praise" or "glory." A great danger the church faces today is to simply repeat these confessions of faith apart from an understanding of Christ's living presence among the early Christians. When the church today confesses its faith in Christ's resurrection, some say, "I cannot possibly believe in the resurrection." Others say, "I do believe in the resurrection." But simply repeating the Christian confessions will not persuade anyone. For one thing, modern science can neither prove nor disprove the statement that Christ rose from the dead. For another, the early Christians did not come to develop their confessions out of detached investigation, but rather as they reflected on the meaning of their experiences of the living Christ. If people today are able to confess with the church that Christ rose from the dead, it is not because of science or because a man named Jesus founded a "sect" long ago, but because Christ is alive and active among human beings today.

What does the Christian faith confess?

What the Christian faith has confessed through the centuries has been authenticated in the lives of Christians. And that which is authenticated for Christians is what they have borne witness to. They were able to stake their lives on it when they were persecuted, and to risk their love for others. And their witness has been primarily that Jesus is risen from the dead. It is mainly out of this faith that the first community of the disciples sprang, whom Jesus had left behind after his death on the cross. If we do not share with them the experience of Jesus as alive in our lives, it profits nothing, for we cannot understand. The presupposition of every other statement which we read in the New Testament has always been the fact that Jesus is risen from the dead. He is with us.

If we do not have this key to the whole story, then we see only words and details. But it is the risen Lord himself who has made possible the church's confession of him in word, symbol, and action. Believers seek to discover the mystery of Jesus and to communicate it. In every church confession of Christ three great questions recur: Who is he? How did he come into the world? What is the meaning of his suffering and death on the cross? These three questions need to be answered from the standpoint of the church's basic confession, "Jesus is risen from the dead."

Why is Jesus called Lord?

One of the oldest Christian confessions is *"Maranatha"* (1 Cor. 16:22). It comes from the Syrian church and was used in Palestine, probably as a prayer in worship. It means, "Our Lord comes!" or "Come, Lord!" Christians confessed both that Jesus was present and that he would come. He came and would come as one like God, yes, as one who *is* God, the Lord of lords. "Lord" was the title in Judaism which was used for God, the Creator and Judge. Both "lord" and "god" were titles borne by the master of the Roman world, Caesar. Whoever named Jesus as his Lord confessed that in him God dwelled and acted—that Jesus brought God's lordship over the world. No power or authority, not even those under which I suffer, are able to remove Christ's lordship from me. This was Paul's message when he quoted an old Christian hymn to the Philippians:

Therefore God has highly exalted him and bestowed on him the name which is above every name, that at the name of Jesus every knee should bow, in heaven and on earth and under the earth, and every tongue confess that Jesus Christ is Lord, to the glory of God the Father (2:9-11).

The early church also called Jesus the Son of God. In the ancient Near East the sons of God were earthly rulers. The Egyptians believed their Pharaoh was a bodily descendant of God. The Hebrews gave this name to their kings, but in a metaphorical sense. They were God's sons because God had chosen them to be representatives and spokesmen for the whole people. The sonship of Jesus also refers to his choice by God, but at the same time to the fact that he lived in complete trust and unity with God. In the man Jesus, who is our Lord and the Lord of all the world, we see God. In his unending love, in his obedience and faithfulness, in his suffering and sacrifice, we recognize the face of God, as one can recognize a father in the face of his son. And at the same time we see the face of humanity as God wills it to be. Thus for Christians Christ is the Mediator between God and human beings.

Why do we celebrate Christmas?

Christians asked quite early how this Lord and Mediator became Son of God and Savior. By the time our Gospels were compiled, stories about the childhood of Jesus were being circulated. Matthew and Luke offer examples of these stories. They are attempts to make the mystery of Jesus—the one in whom God and human beings meet —comprehensible in terms meaningful to that time. How did Jesus— the Messiah, King, Lord, and Son of the Highest—come into the world? Both Matthew and Luke see Jesus as the fulfillment of a centuries-old promise. According to Matthew, Jesus was also a descendant of David (though the fascinating genealogy in the first chapter is historically dubious). For both Matthew and Luke, Jesus was born of Mary by the Holy Spirit. According to Luke, that was a miraculous event—a miracle of God—more wonderful than the birth of Isaac, Samuel, Samson, and John the Baptist. The Apostles' Creed formulates it as "conceived by the power of the Holy Spirit and born of the virgin Mary." From that standpoint, even though we hear little of Mary later in Luke's gospel, she has an important place in it. The fact that she took a humble place and that Jesus later did not give her privileges over other believers (11:27-28) shows what role she plays in Luke. She symbolizes all believers, for she opened herself to God, not claiming the new life but receiving it as a gift.

Mary's prayer was, "The Almighty has done great things for me" (Luke 1:49). She stands in the age-old tradition of the poor, the humble, and the oppressed in Israel. As she looked at the child in her body and then in the manger, she represented a believer waiting in darkness and patiently hoping. Christians should not speak of this woman in any other way than humbly. Don't attempt to improve on the gospel! Yet artists have often depicted her in fanciful ways and theologians have made dogmatic speculations about her, right up to the present day. One can understand a concern to exalt Mary in order to honor her Son, but such speculation steps over the limits set by the New Testament. Only in Christ do we have the Mediator and model of one in whom faith reached maturity.

Christmas and the stories of Jesus' wonderful birth are symbolic of the reality that in Christ God became a human being. And whatever God did in Bethlehem he did in the fullness of his power. Therefore it is a matter of the working of the Spirit. We must leave this secret as it was left by John the evangelist: "The Word became flesh and dwelt among us" (John 1:14). Or, as a recent translation puts it, "The Word became a human being and, full of grace and truth, lived among us" (TEV). The word of God became a human being in Jesus of Nazareth. That is our faith.

Why do we celebrate Good Friday?

The church's Creed appears to overlook the life and work of Jesus. It passes directly from the confession of the wonderful birth of the Lord to "He suffered under Pontius Pilate, was crucified, died, and was buried." Jesus, Mary, and now Pontius Pilate. The church had good reasons for making him part of its Creed. Its faith had to come to grips with the forces of this world. These forces, which brought death to Jesus, are here represented by the man who ruled at that time in Roman Palestine. Condemned to death, Jesus died on a cross, the Roman form of gallows. Our faith springs from this death. The cross is the symbol of Christianity—a stumbling block to many, but a comfort to believers. The Christian church has seen the cross, an instrument of violence and death, as a sign of victory. The cross symbolizes the fact that Jesus' whole life was suffering, that his death was really the most awful human death, and that his grave was a dungeon of the lost, a hell, a sepulchre of corpses.

The meaning of the cross is that we have been crucified with Jesus, laid in the grave with him. Our old humanity is dead. Further, in those places where our lives are like a cross—where we sit in distress, dishonor, and shame, when we see no way out and only death stares us in the face—there Jesus is also. As his cross is our cross, so our cross is also his. We are never alone with our suffering. And he suffers not only by our side, as other friends sometimes do, but he suffers *for* us. That is the Christian explanation of his suffering. The thought becomes sharper as we continue: "He descended into hell." In Israel, and in Christian faith, death above all meant separation from God. Death therefore does not only happen at the end of a person's life. Many people sense that in some hellish moments they are already separated from the God who made them and rescues them. In death one is broken and lost, alienated from light, deprived of love and incapable of loving. Christ is there with us also. We can take this sentence of the Creed as directly as the ancient church did: the dead Christ does not forsake the dead.

Why do we celebrate Easter?

"Jesus our Lord . . . was put to death for our trespasses and raised for our justification" (Rom. 4:24-25). He went to the cross out of love for the godless and continued to pray for their forgiveness (Luke 23:34). In the resurrection of Jesus from the dead, God showed his will to be love. The worst sins of my life cannot separate me from him. It is God himself who forgives. God is Christ with me and was already with me long before I knew it—just as Jesus was on the road to Emmaus with the disciples while they still mourned him as dead. Jesus had proclaimed the kingdom of God among all people and let them share in his wonderful healings and powerful word. But he had been killed. Now they saw their Lord as though there had been no death. This is the Easter message of the church.

At Christmas God humbled himself, becoming a child in a manger. At Easter human beings were united with Christ in his resurrection. God set Jesus free from the grave to redeem the world, so that it could be renewed and its suffering and death ended. Our suffering in these days of our earthly life is not the final meaning of our existence. Behind the crosses of our lives stands the confession that God will not leave us in the grave. In Christ a new time and a new world has dawned. And we belong to it. The resurrection is basic to the church's message. It is a sign under which our life now stands forever. All things will become new with us, in us, around us. And in this new, emerging world there will be no more death. The direction of our lives is no longer ambiguous. Our future has been won.

The Creed of the church completes the Easter message with the sentence, "He ascended into heaven, and is seated at the right hand of the Father. He will come again to judge the living and the dead." These ideas are strange to us. The doctrine of the ascension of Jesus requires interpretation today. We no longer think of an "above" and "below" in the universe, and God's throne has no particular place in space. This sentence is an attempt to make visible something which cannot be visualized. God is not "above," but rather "ahead." Jesus Christ presses through to the depth of time and gains power over our history, our present and our future. All power over us lies with him, our risen Lord. Together with the whole world, we are heading toward him.

Where we have come

The confession of Jesus Christ is the center of the Christian Creed. It is the Second Article, between the first about God the Father and the third about God the Holy Spirit. After reflecting on experiences of Jesus, Christians throughout history have expressed their faith in the short phrases of the Apostles' Creed. This confession is at the same time a confession of the church. It is recited at baptisms, as people enter into the community of Christian believers. It is also recited as a source of strength and solidarity for the faithful. And the risen Lord himself makes the faith of Christians possible. We acknowledge Jesus, who is the Word, with our words (Rom. 10:10). We confess who we are and who he is. The beginning of the church's confession of Christ is his resurrection from the dead. This confession laid the foundation for the longer reports about him in the Gospels. It was the presupposition of the early church and of the entire New Testament. We can only be Christians by means of the risen Christ. He is with us. Day by day he gives life to us, to our neighbors, to the human race, and to all creation. He gives us strength, comfort, and joy. In the Second Article of the Creed the church confesses its faith in Christ: he lives among us as the eternal Son, our Lord, who came into the world by the will of God, was made perfect in suffering, for us was crucified, and with us is risen from the dead. He directs our present. It would be a misunderstanding to think of faith as a demand for us to overcome our difficulties, to accept all the miraculous works and deeds of God, and to intellectually accept the church's confessions. These very confessions point to the living Christ among us. Christmas, Good Friday, Easter, and Ascension become new every year in the celebration of Christianity, because they are symbols for the life of Christ in our midst.

4. Christ Says Yes to Us

What does the Bible teach about judgment?

"He ascended into heaven, and is seated at the right hand of the Father. He will come again to judge the living and the dead." Most people are expressing their basic feelings when they say there must be a judgment of good and evil in the world. Whoever is evil in this life must be punished, and whoever is good must be rewarded. It is as simple and obvious as that. And there is truth in this. The Bible speaks frequently and clearly about judgment. Because of the wickedness of the human race, God sent a great flood which destroyed all. He confused the nations because in their inflated pride they attempted to build a tower that would reach up to the heavens. The problem of punishment, the quest for what is right, and trust in the inexorable justice of God recur page after page in the Bible. After all the temporary punishments here on earth, there must be a final, eternal reckoning at the end of the world.

This is no distant dream. Jesus himself accepted the reality of a final judgment. Shortly before his death he promised to return in glory as a king with all his holy angels to deal with everyone according to their deeds, those both open and hidden (Matthew 25). In the New Testament there is no doubt about this judgment. Paul wrote, "For he who sows to his own flesh will from the flesh reap corruption" (Gal. 6:8), and again, "For we must all appear before the judgment seat of Christ, so that each one may receive good or evil, according to what he has done in the body" (2 Cor. 5:10). According to Jesus, there will certainly be disappointments. Was that which we took to be good in truth really good? Was our devout enthusiasm really piety? Was all the wrong which resulted from such good intentions really deserving of punishment? At the last judgment we hope we will be better known by God than by ourselves. We hope we will be freed from both our own self-judgment and the judgment of others. And our hope will not be in vain.

What does Christ demand in the last judgment?

The gospel completely changes our standards. It is a revolution. When we judge persons, we measure their ability against their achievements. And this means measuring quantity and extent. But Jesus' revolution turns from an examination of quantity to an examination of *quality*. He looks into our hearts. He sees our wills. He tests the motives of our actions. He sees how weak we are. He sees how strong we are, and how much better we could be if we would only make use of our powers. He knows those who talk a great deal but do nothing, and he knows those who say little but apply themselves to their tasks. In his parable of the last judgment Jesus tells us of those brought before the King of the world, who will hold court in great splendor with his holy angels (Matthew 25). He will sit upon his throne and divide the nations and peoples according to this one criterion: "Were you with me in the days of my flesh when I was hungry, imprisoned, weak, naked, and sick? At that time no one recognized me. But you knew that there were poor, imprisoned, and sick people. A single glass of water would have meant so much! It would have been enough for me if you had been with the poor, if you had not turned away from the hungry. Whatever you did to these, you did to me." This is the word of the Lord. We are to be with those around us in their distress. And we are not to exercise mercy simply in the hope of reward in heaven. "Do not let your left hand know what your right hand is doing" (Matt. 6:3). The judgment which Jesus pronounced turns on both great things and such fine distinctions.

What does Christ do in the last judgment?

In the Middle Ages Christians painted the picture of Christ the Judge in such strong colors that people were terrified of him. They fled from his inexorable judgment to mother Mary and the saints, that they might intercede for them and rescue them from his anger. Were they wrong? Who can stand when so penetrating and detailed a judgment is made? Once more the New Testament appears to lay stress on what overwhelms us. Once more the one whom we have called Savior appears to be our Judge. Once more the issue seems to be what we have done and not what he does for us. Is the story of Jesus and the human race in the end one of despair? After so many good words, does the anger and judgment of God have the final word?

This is not what the church confesses. It is Christ who has taken over the lordship of the world, and he is at the right hand of God, whom he calls Father. His compassion rules. And it is Christ and not some thunderous Zeus who is our eternal judge. We are found out by him. He sees through us. But even in judgment he is still what he always is for us: our friend and comforter, Savior and Redeemer, our future and glory, the one who goes on loving us all the way to the cross. And Christians know that it is Christ who will bring us through, even through the last judgment.

Our ultimate judgment will not be pronounced by some anonymous legal power, like that which we meet in our law courts. The judge will be Jesus, and we know him. His yoke is light, for he does not demand punishment, deterrence, or destruction of those who have sinned, but rather brings restoration to people who have already destroyed themselves. Jesus does not allow an impersonal law to take its course any more than he promulgates an abstract command. He gives us new life. Jesus justifies us—declares us righteous, and thereby makes us just, right, and innocent. In our governments we value judges who are strictly impartial. We want every party to receive exactly what they deserve. But this is not what we mean when we say that God justifies us. Instead we mean that God himself loves us enough to create us anew and bring us into right relation to him.

What is the role of the law?

The apostle Paul has most clearly explained what justification means. In doing this he did not promulgate a new doctrine, but only brought together what we can see throughout the Bible and in the teaching and activity of Jesus. It is true that in Paul we find God's salvation through Jesus formulated in legal language. These expressions appear harsh and lifeless to us. Yet the substance is what counts. And that substance is the stuff of our daily lives, of our existence before God in life and death.

Some people think Paul, who was himself a learned Jew, might have misunderstood the basic tradition of his own people. After he became a follower of Christ he held that ancient Israel had known only part of God's righteousness, which now is known entirely. The righteousness of the legal world has clear standards, firmly laid down in the laws of society. Before his encounter with Christ, Paul assumed that it was just the same with God. God judged according to the standard of his laws. Paul thought that was justification. The Judaism of his day had 613 laws, some important and many not so important, all of which had to be fulfilled before a person was considered justified before God.

Paul learned the truth about God's justification after he repented of his persecution of Christians. He learned two important things:

1. A person can perform good works with an evil heart. Such

people are not justified before God. Certainly it is a good thing
when people give 10% of their income to the poor. But is that really
a good work when the purpose is that people praise them, or that
God be pleased with them and reward them? Jesus looks into our
hearts. He tells us what love truly involves.

2. God's kind of love is radical. But we are incapable of fulfilling
Jesus' demand for such unconditional love. I may never have stolen
or committed a serious crime, lied only occasionally, and certainly
never murdered. But have I ever failed to come to the help of someone lying wounded by the side of the road because I could not
bother, was too busy, hadn't the time, or didn't care? In Jesus' story
of the good Samaritan the priest and the Levite acted in the same
way, passing by on the other side of the road. Only the Samaritan,
an outcast from Jewish society, cared for the man (Luke 10).

Thus Paul saw that all of us founder on God's laws. If God's justification of human beings is of the same kind as in human society,
then we are all lost. The law of God condemns us and reveals our
disobedience. This is the effect of God's law on us. It shows us to be
the sinners that we are.

What is given to us in the gospel?

In his law God tells us what we should be. At the same time he
shows us, by means of his law, that we cannot achieve this. We may
want to fulfill his commandments, and may often follow them literally, but in the end we miss their ultimate purpose. Again and again
we founder when it comes to loving God with all our heart and
mind and soul and our neighbor as ourselves. Thus the law condemns us. We despair. Only God can help us. It is before him that
we stand guilty through our disobedience. We separate ourselves
from him because we do not love as he wishes. But God comes to
us in Christ. In the gospel he tells us what he gives to us. He brings
us home, lost as we are, like the father in the parable who brings
his prodigal son back into his home. Christ took our godforsaken
condition upon himself on the cross and showed us the love of God.
The gospel of Jesus Christ is good news. We who are guilty before
the Judge will be declared free and innocent by the Judge.

Justification, or being right before God—that which we try to
achieve ourselves—will be bestowed on us by God himself. We

receive it as a gift from Christ, who died for us and fulfilled the
law in his eternal, invincible love. He is no longer our Judge. He
approaches God for us. He sets us free from our self-assertive will.
He leads us uprightly before God's judgment. Our sin is that we can
never be pure and good; but God gives us righteousness through
faith. Jesus himself shows us faith and gives us faith. In faith we
admit that God is just. And in faith we fulfill the first and most
important commandment, to love God with all our heart. We
acknowledge him as just and give up the attempt to be justified
before him by our own actions. Now at last we gain detachment
from ourselves, our anxieties, our ambitions, and our false pride. For
it is not from ourselves, but from God that our righteousness comes.

What shall we become?

Through the judgment of Jesus we become just persons. What an
incredible verdict! A judgment by which we are changed! Once
again we must ask where we are heading. Who will we be? How
we are justified before God was shown by Jesus in a parable taken
from the simple events of human life:

"Two men went up into the temple to pray, one a Pharisee and the other
a tax collector. The Pharisee stood and prayed thus with himself, 'God,
I thank thee that I am not like other men, extortioners, unjust, adulterers,
or even like this tax collector. I fast twice a week, I give tithes of all that
I get.' But the tax collector, standing far off, would not even lift up his
eyes to heaven, but beat his breast, saying, 'God, be merciful to me a
sinner!' I tell you, this man went down to his house justified rather than
the other; for everyone who exalts himself will be humbled, but he who
humbles himself will be exalted" (Luke 18:10-14).

In the vivid parable of the prodigal son Jesus showed once again
that God brings home the lost. The son who went away, the wicked
son, was able to enjoy the glory of his father's house after his return
and repentance. But the other son, who was upright and always
remained at home, showed a lack of love. A shepherd left 99 sheep
behind in order to find one that was lost. Jesus took children into
his arms and blessed them. He blessed the poor and simple because
in their weakness and inability to help themselves they had to rely
on God. They could not help themselves, so God had to help them.
Jesus certainly doesn't want us to become childish. But he sets chil-

dren before our eyes as examples of the Spirit which fills those whom God has blessed.

Jesus himself was in this sense a child, God's Son. He completely surrendered himself to the Father. He did not seek his own self-realization, but rather sought the thoughts and will of God in the world. He renounced himself in love, all the way to the cross. In everything he wished to be one with God his Father. This Jesus, our Savior, is the one God has set over us and all people. We will be measured against him, but he is the one who measures. He does not desire our death, but our life. Unlike an earthly judge, he does not want to seek out our crimes so he can punish us. He desires that we be acquitted and set free to live with God in freedom. The seriousness of the judgment against us will not be ignored. But to the extent that we accept and acknowledge this judgment we learn who we are. We can only fall into the arms of the Judge, who died for us and brings us into a new relationship with God. A change takes place in us. We become like Christ. God brings the fallen—all of us who are oppressed by guilt—through judgment and home again. He gives us freedom and righteousness. He gives us both the possibility and reality of new life.

All that Jesus did, his words and deeds, came out of his love for the Father and for us. He offended the religious people of his day by loving the unlovable. He sought out the poor, the crippled, the guilty, and the outcasts of society. He encouraged them and ate with them. He told them that God was greater than all their sin and made new beginnings possible, even in the darkest valleys of life. Those who believed in this new beginning and trusted themselves completely to God would find the power of evil taken away, guilt and sin forgiven. They would find reconciliation. But the most important thing Jesus did for human beings was to suffer and die. And when God said yes to Jesus by raising him from the dead, he also said yes to us. Some early Christians expressed this in the language of Jewish worship. Christ was the "high priest" for all people before God, and was at the same time the lamb to be sacrificed. He both offered the sacrifice *for* sin and at the same time *was* the sacrifice. Thus God reconciled the world to himself (2 Cor. 5:19). By Christ's death the human race has been cleansed from its works of death. Christ has said yes to us. We have been called into the presence of God, who is both Judge and Redeemer. He makes the highest possible demands of us, and yet takes our sin from us so that we can become new people.

Where we have come

Jesus turns everything upside down. Our thoughts about God and ourselves become quite different after we know him. He says yes to those who trust him, giving them his example and the power of his love. That love was proved by his death on the cross. He says yes by opening a way to God for us and setting us free from the condemnation we have earned for ourselves. He says yes by breaking our ambition to become God's equals. We may take God's law quite seriously, but it will lead us only to despair. We want to be lords over our lives. But Jesus, the Word of God, reveals that the meaning, certainty, and continuance of life and existence do not lie in ourselves. We flee from ourselves, for we cannot stand before God. We flee from God the Judge to the God we know in Jesus Christ. "Come to me, all who labor and are heavy laden, and I will give you rest" (Matt. 11:28). Jesus says yes to us by entering our lives and taking upon himself the anguish of our consciences and the poverty of our love. No longer do we have to bear that which we are not able to bear. Jesus says yes to us in that we may come to him and forever believe in him. He wants us to be freed by his love and to be able to love God—the Lord, Creator, Father, Judge, and Perfector of all things. All this is ours in the one who is God's beloved Son.

5. The Spirit of Jesus and the Triune God

By grace alone, by faith alone?

Christ says yes to us. This one short, brief sentence has many implications. We recognize who Christ is, and we recognize who we truly are. And we become different. Christ accepts us. The Bible uses the word *grace* to describe this acceptance. It is not through what we do that we become pleasing to God and justified before him, but because God himself has dealt with us in love—by grace alone. We know we are not the persons we were meant to be. Our end is not life but death, not success but failure. But Christ accepts us and represents us before God. He came from God, took flesh, and fulfilled all through his unending love. Now he is with God. The Bible uses the term *faith* to describe our acceptance of Christ as our Mediator and Savior.

But we must not be satisfied with any narrow understanding of grace and faith. They can indeed be seriously misunderstood. We misuse these words when we take them lightly and let them fall too easily from our lips. To believe means more than intellectual understanding or memorization. Jesus is the Lord who daily accompanies us, who comes again and again. In him God comes close to us. From him the Spirit of God comes to us. He works in our hearts. We have not been justified through Christ in order that we should take that fact lightly. God's grace is not cheap grace. It leads to faith. And faith involves self-knowledge, true commitment, and action.

In Christ we discover who we are. And we know what we must do. We need to change our lives. God's command that we should love him with our whole heart and our neighbor as ourselves now stands clearly before us. But we also know that Christ gives us such love. God is with us in Jesus; without him we cannot live a life pleasing to God. In faith we surrender all that we have and are to God. Faith sets us free from the illusion that we ourselves must be all-powerful, all-knowing, and all-capable. In faith we finally win detachment from ourselves. We can stand outside of our ambition, guilt, and pain. Christ achieves for us what we thought we could achieve for ourselves, but we are not thereby unclaimed. When we believe in Christ the Spirit of Jesus claims us. He lights the way as we go forward. It is no longer our ambition and pride that drives us—in freedom we do what God wills for us.

How did the doctrine of the Trinity develop?

Jesus is more than a teacher, more than a model, more than the one by whose mouth God speaks to us. He is more than a Jewish Messiah, God's anticipated King in the last days. It is true that today we strongly emphasize his humanity. Jesus of Nazareth deals with human beings as a human being. He gives us a new image of humanity, in which we can find ourselves amid all the pressures of our time. But the early church was in a much different situation. Many different gods were worshiped at that time. Which god was really God? Was it enough to select the best from all the different presentations of God? Is "god" simply the title we give to the sum of all our greatest longings, wishes, and ideas? No. The Jewish people knew God to be the power who guides world history, who tests and renews our lives, and who guarantees a future for us—we human beings who were made for eternity. God spoke through the Law and the Prophets. God is the eternal Father to whom we can trust ourselves. This is what the people of God had learned. A basic Jewish confession was, "Hear, O Israel: The Lord our God is one Lord" (Deut. 6:4). But those who believed in Christ saw something else as well: God so loved the world that he took flesh in the man Jesus of Nazareth. Christians believed in the unity of the Father and the Son. Against the background of the Old Testament, that was a staggering thought. And the first generations of Christians had to do some very hard thinking to work through the meaning of it. The doctrine of the triune God came out of those efforts. This doctrine remains a stumbling block to Moslems, Jews, and many Christians as well. We may wish to accept Jesus, but perhaps not the doctrine of the Trinity. But we understand Jesus much better by means of that doctrine.

Why three and still a unity?

The church develops doctrines in order to reject errors in understanding the faith. As the early believers considered the meaning of the Christian faith, they discovered that numerous errors were possible. They asked themselves, "How can we hold together our faith in God, whom the Old Testament names as the one and only God, and Jesus, in whom we experience God's presence?" God surrounds us as the origin and aim of the universe, the Lord of the world, the Father and Creator of all things. But he also encounters us in Jesus of Nazareth. And his Spirit speaks to our hearts, bringing us faith and the ability to love God. We experience three *forms* of the one and only God. They cannot be separated from one another. Each is related to the others. We speak of three "persons" because the one and only God meets us in three ways. Together with any Moslem, Jehovah's Witness, or Unitarian we can confess a faith in the Creator of the heavens and the earth. But we experience God in three ways in his creation, including God the Son and God the Spirit. The Spirit kindles in us the flame of faith and obedience. This Spirit unites us with our brothers and sisters, and helps us to overcome our own spirit of selfishness. He renews the world and announces to us God the Son, who will come again to renew the earth.

What does the Spirit do?

When Jesus came up out of the water after his baptism in the Jordan River the voice from heaven said, "Thou art my beloved Son; with thee I am well pleased" (Mark 1:11). The highest is bound up with the deepest. God in the highest is near to the one who goes down into the deep. The Son stood in between the "upper" world and the "lower" world. And the Mediator was the Spirit. We can only speak of the Spirit in metaphors. In Mark's story of Christ's baptism the metaphor of a dove is used. We cannot catch a dove in our hand. It comes and goes as it wills. And no one can capture the Spirit of God. We must wait and pray that it will come. We may feel empty and forsaken. We may give up hope that he will come back. We must pray for him. He may not come. But suddenly, when we least expect it, he is present and seeks us out. That is the form of God from which no one can flee.

We are not satisfied with our strife-filled lives. We want peace, but we cannot find it. We long for it and pray for it. But it evades us. Then, when we have done nothing to merit peace, it comes like a dove. It suddenly flies down and settles on the roof of our house as though it always belonged there. The presence of God's Spirit is a matter of life and death. For the Spirit of God is not uninvolved with the world. "The Spirit of God was moving over the face of the waters" (Gen. 1:2). From the beginning, the Spirit has been involved in creation. Where the Spirit of God is absent, there is chaos. If God does not seek us out with his Spirit, then we are lost. His Spirit must rescue us from the self-destructive results of our separation from God. Christians have been baptized like Christ, with Christ, and in Christ. He goes before us into deep darkness, into the destruction and suffering of our world. He calls out to God his Father. And we are united with him in that, for he is our Brother and gives us his Spirit—the Spirit of God.

Who is the Spirit?

The Spirit of God is close to us. He is the God who comes to us and is in us. God the Creator rules over us, God the Redeemer is for us, and God the Spirit is in us. That has been the experience of Christians. And that is what we celebrate at Pentecost. Christians are to be filled with the gifts of the Holy Spirit: to speak the truth, proclaim salvation, glorify God, bring comfort to those who hurt, heal the sick, care for the dying, visit the imprisoned, give children a home, bring hope to those in despair, and spread joy. But far too often while pious speculations flourish and critical scholarship digs deep into the ancient biblical texts, there are few works of love. God wants to be formed in us, not just to be doctrinally acknowledged. The Spirit of God wants to enliven us and give us faith active in love. But for this reason the Spirit can be dangerous. Love, when it truly exists, can consume the lover. In Baptism God puts to death our old, self-centered natures. We are brought up out of the water as those who were dead and are now restored to life. We are baptized into the death of Christ in order to receive new life.

What is the communion of saints?

It is the Holy Spirit who has built the church. We know this not only from the events of Pentecost, when church history began, but also from the continuing experience of Christians today. The Spirit of love is the Spirit of community. Spiritual community means caring for and listening to one another. The Spirit of God in Jesus first appeared in the community of his disciples. Jesus says yes to us when he builds us into his church. This church is found in the worship of a local congregation or gathering, in missionary work, social service, or a discussion group. What is decisive is the Spirit of community. We like to live with people who understand us. Otherwise life gets too confusing. Understanding others and being understood by them brings happiness. God comes to us in the Holy Spirit, and by that Spirit we understand God. For we cannot understand him on our own. The great eternal God is now within us, and he guides our thoughts and actions. And it is through the Holy Spirit that we are understood by other people who know God. It is a marvelous experience to realize that God himself understands us. He comes nearer to us than the dearest person we know. He becomes a fire in our breast and constrains us to speak out about what he has given us. He constrains us to pray—to ask, thank, praise, and carry out his will. And he urges us to act together with others who are understood by God and understand him in the Spirit. It is this miracle that we acknowledge in the church's Creed when we speak of the "communion of saints."

Where we have come

The yes of God to us is the work of his love. We have not earned it. Our faith can only accept it. It works without us, through the free grace of God alone. Through God's love we see ourselves anew. We are God's creatures, but have drawn away from him. Now God relates to us through Christ, in whom he became a person but remained God. This relationship comes through faith. The early church's doctrine of the Trinity was intended to protect against errors, which are always lurking in the background in this matter and in all our talk about God. The three persons of the Trinity cannot be separated from each other. They belong together. We do not experience one without the other. It is Jesus who says yes to us. It is he who was born of Mary. He is the Son of God. His name stands in the middle of the church's Creed. We know God the Father because he is the Father of Jesus Christ, and we know God the Spirit because Jesus received the Spirit and sent him to us. We celebrate Pentecost as the descent of the Holy Spirit upon the disciples. The Spirit is the flame and storm in our hearts. He creates love and human community, declaring the will of God to the church. We celebrate the Holy Spirit because through Christ he recreates our lives. He is God's creative Spirit, by whom we came into being, exist now, and will be in the future. It is by the Spirit that we are able to respond to the Father as his children.

6. The Coming Lord

How does faith look into the future?

Christians recognize Easter and the Ascension—Jesus' resurrection and assumption of power at the right hand of God—as the definitive miracles of Christ's life. In them we see that our reality is pervaded by the reality of God. The old is only provisional. Our lostness, anxiety, sin, and separation from God is shown to be passing away. In the Gospels we can see that this was already happening in Jesus' life. He was different from us. There was an outward calm about him, and yet also an invincible power. He seemed to have unlimited time, and yet pressed on relentlessly. He talked about that which was new: the kingdom of God was at hand and people needed to be vigilant.

Jesus knew people like us: people who were oppressed, troubled, anxious, always wanting something better and yet spoiling that which is good—people entangled in painful guilt. But the picture of Jesus given to us in the Gospels is a contradiction of all that. He sat in a boat with his disciples and slept through a storm that severely frightened them (Mark 4:35-41). The experience of those disciples, like the experience of Jesus' disciples today, was an experience of God. When we follow Jesus, we follow God. When we come to Jesus, we come to God. And when Jesus comes to us, God comes to us. Jesus himself said he would come to us. He would return to us after his victory over death. We see a future in Christ. Despite all the shadows of death and the oppressive catastrophes of life, there is an unconquerable hope for the world. Whatever predictions about the future are put forward by science, Christians know nothing that happens can separate us from the love of God.

When will Jesus come?

Again and again the disciples asked the Lord when the future events he spoke of would take place (Luke 21:7). In this book we are seeing how the eternal future is drawn into time. We retell the past in order to strengthen faith in the future. And this faith is trust in the God who promises the fulfillment of salvation. God himself is the future becoming the present. The story of his people is the story of waiting for his kingdom, for the fulfillment of his new covenant. The Old Testament promised this fulfillment and strengthens Christian faith. We celebrate the coming of God's Christ in the festival of Advent. With the disciples we believe that Jesus' earthly life was not the end. He will come in glory as Judge.

But when will be come? The longing of God's people stretches out through time. *"Maranatha!"* was the cry of the ancient church: "Come, Lord!" And in the last verse of the Bible Jesus answers, " 'Surely I am coming soon.' Amen. Come, Lord Jesus!" (Rev. 22:20). When we ask when this will be, Jesus does not give us a date. It will be soon. God's coming, his judgment and glory, stand before us. Therefore make haste! Jesus spoke about the signs of the end, and over the past 2000 years people have looked eagerly for those signs. We have seen wars and revolutions, the falling away of the faithful, earthquakes and plagues, and other natural disasters. And yet all they have pointed to is that the end is coming. They have not yet brought the end. We should not let ourselves be confused by those who take their divining rods and instruct us how to read God's calendar (Luke 21:7-9). Here is the contradiction. The end will be soon, and then again it won't be. The first Christians anxiously expected the end, and in one of the oldest parts of the New Testament Paul said the power of evil in the world was delaying the Lord's coming (2 Thess. 2:7). Other Christians believed it was due to God's compassion for the human race. Whatever science says about the future of the world, both Jesus and the church call us to repentance. While there is time, we must make use of it!

Is Jesus already our Judge?

There are other texts in the New Testament which speak of judgment quite differently from those we have heard so far, particularly parts of John's gospel. They declare that the judgment which is to come is already here. The coming Savior of the world is also here now, working among us. Whoever has had an authentic encounter with Christ understands the deep truth of these words. Our whole lives as Christians are caught in this tension. The apparent contradiction is the continuing experience of Christians. The Christ for whom I wait is already with me in my need. And he who is with me is also coming. His coming is the moment in which salvation takes place. I reach out, but I am imprisoned. I long for salvation, but I am already saved and made holy in Jesus Christ. Everywhere I see the signs of his coming. My life and the history of the world are not going around in circles, but are unrepeatable moments in time, leading on to a goal. At every point on the way, however, the goal is also reached.

Jesus is indeed present now. And as the Lord is already present, so also is his judgment. The children of this world speak of accidents, blows of fate, loss, and damage. Faith speaks to us of judgment. But the Christian faith also gives certainty of deliverance from judgment. "He who believes in him is not condemned" (John 3:18). Jesus brings judgment now. Just as a judge seeks out the deeds and motives of the accused, so Jesus unmasks us when he reveals himself to us. The coming of his light into the world is judgment. When we step out of the darkness in which we live into that light, we have eternal life. No one who believes in him will be lost. God wills that all should be saved through Christ. This shows us that the coming judgment is already here, and every hour is an hour of decision for or against the Lord, our Judge and Deliverer.

What are the consequences for faith?

Christians do not believe in some particular theory or explanation of the world. Faith is not determined so much by knowledge of the past as by the future. Because Christ will come, existence acquires a new form. Christian faith is hope rooted in love. We go through life in the strength of that faith. But we must not confuse our hope with optimism. Optimism is a refusal to see reality. Christians must keep their eyes wide open. They must not overlook or forget how deep humanity has fallen. But at the same time Christians see the magnitude of our hope. Our existence stands under the yes that God has spoken to us. Our faith answers this yes with "amen," "Let it be so." God has spoken this yes to us in such a way that we can understand and respond. He speaks every day anew and will speak to us until the last day. The Christ who comes is the same Savior we encounter in the Gospels and who accompanies us. Jesus compared himself to a bridegroom of ancient times. The church is like a bride who waits for him. For a bride in Israel, the coming of the bridegroom changed everything. But even in waiting we are not what we used to be. Joy changes us. We are already wearing festive clothing.

What is the sign of the Son of man?

The coming of the Lord will be irresistible. We will not be able to ignore it. All our work is on its way toward his coming, just as our lives are. The Christian community is being formed by its hope in the coming Lord, who is here now and yet will one day be revealed. The coming kingdom of God is the kingdom of the Son of man. Jesus said the "sign of the Son of man" will appear in heaven (Matt. 24:30). It is no longer clear what this meant to Jewish Christians in the first century. But the Gospels leave no doubt about the fact that Jesus spoke of himself when he talked about the Son of man, the Messiah. And this returning Lord, himself born of a woman, will renew our humanity in his own image. The man Jesus gives us a measure of what human beings are to be. We trust in the one who is a sign of the new world, already seen and made visible. We look to the one who "emptied himself, taking the form of a servant . . . . and became obedient unto death, even death on a cross" (Phil. 2:7-8).

Is Jesus always a mystery?

Did Jesus actually deliver us, or was he only a visionary who wanted the best (as many do) and failed (as many do)? People are divided about Jesus. But if we cannot believe what Christians believe, then we must know who we are refusing to believe in. And if we believe that this Jesus is the Christ, our Savior, we must know who we are believing in. There is a mystery about Jesus. And no one can solve it. Every generation of researchers and believers takes up the task afresh. But the New Testament presents the words and deeds of Jesus as an inseparable unity. There is no fragmentation of his personality such as we find in all other human beings. Jesus was obedient to God. He knew that the future depended on it, and in his obedience he struggled with human evil. The New Testament prevents us from understanding this man as a Prometheus or a hero. God has acted in him. And God has not acted in him by endowing him with miraculous powers and great splendor, but rather by allowing him to be lowly and weak, poor and humble. That God should be active in the violent death of this man, and by his very death free us from sin, was as much of an offense to the people of the first century as it is today. And it will always be an offense.

Jesus can only be understood by one who is in relationship with him. If we try to approach him "objectively," he will elude us again and again. He is a part of history, but can we classify him with the other parts? Did he institute a new religion, found a church, or introduce a new form of worship? No. He did nothing that can be detached from who he was. He was and is himself the life of the Christian church. He himself is the means by which people can come to God anew. Much of what he said can also be found in other Jewish traditions. And yet people were different after they had known him. Jesus desires that we should know him and his mystery. And the only way we can do that is to give ourselves over to his love.

Where we have come

Christ comes as the Judge in whose judgment we find our deliverance. He comes to bring the world to an end, receiving it in distress, and reestablishing creation. He who was humble and poor, the Lamb who was led to the slaughter, who gave himself for us, comes as the one God has made his Son and heir. He is the victor. We shall not know the times or seasons of the end of the world and Christ's coming. But he who is with us to the end of the world will come to us. We are to be with him in the fulfillment of who we are. And after our death and departure from this world we are to be made like him. We will be with God. Christ will represent us before God as he represented us on the cross. This coming Lord is always present. If we follow him, we follow God. Not tomorrow, but already today, this Lord has become my Judge and Deliverer. The judgment on me and the world has already been executed. And I have been delivered. I have been delivered by leaving myself in the hands of this Judge and Deliverer. Whoever believes in him will not perish (John 3:16). My faith penetrates ever deeper into the mystery of Jesus of Nazareth, whom God sent for our deliverance, but without ever being able to understand him completely. I never resolve this mystery. I can only participate in it. Jesus is continually nourishing my soul. That is what God has done for the world in Christ.

Summary

I experience

I experience a lack of meaning in my life. Some days I am happy. A job was well done, I passed an examination, or I met a person I could help. My job brings me payment, my examination will take me further, and that person has become my friend. But how seldom I can lay a piece of work aside as finished! How seldom is my study completed! And how seldom do I find a true friend!

I experience frustration in my efforts and lack of hope. And my little moments of happiness do not compensate me for the greater loss. The greatest happiness is always beyond me. Every day I experience a longing for that greatest happiness—one that will give meaning not only to one day, but to my whole life.

There are so many explanations of life. I can select from the world's religions. Sects try to get my support. But all seem too busy to tell me about ultimate meaning, the meaning of the whole. Have they really made sense of the whole when they are too busy to share their answers with me?

I seek one who not only gives meaning, not only offers love, but who *is* love. I seek one who not only talks about peace, but *is* peace.

I experience my longing for a physician who can make me well, for a deliverer from this world, for someone who is powerful and good to conquer the evil in me, in society, and in the nations. I experience what Israel felt when it cried out for God's Messiah in the distress of its darkest days. How often I have been oppressed by the fact that while I hear of God, I do not know him. I feel as one who has lost a home. Someone must take me by the hand and lead me back.

I question

Who will give meaning to my life? Who can give meaning to my pursuits, my daily troubles and agitations? Is it really the ultimate meaning of life for one person to gain power over another? What remains at the end? And why?

Are graves the last word of our existence? Who will heal us? Who will bring rest to our hearts? Who heals nations, communities, and families? Who will keep us from consuming one another? Who is this peace that we all seek? Who is willing? Who is able?

Who has the power to give us peace forever? Who takes people by the hand and makes them still, so they can once again hear their own hearts and the God who satisfies their hearts?

Who frees us from the demands that hang over us? Who takes away our sin, removing that which separates us from God? We cannot carry the burden. Who will carry it for us?

I believe

I believe that the God who made me and daily creates me anew in his love has also seen my distress. The unique God has chosen a unique man to complete his work in me and in the whole of humanity.

I believe in Jesus, the carpenter's Son from Nazareth. In him God sent his Word, which was with him from the beginning. He announced the nearness of God's kingdom. He is God's Judge, who himself makes me righteous in God's sight.

I believe that Jesus, the Messiah and Christ, the anointed King, came into this world as a lowly man among lowly people. He preached the coming of the kingdom of God, suffered, was condemned, and died on the cross for us.

I believe, together with the apostles and disciples, that Jesus fulfilled the law of God for me. He became a model of love. I believe Jesus has made me right with God so that I am now free to live for God and my neighbor.

I believe that the law of God is a mirror of my heart, in which I know who I am, and who I would be if Jesus had not delivered me. On him I cast all my hope.

I believe in God's judgment. Christ the coming Lord is judgment, Judge, and Deliverer all in one. He is judgment, for darkness and light are already among people in him; he is the Judge, for he alone can justify us before God; he is the Deliverer, for he will do what he has promised.

I believe that Christ my Lord has been raised from the dead by God. He rules with God both now and in the future. He will bring me through death to himself, just as he now through faith draws me out of darkness and into the light of his presence.

I believe that the three are one: God, my Creator; God, my Deliverer; and God, the Holy Spirit. I believe that those who believe in Jesus partake of the Spirit.

I believe Jesus instituted no religion. He himself is spirit. Jesus founded no church. He himself is life. Jesus contrived no piety. He himself is what it means to be pious. Jesus invented no means of salvation. He himself is both Savior and salvation.

I believe and base my life on the fact that Christ is the salvation of the world and the Redeemer of my life. In him I shall not die, but will have eternal life. In him the world, with all its confusion, meaninglessness, and sin, will nonetheless be drawn back home to God. Jesus is the future of the world. I believe that he will come again. And I believe that all people will see him.

5

HOW
WE LIVE

**We Are Freed
and Claimed:**

Law and Gospel

1. The Good News

Can the good news reach us in our world?

What we have said about Jesus is what the church calls the gospel, the good news. Indeed, nothing can bring more joy to a person than to be able to say, "You are no longer evil and guilty, but are now righteous and whole." And God freely gave us this wholeness when he sent his Son to suffer and die for us. But isn't this too good to be true? People used to believe this message, but is it possible today? Others have believed it, but is it true for us? How can Jesus come into our lives? The good news which the church proclaims seems to have little to do with the reality of our modern world. Everywhere around us we see quite different questions, sentiments, traditions, and needs. Our day-to-day attempts to live our lives seem to leave the church's message far behind.

But the good news of Jesus Christ is good news for us precisely because it is still valid today. Jesus did not only bring salvation to people in the past, but also to us. How are we to live in light of that good news? We need to discuss the relationship between the history of Jesus and our own history. Of course, much history also lies in between. We are heirs to a very confusing history of the life of the church in the world. The history of Jesus has been overlaid with many experiences of Christians, both good and bad. But Jesus still comes to each generation anew. He reveals himself to all who seek him. Let yourself be touched by the one who said, "Everyone who is of the truth hears my voice" (John 18:37). If we participate in the best of our modern trends—namely, the longing for truth and reality—we can gain access to Jesus himself. None of the mistakes and problems of the church can obscure him. Set those aside for now! Seek the one by whom you can live.

The apostle Paul said the gospel is "the power of God" (Rom. 1:16). But we learn this only when we commit ourselves to Christ. Jesus compared himself to a shepherd. Shepherds direct their sheep with their voices. "My sheep hear my voice, and I know them, and they follow me; and I give them eternal life . . ." (John 10:27-28). He also compared himself to a shepherd who sought sheep who had strayed away. For one lost sheep a shepherd would leave the entire flock in the fold (Luke 15:4-7). Jesus seeks us today. That is the gospel. And because he has sought us, we can follow him. We need not follow him in some distant past, for he is present here and now. He reaches us today, in our own lives. He is with us at home, on the highway, at school, at work, and at play.

What is discipleship?

Discipleship is life with Christ. Jesus is with us now in a saving way. He stands in our place. He is working in us, renewing and directing our lives. He suffers for us and heals us. He continues to work as he did during his earthly ministry. By faith we experience his presence. In fact, faith *is* the experience of Christ's presence. He lives among us, calling us to welcome the poor and the outcast. He does not seek power or riches as we do. Rather he gives us love and a desire to change our lives and improve society. He strengthens us when we are tempted. For us he suffers in body and spirit. In our place he dies. This is the Jesus whom Christians follow. He goes on ahead of us in love. He calls us and draws us to him. To live in his presence means to accept the ups and downs, the splendor and the pain, both life and death.

Life with Jesus can be threatening. He accepts us without qualification, but the going can be rough. He forgives and saves us, but he also claims us. He makes demands. He wants us entirely and all the time; not perhaps today or tomorrow, but *both* today *and* tomorrow. Jesus is not an example or a guru whom we are free to exchange for other examples and gurus. Because the gift he gives us is so great, so also are his claims on us. "He who does not take his cross and follow me is not worthy of me" (Matt. 10:38). Thus discipleship is both a duty and a promise. We are to live as Christ lived, and we are enabled to do that by his presence in us.

What do I experience with Jesus?

Discipleship is life with Christ. What results from this life? In the church's traditional terminology we say that Jesus works out our *sanctification*. After reconciling us with God he gives us what we need to live as reconciled people. When we live with God we experience a number of things:

1. In the presence of Christ we are revealed to ourselves much

more clearly than before. We recognize our weak points, imperfections, and the inroads of evil in us. We find that we cannot view ourselves with the friendly objectivity of a doctor. We cannot be satisfied by saying this is just the way we are. We develop a much finer sense of our own weaknesses and possibilities, our potential for both good and evil. We begin to ask whether that which we have always found satisfactory in ourselves is really good enough. Therefore we learn to understand others better.

2. In the presence of Christ we also grow in freedom. For Jesus teaches us freedom. He reverently acknowledged the traditions of his people and religion, and yet he established over against them a freedom which cost him his life. Christians need to see obedience *to* the law together with freedom *from* the law.

3. In the presence of Jesus we learn that we can exercise freedom in the context of constraint. When we step out of ourselves and see ourselves with detachment, we recognize much more clearly who our neighbors are. Together with Jesus we learn the meaning of community.

4. These three experiences that grow out of Christ's presence with us occur only when we have known a fourth experience—when we have learned to give of ourselves. We reach beyond ourselves when we are united with the Spirit, which Jesus sent to free us. The presence of Jesus is in his Spirit. Jesus depended on God completely. He expressed this dependence both through his constant life of prayer and the resulting actions. If we follow Jesus, we follow also in his conversation with God. We, too, will become people of prayer.

How are we to act?

Whoever follows Jesus will have a desire to act as he did. If he is with us every day as our Savior, if he guides our lives—living and suffering in us—then we will indeed act differently than before. Because our world is complicated, this will not always be a simple matter. For this reason we need to know something about Christian ethical teachings—about how to make decisions when we are in doubt. It is comforting to know that before we act, God has acted for us. We may long to do what is right, to be set free from all that stands between us and God; but before this longing to be holy came over us, God had acted for us. Our longing to be holy is really awe over the work that our Savior has already done in us. All our questions about right conduct presuppose the good news. In Christ God has already done what is needed both in us and in the whole world. When we understand this, we are able to see the question of how we should live and act quite differently.

What is the first consequence of the gospel?

The gospel—that which God has done for us even before we could act—gives us first of all balance, certainty, and calmness. We are naturally restless, excited, and full of sorrows. We think we have to do everything ourselves. We have to think about so many things. There is never enough time. Most things are left unfinished. And we can see that even on our dying day there will still be much left undone. But as we have seen, part of what it means to be human is that our lives remain open and unsettled, even to the very end. And God has accepted us open creatures with all our problems. How shall we then live? We do need to explore that. But we also need to realize that it doesn't all depend on us. Perhaps we can help to change that part of the world in which we live. But we do not have to be saviors of our world. For the Savior is already here and at work. His presence causes us to see more clearly what is important and what is unimportant. We see things in their proper place—in perspective. Our daily lives, which are so often enveloped in a dense fog, are illuminated. And we can step out of the oppression of want and fear, joy and sorrow, into the clear air of Christ's presence. With him there is joy. We can step back from our mechanical routines and frantic pace, rejoicing in what he has said to us: "In the world you have tribulation; but be of good cheer, I have overcome the world" (John 16:33).

How do we become new persons?

Every alert person who has truly encountered God's judgment knows that he or she is guilty. There is no one who is not a sinner. We have all gambled away our freedom. We have made room for evil and destroyed God's good creation. The pollution from our consumer-oriented society threatens land and water life with destruction. Never has the biblical witness been more true: "The imagination of man's heart is evil from his youth" (Gen. 8:21). We cannot take this simply as a general complaint. We must rather take it personally. And we know it. A single glance at our diary for the past year will lead us to confess our guilt. We have separated ourselves from God. We have looked at our neighbors with evil. We have not thanked God for his gifts, but have abused them as though we earned them.

But Christ has declared the coming of God's kingdom—a new beginning. We have been redeemed and set free. What lies behind us is forgotten. Sin is forgiven. Our separation from God is ended. Jesus makes possible a new relationship when he says, "Your sins are forgiven" (Matt. 9:2). This applies not only to individuals, to our personal histories that need redemption, but to all of sinful human history. Christ not only forgives us and creates us anew, but renews the world. He is at work in the world, and it is no longer necessary for us to act as we have in the past. The world is old in sin, but God has declared it new and transformed it. And although we, too, are old and plagued by sin, Christ has created us anew. He is transforming our lives.

Where we have come

The good news of Jesus is that we have been rescued. How must our lives be changed so we may walk in the light of Christ and his truth? Jesus of Nazareth, who lived 2000 years ago, can enter our lives. That is what he wants to do. And generations of people have experienced his presence. He seeks us today and wants us to follow him. And we *can* follow him because he is not far away, but stands in our place. To follow him means to experience his love and suffering. Jesus sees through us and sets us free from everything that prejudices us against our neighbors. He frees us from feeling we have to do everything, and so we are able to actually love and care for others in the places he points out to us. He gives us detachment from things and from ourselves, and shows us that we are totally free only when we are bound completely to God. We can be free in his presence because we no longer have to accomplish our wholeness and salvation ourselves. He has already seen to that. Before we could love, he had already loved us. We need no longer panic about our lives. He gives us calmness and a sense of direction.

We have separated ourselves from God. But Christ has overcome this separation. In him we see the new persons we are to be. Now we can ask in quietness how we are to act in our world. We are creations of Christ's love, examples of that newness which comes into the world by him. But we do not have to redeem the world. He has already redeemed it.

2. God's Law

Which law is God's?

Our laws are written by our representatives and enforced by the government. We deliberate about how we wish to live with each other, what individuals should do for their communities, what taxes citizens should pay, and what services they should render. Every nation has its own laws. But the Bible speaks of law in a quite different way. God's law, expressed especially in the Ten Commandments, applies equally to all nations. It is simple, clear, and as unalterable as the laws of nature. God's law is not subject to our wills. In fact it exists over against our wills. For that reason the Ten Commandments are expressed mostly in negative terms: "You shall not steal"; "You shall not kill"; "You shall not commit adultery."

We are free to do what is right, but we are not free to do everything. God has decreed our limits. In Christ he has said yes to us, but in his law he clearly tells us what he expects of us. According to tradition the Ten Commandments were revealed to the people of Israel after they had been freed from slavery in Egypt (Exodus 19-20). They constitute the basic law of Judaism and Christianity. Today they are known in all countries. The authority of these Commandments rests in the God who gave them on his holy mountain, accompanied by powerful signs of thunder and lightning (Exodus 19). In this way the seriousness of the law and the terrible, far-reaching power of the Lawgiver is expressed. God's law is a life-and-death issue for the human race.

How do we interpret the law?

The problem with any law is its interpretation. But laws *must* be interpreted, because they exist in human history. The texts of laws remain the same while people and situations change. If we ask how Christians today should live, the answer must involve an interpretation of the Ten Commandments. Like human laws, God's laws cannot be properly understood in isolation from their historical contexts. This does not mean that any human being can change God's law. That is impossible. But the law must be interpreted and applied to different situations.

Some people set aside portions or all of God's commandments as not applicable to them. They consider any authority to be bad. They do not want anyone to tell them what to do. And there are others who want God's law without the God who gave it. They want the Ten Commandments without Jesus. They try to live by the hard letter of the law, without love and mercy, opposing those who interpret the law differently. Both ways are mistaken. One seeks freedom without law and the other law without freedom. Jesus said, "Till heaven and earth pass away, not an iota, not a dot, will pass from the law until all is accomplished" (Matt. 5:18). But at the same time he exhibited an amazing freedom in his faithfulness to the law.

What is the freedom of Christ? When we understand that, we have understood the whole gospel. Those who do not understand the freedom of Christ may be devout, but their faith has nothing to do with Christ. I am a Christian because I acknowledge that everything given to me is a gift from Christ. He is both promise and fulfillment. And I also understand God's commandments in light of him. It is in Jesus, who is without sin, that I see what God desires in his law. God does not want to destroy me, but to make my life new. Much of the offense Jesus gave to devout people of his day was caused by his refusal to interpret the law in the abstract. He always interpreted it in terms of people. That was his secret. In Christ the law was never something from the past, but always a living reality in the present. As Paul said, Christians are free *from* past laws, which were once valid but are now dead. But we are free *for* the living law, which is nothing less than God's will in Christ. Great evil is continually done in the world in the name of laws that are unrelated to people's true situations, and which lack the forgiveness that Christ gives. Jesus offers us a law in the present. He wants God's commandments to lead us to him. The law of God is not unbreakable rules, but an assurance to people that God loves them through all eternity. This love will achieve its goal. That is the freedom of Christ.

Why do we speak of two tables of the law?

We live our life in the world in three ways. We are first persons in our own right, and have our inner selves into which no one apart from God can quite enter. We are also in relationship with other persons who trust us, encounter us, and talk with us. And we are finally part of a larger community, nation, and world. But all three aspects of our life in the world belong together. When we sink back into our own thoughts we find that our colleagues are still present in our minds. And when we are in public we achieve nothing unless someone gives us support. All three aspects are dealt with in the seven last commandments. These protect human life in the world, while the first three speak of our relationship to God. According to tradition, Moses wrote the first three on one stone tablet and the last seven on a second. But we must never forget that the two tables of the law belong together. Jesus has shown us that we cannot separate God from our neighbors. Only in our neighbors do we rightly see God.

What is the First Commandment?

The First Commandment sets before our eyes the power and unity of God: "I am the Lord your God, who brought you out of the land of Egypt, out of the house of bondage. You shall have no other gods before me" (Exod. 20:2-3). In this confession the people of Israel found their identity. And this First Commandment remains the foundation of God's people, the presupposition of all other commandments. God wants our exclusive worship and service. The Bible adds that no one is to make a graven image or idol. For an idol is an attempt to represent God, which is impossible.

We have already spoken of the claims made today by different religions. But these are not all that are meant here. In the gods of ancient and modern religions we can in fact discover a longing for the one, true God of heaven and earth—pointers rather than competitors. Far more dangerous are anonymous powers and idols, the collective wishes of modern secular society which rob us of our freedom and exclude God. We desire to have what everyone else has, and, despite the cost, to live as they live. At that point God dies in us.

We may well ask, "How can we bear witness to the uniqueness of God and his power over our lives in a society which lives by creating desires for more and more material possessions? How can we take a stand in the world in which these powers speak so loudly, where we can speak of God only in an embarrassed and peripheral way? How can we hold our hearts free for God when so many others want to possess them? Everyone tells us we will be happy if we only buy this or that product. How can we serve God only?"

But God says we shall have no other gods before him. For otherwise we cannot live. With other gods we will die, even if we make ourselves millionaires. We can only live with God when we put other gods behind us. God's creation is good, and is to be appreciated. But nothing may sit in God's place. If we serve anything or anyone but God, he is no longer our Lord. We live in a world in which God's absolute lordship is contested. We are to testify by our lives that God alone is our Lord. We belong only to him.

What is the Second Commandment?

The Second Commandment is closely related to the first: "You shall not take the name of the Lord your God in vain" (Exod. 20:7). People in the ancient Near East saw persons in their names in much the same way we see them in their pictures. God is present in his name. Whoever speaks ill, falsely, or contemptuously of God's name attacks God himself. We have no image of the invisible God, but he has entrusted us with his name. In it he gives us himself. "The Lord will not hold him guiltless who takes his name in vain" (Exod. 20:7). But such guilt is incurred around us every day, and we ourselves have our part in it. Most of us have spoken of God as if there really were no God.

And yet isn't it also an emptying of the word *God* to babble devoutly and pray endlessly with it? We use our time-honored forms of prayer inattentively, disguising our lies and deceit, our prophesying and magic with God's name. We have made his name into a meaningless piece of our religious and irreligious language. It seems that God's name has ceased to be a name and has become merely a concept. We *use* it much more than we *call* on it. God wants to be called on. Otherwise his name is taken in vain. When we hear people's names, we link thoughts with them and picture those who bear them. But with God no such separation is possible. If we make his name into an idea, we have lost him. The Second Commandment charges us to struggle against this misuse. We do this when we learn again to pray with those who pray in the Bible, to call God by his name and to earnestly expect his help. That is what it means to say God's power is in his name.

What is the Third Commandment?

When God gave human beings the task of caring for the earth, he thereby made working days holy. The Third Commandment establishes a day of rest. The Bible prohibits all work on the seventh day of the week. According to Genesis God rested on the seventh day, after his work of creation was completed. He blessed that day and made it holy. The Sabbath was the Jewish day of rest. Christians have traditionally rested on Sunday, because they were accustomed to gathering on the first day of the week—the day Jesus rose from the dead. So Sunday was a day for both celebration of God's creation of the world and his new creation in Christ. We are free to rest after a week of labor. It is not a useless rest which God commands, but a creative one. He calls us to celebrate the wonderful deeds of creation.

It has been said that this old rhythm of work and rest dates back to an agrarian society. Today our industrial society is never free from work, and we can make free time whenever we like. But whoever has the good of workers at heart cannot talk of scattered free time or a staggered week. The Third Commandment was given for the sake of workers. On a common day of rest there can be true celebration, both with one's family and the entire community. Our leaders promise to further reduce our hours of work, and futurologists paint a picture of a world in which it will be a luxury to work. This should mean that the worth of rest, play, and celebration are increasingly seen among us. But the opposite is the case. Sunday is desolate.

Most of us do not know what to do with our free time. We do not know how to celebrate. Our work is not blessed, and our celebration is not sanctified.

It is true that observance of Sunday has often been made into a burden. Jesus had to bring the Third Commandment face to face with freedom and joy. "The sabbath was made for man, not man for the sabbath" (Mark 2:27). Worship is less a duty than celebration, and our celebration of God is what defines our day of rest. Sunday should be free from compulsory, joyless work not so that we do nothing, but rather that we celebrate in a meaningful way. And the goal of all celebration is freedom.

In our work we find fulfillment as we experience the preservation and unfolding of creation. God has given us the gift of being creators with him. But at the same time all human work is overshadowed by the curse of toil and transitoriness, uselessness and ruin. We can no longer trust in our dreams of progress. We suffer from the fact that our work is alienated from God. This reveals the deepest meaning of a day of rest, and why we cannot live without one. Here we can be free for a time from aims and objects, uses and purposes. We need to learn this kind of rest from the Old Testament, from the Psalms and the prophetic books. We can learn it also from Jesus' life, and from the hymns of the early church.

The most audacious and humble of acts is ours as we honor and praise God, as we sing and play in his sight. The joy and gladness of seemingly useless play can be a reflection of the celebration God intends for us on his day of rest. Art, music, poetry, and sports can all be seen in this light. Genesis uses the daring image of God himself celebrating on the seventh day. In other places biblical writers speak not only of the whole creation singing and playing in God's sight, but even of God himself playing with his creation (see Psalm 104). He plays with his people as a bridegroom plays with his bride. The coming of Christ is therefore compared to the joy of a marriage feast. On Sundays we celebrate our Lord's coming among us. We plunge into the "game" of the church's liturgy, into the realm of the unimaginable. There we encounter a power which can tear us away from ourselves and give us strength we do not have. That power is the proclaimed Word of God. In the first three commandments we see how we are to encounter God. We should acknowledge him, honor him before people, and give him space in our time—all of which belongs to him.

Where we have come

As part of the old creation we are separated from God. We cannot recognize God's will, let alone fulfill it. For our hearts are evil apart from God, even when we try to follow the letter of the law. So the law condemns us. It convinces us of our powerlessness. We are not God. The law shows us that we cannot justify ourselves. Only God can save us. In God's new, redeemed creation he frees us from the law and gives us the love and creative freedom Jesus identified as the heart of our relationship with God.

In the light of this love and freedom the Ten Commandments need to be interpreted anew for every generation. We know God's will and Commandments only in the setting of the love Jesus shows and is. And our freedom remains bound to the love God offers us. We are justified by faith in Christ, made right before God, accepted and set free, in order that we may do his will. And God's will, as expressed in the ancient Commandments, affects all areas of our existence: our inner selves, our relationships with our neighbors, and our life in society. And yet all these areas are one in our life with God.

The first three commandments deal specifically with our relationship to God. We are to acknowledge him as the one and only God, the almighty Creator of the world, the ground and sustainer of our existence. The First Commandment is directed against a thousand different temptations of our time: idols, fetishes, ideologies, substitutes for religion, heresies, greed, passions, violence, and all the other demons which today would conquer our hearts. But God says, "I am for you. I am the Lord your God. You need no other gods." Whenever in the other commandments we hear the stern "You shall not . . . , " we need to remember this First Commandment: "I am for you. I am your Lord."

The Second Commandment forbids us to dishonor God's holy name. Jesus entrusted God's name to us and interpreted it anew: Father, King, and Lord. In Jesus Christ God has become known and is brought near us. We should know and confess before others that there is no name above the name of Jesus in heaven and on earth

(Phil. 2:9-11). But if we honor God by calling on the name which he himself has imparted to us, then we will not make an image of him and try to replace him with anything we have made. We will not pretend we can replace him with idols of our own making and gods of our imagination.

The Third Commandment reminds us that together with the world, God created time and gave order to it. We are part of this order; it is sacred. It makes us whole, for it comes from God. We can accept our working days because we have days of rest, and our days of rest are important and meaningful because of our work during the week. We need to recognize our limitations: six days of the week we can give; on the seventh day we need to receive. On Sunday we can then celebrate God's coming to us in Christ. We who are weary and heavy-laden can be restored in body and spirit. Our society would like to level the calendar, making all days the same. But we need to resist such pressure. We need to separate our work and play in a healthy way, so that each might enrich the other. Week by week we need to give our lives breadth and depth, handing over to God our sorrow, anxiety, and joy. To honor the Sabbath means to take time to consider our health and let our lives be ordered with appropriate time for thanking, praising, and honoring God.

3. Our Social Life

What is the Fourth Commandment?

Jesus said that even if we praise and honor God, give reverence to his name, and celebrate his day of rest, we are far from him if we do not love our neighbors. Our obedience to the first table of commandments includes obedience to the second table. Confused and disappointed, we ask again and again, "How can I love my neighbor?" The Bible clearly points the way. We start with ourselves and move outward. We first discover ourselves as persons who live with others. We are encompassed and influenced by larger communities: nations, societies, groups, and families. We do not initially seek out such communities; we are born into them.

The first people who represent humanity as a whole to us are our parents. The Scriptures say we can only lead a good life if we recognize what we owe them. This applies not only to our physical parents, whom we often resent, but also to all our other parents. Our lives do not come from ourselves. We have inherited all that we physically and spiritually are, including most of our material goods. We can do very little alone. Every day we need others who know more than we do and who are more than we are. We have been entrusted to them.

Crises, protests, and the rejection of elders' authority are stages in the development of young people. It is not without reason that many ask why they should honor their parents. Like other authorities, parents can become rigid—or what is more common today, confused and weak. They may have no standards and therefore no courage, being happy to look only at themselves while pushing their children away. Fathers and mothers must not make their children orphans in their own homes. And children must obey their parents even when they make mistakes. Equally important, they must not turn away from their parents when they are old and weak. We are in partnership with our parents in the search for meaning and values in our lives.

Apart from parents there are many other carriers of tradition with whom young people have to deal, including teachers and civil authorities. Obedience to such authorities is unpopular in a day when *liberation* is the universal catchword. But the Bible says obedience is the *second* thing we owe to parents. The first is honor, attention, trust, love, and understanding. Whoever practices these has no trouble obeying. The Fourth Commandment is the only one with a promise attached to it: "Honor your father and your mother, that your days may be long in the land which the Lord your God gives you" (Exod. 20:12).

When we think we can overcome the future without understanding our past or even resisting it, without recognizing the heritage of our nation, society, and family, then our roots do not go down deep into the earth but rather spread merely along the surface. When we think no one is better and wiser than we are, that no age or position puts anyone above us, then we don't know what we are talking about. We like to think that all which came before us was worse than what we experience today. We naturally want to reject all authority as such. But authority is not arbitrary. It is firmly based on the experience of the past.

Fathers and mothers are participants in God's creation. The fullness of God's creation is seen in the Lord's good land, in children of promise who honor their parents, and in the Lord himself, the Almighty One who allows himself to be called Father. The people of Israel were indebted to their faithful fathers and mothers for their continued existence. It is no different for us today. Every generation of Christians has an earlier generation to thank for its faith. Therefore faith is also a turning back; it exists in the tension between going forward and returning home, between our visions and our origins. In the last verses of the Old Testament Malachi prophesied something that the Christian church recognized as fulfilled in Jesus: "He will turn the hearts of fathers to their children and the hearts of children to their fathers, lest I come and smite the land with a curse" (4:6).

How do we live in community?

The relationship between young people and old people is only one example of life in a human community. The Bible gives us very little direct advice about how to live as citizens of our nations and also as members of complex societies. We can find political mandates only indirectly in the Scriptures. Attitudes of both world affirmation and renunciation are frequently developed from the Bible. Extremes in either direction can lead to errors and fanaticism. Such views can conflict with the First Commandment by robbing God of his honor and setting another god in his place. Christ would never have given divine honor to a nation, party, or person, as has so often been done. Christians are to hold two things firmly together: We are both citizens of God's kingdom and of our own countries. We are to work for the improvement of our societies, and we will do this well only if we acknowledge the lordship of Christ. But when we ask by what means our nations will be bettered, the Bible is silent. Only the goal is clear: the human race should live together according to God's will. It is not his will that people starve and suffer, are persecuted and imprisoned. God wills justice, compassion, and love. All who hold office, administer laws, and exercise authority must know that their power is given to them by God. All authorities must therefore act by God's standards. But when governments act in opposition to God's will, Christians must not give up exercising love and bearing witness to the power of Christ.

Is democracy the most Christian form of government?

Democracy is rule by the people. It takes many forms, not all of which can be reconciled with Christian faith. Modern democracy certainly does not have purely Christian roots. But the civil rights granted in modern democracies do offer a great amount of freedom to the church. Democracies are also among the first to call for efforts to safeguard the freedom of citizens, to prevent the seizure of power by a few, and to support justice for all. Democracies have supported international conventions such as the Universal Declaration of Human Rights, accepted by the United Nations in 1948, in which the following rights were upheld: equal political rights and freedoms for all people regardless of physical and cultural differences; equal rights before the law; equal rights to education; freedom of religion and expression; rights of parents over their children; prohibition of arbitrary arrests, illegal punishment, exile, and torture. Such rights are in harmony with the gospel and allow the church freedom in carrying out its mission.

Modern democracy is also a form of government which makes it possible to better one's situation in life. Christians living in democracies can work to improve their countries. That means above all to press for justice for all and to seek the mutual help and well-being of all citizens. The efforts of Christians living in countries with few personal freedoms may encounter more hindrances, and the question of obedience to the state will more frequently arise. Christians in such countries may suffer a great deal. This was the case for the first three centuries of the church's existence. The early Christians saw clearly that the state was provisional, limited to this world, existing only to give order to the human community. The proper relationship of early Christians to the state was defined by two complementary statements: "Let every person be subject to the governing authorities. For there is no authority except from God" (Rom. 13:1), and "We must obey God rather than men" (Acts 5:29). The experience of German Christians with National Socialism in this century has taught us that the second of these is no less important than the first.

What is the Seventh Commandment?

The Seventh Commandment reads, "You shall not steal" (Exod. 20:15). We must discuss this commandment here because it has much to do with life in our human community today. We may say, "That commandment has nothing to do with me! I'm not a thief!" But it is not as simple as that. In primitive rural communities it might well have been possible for every piece of property to have its rightful owner. But that is often very doubtful today. Most people have wondered whether God was responsible for giving some so much, others too much, and the majority of the world little or nothing except their own hunger and thirst. Today we are painfully conscious of those people who live in the so-called Third World. The gap between the poor majority in those countries and the rich majority in our industrialized nations is becoming ever wider. We cannot continue like this. God cannot will it. We may feel as though our possessions are rightfully ours. We may have worked very hard and made great sacrifices to obtain them. But the Old Testament brings us face to face with the very nature of possessions.

Who owns the land and its produce? The Bible gives a consistent answer: God alone. Human beings only manage his possessions for him. The New Testament also tells us that all we have is lent us by God. We own nothing forever, and nothing we possess is ours to do with as we please. We have the responsibility to use our possessions in accordance with God's will. And we are not to become slaves to them. Christians are to be recognized not by what they have, but by how they have it; not by what they earn, but by what they give away. In this sense the Bible approves of possessions. But how difficult it is to distinguish between that which has been justly earned and that which has not! There is the merchant who sells shoddy goods at high prices; the worker who takes good wages for poor and inefficient labor; the landlord who lets property for too much rent; the banker who speculates at others' risk; the government official who wastes taxpayers' savings. Are not all these under the judgment of the Seventh Commandment?

Many people say that all private property constitutes theft. Many think that large properties and industries should be nationalized. In a world of morally bankrupt conglomerates and multinational corporations, should not the means of production belong to the workers in common? Should not the necessities of life be guaranteed to all citizens? These questions are posed everywhere today. People have become unsure about the proper place and legitimacy of property. There are great differences among the countries of the Third World and the industrialized nations of the West and East. Nowhere is there either pure Communism or pure capitalism. All limit the power of property holders to some degree, and all acknowledge the need for individuals to control a certain amount of property and have some responsibility.

The Bible insists on our right use of property. We should be careful of every kind of possessions, not letting ourselves be enslaved by them like the rich young man in Matthew 19. It seemed as though he would do anything to be with Jesus. It appeared he thought less about this life than about joy in God's kingdom. But then the demonic power of possessions pulled him away from Jesus. He could not follow him. Jesus can be very difficult for us. When we want to remain rich, he asks us to become poor. But he also says, "Everyone who has left houses or brothers or sisters or father or mother or children or lands, for my name's sake, will receive a hundredfold, and inherit eternal life" (Matt. 19:29).

What do we have to do with other countries?

The question of how possessions are to be shared justly among people is really secondary. What worries us more is the thought that we might then not have enough of the good things of life to survive and safeguard our corner of the world. Creation is finite and limited. We can use our power and technical skill to subdue the earth and make use of it, but we cannot increase the amount of raw materials that exist. We cannot invent any more land, water, air, metals, or oil. We must use what we have been given. And those supplies are fast running out. We don't mind sharing what we have so long as we don't need it anymore. But anyone who takes for themselves what God has provided for all is stealing. Anyone who destroys God's creation, which he made good and pure and beautiful, commits murder. And anyone who does not think of those who are far away and powerless has not recognized their neighbors.

The Seventh Commandment was formulated for a society which knew poverty and hunger, but could not easily look across the

boundaries of its own land. Now each day we receive news from all
over the world. Therefore we must ask what God's will is for all
people. The question of what one has and another does not have no
longer stops at the border. Christians cannot shut themselves off.
We must ask how we manage our possessions. Do we keep them for
ourselves, or do we use them for others as well? Do we squander
irreplaceable energy and raw materials? Our individual actions may
seem very small matters, but they are what make up the whole.
Leaders of nations, industrialists, and political parties must be
pressed to consider the well-being of all nations in their decisions.

God's will for his creation allows provincial egotism of nations as
little as the selfishness of individuals and families. The Seventh
Commandment has in mind not only the movement of money, but
far more the general welfare of all people. When we interpret "You
shall not steal" for today, it also means we should share our privileges with others. We should share our knowledge and riches with
the poor, both at home and in other countries. The Bible says God is
nearer to the poor than to the rich. This is not just because they are
poor or rich, but because the poor cry unto him and the rich find it
difficult to keep their hearts free from greed.

Must the world remain as it is?

From earliest times human beings have had a longing for equality and a redistribution of land and possessions. Could not good
come from a radical (and perhaps bloody) revolution? Such longing is very strong in our day, for in spite of our great knowledge
and technical ability we do not want to care for the poor and those
who suffer. Can Christians be revolutionaries? Jesus and the apostles showed little interest in government, and none at all in altering
the social order. Jesus was no political revolutionary. But people
have used him to justify both revolution and the utmost in conserva-
tism. Some say Jesus would leave things just as they are. There will
be no real change so long as this present world exists. Others say
Jesus' vision of justice and community was a radical one, that we
cannot leave the world as it is. Who is right?

Jesus and his earliest followers expected an imminent end to the
world. Only because of that expectation did they choose to let so-

ciety remain as it is. But we have no authority from God to throw all order away, answering evil with evil and giving violence a Christian permit. Violent revolution always transgresses other important commandments of God. The real question is whether such action serves love. Many Christians who opposed Hitler chose to use violence as a last resort. They used violence against the violent. Such actions are sometimes necessary. Christians must resist when people are robbed of their freedom, rights, and dignity. Our consciences must determine how such resistance is to be carried out. But no end can justify every means. Christians cannot stand in the ranks of either conservative or revolutionary fanatics.

Today we are able to help people throughout the world because of our rapid communication and transportation system. And we are able to pursue tolerance and justice right where we live. We must set ourselves against the use of arbitrary force; we must see through shallow motives; we must promote understanding between neighbors. Many of us today have everything we need for a comfortable life, but our lives often have no meaning or purpose. The gospel of Jesus Christ addresses our deepest needs. By bearing witness to it we can change the world without having to become political leaders or officeholders.

Where we have come

The Fourth Commandment says we must not break off conversation with each other. Both young and old are partners who must seek together, for the future can never be separated from the past. And there is no freedom which is not bound up with authority and tradition. God desires that the old should encompass the young, that the young should lead the old. Jesus called God "Father." The relationship between parent and child is a model for all human relationships. Government must concern itself with the care of its citizens, and Christians are to be concerned about their families, schools, communities, friends, colleagues, and peoples of other nations. Caring for others involves tolerance, self-renunciation, and specific kinds of help.

Negatively expressed, the Seventh Commandment forbids us to rob others of their property. But in today's context we must apply this commandment not only to private theft, but also to corporate theft. If we grasp the radicality of Jesus' message, we will describe all refusals to help the poor and the suffering as theft. Christians know that the world cannot remain as it is. It is full of violence, deceit, lies, robbery, and cruelty—often perpetrated by "respectable" corporations and governments. Can God lead us back on the path of mutual care and concern? Should we march for revolution, or should we patiently work with others for necessary reforms of our complicated political, industrial, and technical systems? This question is posed everywhere today. And Christians can only answer it in light of God's commandments. Before we embark on any course of social change we must ask, Will we be honoring and respecting others? Will we be adding to their life? Will we be caring for them by what we do and how we do it? Will we leave their lives better than they are now?

4. I and Thou

Who is my neighbor?

Jesus said there are two commandments on which depend "all the law and the prophets" (Matt. 22:40). In these two commandments are included all God's expectations of his people. "You shall love the Lord your God with all your heart, and with all your soul, and with all your might" (Deut. 6:5) and "You shall love your neighbor as yourself" (Lev. 19:18). The first is "the great and first commandment," and the second is like it (Matt. 22:38-39). We fulfill the first three commandments, which concern our relationship with God, only when we love our neighbors. We are members of small and large human communities, and we have duties and responsibilities toward them. To the question, "Who is my neighbor?" Jesus responded that our neighbors are those closest to us (Luke 10:25-37). We are neighbors to each other when we stand with each other in times of need and trouble. When we help each other, we act as God acts toward us. Many people need us today, perhaps in our immediate neighborhoods, but also in faraway places. In our ever-shrinking world, those in other nations are also our neighbors. And we become their neighbors by helping them.

What is the Fifth Commandment?

Helping other people keeps them alive. If we withhold that help, we kill our neighbors. Jesus interpreted the Fifth Commandment—"You shall not kill" (Exod. 20:13)—with unsurpassed severity. Not only the withholding of assistance is murder, but also anger, abuse, and lack of reconciliation. As such they deserve punishment (Matt. 5:21-26). When we read of the many murders committed daily, we are reminded that death always happens to individuals. In death each person is an individual. The same is true in war. Those who discuss war or prepare for war must remember they are discussing and planning the killing of individual people. Killing is the ultimate and most extreme form of lovelessness. Every year thousands are killed on our highways through no fault of their own or any mechanical failure, but simply because others are careless. We must sharpen our consciences so we can recognize the occasions when we deny our love to our neighbors. Jesus said to deny them love is murder. For those who do not love their neighbors do not see them as human beings. A child in its mother's womb is called to be human. Whoever needlessly kills it is guilty of murder. The radical nature of Jesus' message is revealed by the fact that he not only said killing includes anger and the withholding of consideration and forgiveness, but he also placed these on the same level as physical killing. To refuse to be reconciled to one's neighbor, says the Lord, deserves the same punishment as striking him or her down with a weapon.

What is the Sixth Commandment?

Children eventually grow up, leave their parents, and cease to be totally dependent on them. But in a healthy marriage a wife and husband continually grow closer to each other. All the Commandments speak of love in the full biblical sense, but the Sixth Commandment speaks of it in the sense of faithfulness: "You shall not commit adultery" (Exod. 20:14). For marriage is only another word for faithfulness. From very early times God's love for his people has been compared with a marriage. God desires to be with his people, and we need him. Through all eternity God is the partner of those who believe.

Ever since the writing of the Song of Solomon, mystics have spoken of God's love for his people as the love of a bridegroom for his bride. The apostle Paul said husbands must love their wives as Christ loved the church and sanctified it (Eph. 5:25-33). God has given sexuality to us as an expression of married love. Through sexuality the unity of men and women is symbolized—the embarrassment of being different gives way to the joy of union. Our generation prides itself on having overcome the church's age-old hostility to the body. Psychologists remind us that sexuality accompanies us all our lives. It is a gift we are to use responsibly. The expression of our sexuality must be understood within the context of love for one's neighbor. An intimate relationship between a man and a woman is intended to express that love in a unique way. Without love, sex becomes impersonal sensuality. This is the most important thing to keep in mind when dealing with questions of sexuality.

The Sixth Commandment is understood much too narrowly if we read it as applying only to the prohibition of sexual infidelity. Marriage vows are broken by every failure of love, and many of these are more serious than a casual affair. Every failure of love toward our neighbors is adultery: regarding them as stupid; preventing their proper development; denying them real security; concentrating on our own concerns; or simply refusing to help them. In each case we fail to treat our neighbors with love. If we are faithful to our spouses in the physical sense and yet do not want to incur even greater guilt, we must learn to forgive both the great moral failures and all those little daily betrayals. And we must learn to ask forgiveness when we are guilty of the same. It is in this way that marriages mature through crises.

Many people today think the institution of marriage itself is in trouble. Young people hesitate to get married, and the number of divorces has skyrocketed. People today are reluctant to accept the heavy responsibilities of family life. Marriages suffer from our society's ubiquitous egotism, and anyone who wishes to find fulfillment in married life will have to struggle against opposing pressures from both within and without. Marriage involves living for another person for the rest of one's life. Through marriage we offer help to the one closest to us (see Gen. 2:18).

What is the Eighth Commandment?

The most important bridge between people is language. According to the Bible, God himself wants to be linked with us through language. Language is of course not just words, but every form of communication. Our language is an expression of our spirits, and it must be truthful. The Eighth Commandment expresses this negatively: "You shall not bear false witness against your neighbor" (Exod. 20:16). This refers first of all to witnesses in court, but the claims of the New Testament go much further. It is not only in court that we can inflict severe injury through our language. Truthfulness, or a life of truth, is a presupposition of every human community. Jesus called himself the Truth. To be his disciple means to renounce lies (Eph. 4:25), to accept the Spirit of truth (John 14:17), and to become open to the truth.

It is not profitable to speak every truth, however. The expression of some truths can unjustly injure others. It is not only false witness that can kill, but also truth divorced from humanity. When our children lie, we must find out why they are doing it. We should be careful before we punish them. Are they expecting praise or rewards which we are not giving them? Are we responsible for their bad consciences? And what are we trying to avoid with our *own* lies? Why does it please us so much to gossip behind our neighbor's back? Why do we gladly get mixed up in our neighbor's private affairs?

It is a very small step from occasional lying in order to be popular to regular lying. In the course of our daily traffic with others, individual errors occur because we do not know enough, are inconsiderate, or are challenged. But Jesus digs much deeper when he asks if we are *in the truth*. One who is in the truth is free *for* the truth, a friend *of* the truth, and one in whom *love* is present. When we look at our lives from this point of view, we may well be startled. Jesus said, "You will know the truth, and the truth will make you free" (John 8:32). But truth is also an expression of freedom.

Many nations today suffer from situations in which not a single free word is allowed to appear in public. Political and commercial interests stand in continuing opposition to the free expression of truth. When we read or listen uncritically, we are capitulating in this struggle. Politicians often think they can speak only part of the truth, obscure the issues with unimportant details, misrepresent their opponents' views, or lie outright—all in the name of some greater good. As citizens we must challenge such practices with a steadfast and critical search for the truth. In the Sermon on the Mount Jesus sharpened our duty to search out the truth by prohibiting oaths. He said we have no need of them if we are in the truth (Matt. 5:33-37). Only when we cannot trust our neighbors must we use oaths. And even then an oath is no guarantee of truth.

The Eighth Commandment can also be expressed in a positive fashion. Although our language can often be described as character assassination—because slander can literally destroy our neighbors— our words can also be used for good. But how often do we do this in a day? Are we concerned to reconcile, heal, and comfort our neighbors? Is our desire to establish trust between us and others? Can we lay aside our lies and slander? This is a powerful way we can express love for our neighbors.

What are the Ninth and Tenth Commandments?

"Honor your father and your mother. . . . You shall not kill. You shall not commit adultery. You shall not steal. You shall not bear false witness against your neighbor." These are clear commandments. And sometimes we feel as though we keep them. But when we read the Ninth and Tenth Commandments, the ground sinks beneath us. Here we are asked to eliminate that which seems beyond our control: our desires. "You shall not covet . . ." (Exod. 20:17). This command is far more important than the list of objects named, which represent familiar properties in ancient Israel: a house, wife, manservant, maidservant, ox, or ass. The commandment also forbids coveting "anything that is your neighbor's."

From what we know about human beings, this is an impossible demand. We are all filled with desires and drives. It is impossible for us *not* to covet. It goes against our nature. For we always want something. We always want what our neighbors have. Envy, we are told, is not a burden but rather the means by which our society functions. It is said there would be no incentive for economic advancement if people did not envy each other's goods. More than any of the other commandments, these two disturb us. And like the other commandments, Jesus took these ancient words and extended and sharpened them: "But I say to you that every one who looks at a woman lustfully has already committed adultery with her in his heart" (Matt. 5:28). Sin does not begin with actions, but with our wishes and wills. "The imagination of man's heart is evil from his youth" (Gen. 8:21). But why then do we sometimes want to do what is right?

We must ultimately come back to the First Commandment: "I am the Lord your God" (Exod. 20:2). God himself has given the Commandments. They are not of human origin. But we know God not only as one who directs our lives with relentless severity, but also as the one who makes us new every day through his immeasurable goodness. The one who gives us the Commandments also sets us free to keep them. The roots of our actions lie deep in darkness, but God leads us into his light. Because he is the Lord, we can trust everything to him: our deeds and the motives that lie behind them; our good intentions and their meager results; our tormenting passions, which would make us slaves of envy and hate; all that we do not want to do, but yet in our weakness do. God loves us, comforts us, sets us free from ourselves, and saves us. His Commandments are not intended to burden or cramp us. They are the flares which make his love visible before the world. God wants the world to be sound and holy, because it belongs to him.

What is the meaning of work?

The Third Commandment speaks of a day of rest. But none of the Ten Commandments speak of work, that which seems of first importance in our world. Our labor claims the greatest part of our day. We are God's creatures, and he wills that we engage in creative activity. We support ourselves through our labor. That is the material significance of work. Its personal significance, however, consists of the fact that it is not for us, but for others. If we were concerned only with the present day and ourselves alone, we would not work as we do. For work is provision and care.

But we also seek recognition through our work. We want our employers, at least, to recognize its value. Our wages help support our families. But money alone cannot be the full significance of our work. And often our labor seems so empty. Wise factory owners are getting rid of assembly lines, because they know from experience they do not produce the best results. Craftspersons work longer hours, take greater risks, and put themselves more completely into their work than factory workers—usually for less income. But they find satisfaction in their independence. Their work is much more significant for them.

More and more people in our industrial societies are finding their work to be weary toil, a curse. It is true that work never quite loses the character of toil (see Gen. 3:17), but God wants our labor to be worthy of our efforts. We should not earn our wages as strangers on a treadmill, and our achievements should not be measured simply by their productivity or by a stopwatch. Our societies are full of soulless competition—industries and businesses which produce and expand madly. It is becoming more and more difficult for people to feel called to a vocation. A lack of joy hangs over much of our labor. And at retirement many are forced into destructive inactivity. Frequently they become sick from facing such a life.

Today workers are employed without compassion, and are given little respect aside from wages and fringe benefits. Large corporations treat all alike, paying little attention to quality of work or individual differences. Our economic systems deprive us of the possibility of working for people we can trust, who take seriously our intentions, diligence, strength, and faithfulness. We must be on our guard lest our professional lives become more and more divorced from our personal lives. But there are forces now in motion from which we can hardly escape. Modern industrial societies have rendered the ideal of a God-ordained, life-long vocation all but impossible to achieve. And even though our workload is lighter than in past generations, it oppresses us more. We can no longer see our labor as something God has chosen for us.

Jesus praised faithfulness in little things (Luke 16:10; 19:17). The apostle Paul urged diligence in work (2 Thess. 3:6-12), particularly that we may help those in need (Eph. 4:28). All of Jesus' disciples had trades. But the gospel offers no solution for the troubles and conflicts of our work today, for our emptiness, alienation, and personal devaluation. And yet Jesus says to us, "Do not be anxious about your life, what you shall eat or what you shall drink, nor about your body, what you shall put on. Is not life more than food, and the body more than clothing? Look at the birds of the air: they neither sow nor reap nor gather into barns, and yet your heavenly Father feeds them. Are you not of more value than they?" (Matt. 6:25-26). We must test whether we have become slaves of money. The working week leads to Sunday, when we can celebrate the fact that Jesus has set us free. We are called to that! There is no part of our lives in which Jesus is not by our side. That which troubles us has already been overcome. And there is no work in which we deal only with things and not with people. Let those who work with us recognize in us the freedom from sorrow, haste, and anxiety which we see in Jesus!

Where we have come

A man and a woman can become one in the deepest sense. And this means more than just sexual union. Sexuality must be united with love—with trust, faithfulness, care, forgiveness, and unity in spirit and faith. The marriage of a man and a woman is an image of the love of God and a parable of love for all who are our neighbors. There cannot be faith without love. But neither can there be faith without truth. The Ten Commandments forbid the breaking of faith through a lack of love in our lives. Living in the truth means living in a relationship of love with God and our neighbors. But abstract or general truth can be a depersonalizing lie. We must heal and comfort others through words of reconciliation. We must beware of lies, gossip, and slander. Jesus talked of love for others in the same breath as love for God. Our love is authentic only if it is not something put on for Sundays, but is allowed to rule over us every day, accompanying us in our daily work, rest, and play. We must seek the dignity and freedom of our neighbors. We must direct our attention to those who stand near us. We must not covet what they have. And when we are tempted to turn the Ten Commandments into a superficial legalism, we must be reminded that God sees into our hearts.

5. Our Selves

How do we become blessed?

The word *blessed* has almost died out among us, but its substance is familiar. We ask, "What is happiness?" Jesus spoke of being blessed. The same thing is meant. Jesus named those who are blessed; the poor; the suffering; the gentle; those who seek righteousness; the compassionate; the pure; peacemakers; those who are persecuted (Matt. 5:3-11). These are promised happiness. They will be comforted and satisfied. They will see God and find his mercy. They will be called the children of God.

Does this mean that only the poor, the needy, the humble, and the unimportant will achieve that end for which we all strive? If we look carefully at the Beatitudes in Matthew 5, we will see that they portray Jesus himself. How do we become blessed? By becoming as Jesus was. But since none of us can do that, are we then cut off from happiness? Is all meaning and purpose taken from us? To be a disciple means to live with Jesus. It is in company with *him* that we find happiness. And the happiness that comes from life with him is the only kind that endures.

Jesus was a person who lived for others. The love of a parent or a marriage partner is, at its best, truly love for another. Such love brings happiness. And Jesus' entire life was and is an expression of such love. Through poverty, suffering, and persecution he remained at peace and loved his enemies. In the face of this blessedness of Jesus we are poor indeed. We are not like him. But Christians know ultimate happiness cannot be achieved, but can only be given. We who are poor must expect everything from God. Then Jesus will bless us.

How do we learn to play?

Jesus points us to the birds, which have nothing and yet sing. He points us to the lilies of the field, which are clothed more magnificently than King Solomon, even though they do not work. Again and again Jesus forbade anxiety about the future. Like a child at play, he lived totally in the present. And yet he never lost sight of eternity. If we want to learn from him, we must also learn this. It belongs to blessedness to accept this day and hour. Play can light up creation, show us the path of freedom, and bring God near. In our work we use our energies and diligence. But in our play we can be ourselves, delighting in the fullness of God's world. Prayer is also play. We speak to God even though he knows everything; we ask things of him although he foresees all that will happen; we sing songs to him even though he is not a child. Art is a special way of playing, too. A Catholic theologian has called art "God's grandchild." It plays like a jester at his feet. Jesus himself gives us the gift of play, teaching us to forget the world for a time, to relax and enjoy old stories, and to praise the God of heaven and earth.

How do we become mature?

We grow older all the time. Our culture dislikes old people, and we are afraid of wrinkles. Our fear of aging makes it very difficult to mature. We refuse to accept our mortality with grace. Jesus did not live to grow old in the biological sense, but he lived as a mature person. He rejected the struggle for other people's possessions, and resisted those passions which destroy the human spirit. Mature people become free by accepting themselves as they are and recognizing their true possibilities. That which is unimportant no longer oppresses them. They turn away from petty details toward that on which their lives depend. Mature persons have found their identity. They are congruent with themselves. In the vocabulary of the church, the process of maturing is one of growth in *holiness*. With the apostle Paul we know we have not yet attained to the fullness of new life, but Jesus has made us his own (Phil. 3:12). From Jesus we learn calmness in all things. We cannot become mature on our own. But God accepts and forgives us. When we are forgiven we no longer see ourselves as the gods we imagined ourselves to be in our youth. We can think of ourselves soberly, do our work without illusions, and be patient with others, for God has already taken the last step for us.

How do we bear suffering?

Christians see the cross of Christ hanging over the world. Jesus' cross is a sign not only of his own suffering, but of the suffering endured by the entire world. While animals bear physical pain, human beings must endure suffering in a much deeper fashion. Jesus' cross is a sign of victory over suffering. We dislike pain, and we try to quench every evidence of it with drugs. We are also sensitive to the suffering produced by evil and injustice among nations. In suffering, our death is anticipated and recognized as part of creation. In suffering we sense the conflict between our mortality and our longing for eternal life. We cry out against the boundary of death. Jesus said, "Blessed are those who mourn . . ." (Matt. 5:4). Those who suffer are blessed because their cries are a sign that human beings are intended for something beyond death. And in the cross of Christ suffering is turned into a victory over death. Eastern religions proclaim a salvation involving renunciation of our longings and independent selves. But Jesus suffers with us, and through his suffering and death God gives us help, healing, and blessing. Suffering throws us on the mercy of God, teaching us to hope only in him.

How do we gain peace?

Everyone wants to be happy. How must we live if we are to find happiness? Christians answer this question by saying we must pursue *peace*. But true peace is more than what can be written into political treaties. Such peace comes through the gospel. Only with Jesus can we live in true peace. Jesus not only taught us about peace, he was and is peace, the Prince of peace. The apostle Paul called him "our peace" (Eph. 2:14). God's peace comes in the face of what we have, what we are, and what we expect. God's peace is not that corrupt and tired peace nations conclude when they are no longer able to fight. It is not the kind of peace that says, "Let it be. You can't change it." This is not the peace brought by Jesus. He does not sacrifice truth for peace, but rather himself. We always turn that around, which is the reason we have no peace between nations, groups, and families. We are not prepared to sacrifice ourselves. Every small step along this path brings peace nearer to us— the kind of peace Jesus teaches and is. His peace gives happiness.

How can we die?

The story of Jesus is the story of his suffering. And it was his death that made world history. Because of him, our death leads to peace.

Only death makes our peace complete. For in death we confront the limits of all our questions. In the face of death all language is ambiguous. For Christians, happiness is not hitting the jackpot and freedom from the need to work. Some happiness might come from that, but not true happiness. True happiness is being able to live with Jesus. And we need to see the depth of what that means. As we live with Jesus, he shows us what it is to give ourselves away. We can see a little of that in our lives now. But in death everything comes to a conclusion. In death we give away not only our goods and possessions, but our very selves. Jesus died not because he had to, but of his own free will. His suffering was an offering to God, the "travail of his soul" (Isa. 53:11). In death he gave himself for us. In his abandonment he threw himself into the arms of God, opening the door for us. In life and death, suffering and joy we can now pass through that door into God's kingdom.

Where we have come

Alone we are nothing. Left alone we suffer. Left alone we cannot become persons. To deliver ourselves from our loneliness is a never-ending task. Every step toward others requires the sacrifice of a bit of ourselves. We want to close ourselves up, but we must become open. Those who do not sacrifice themselves do not expose their weaknesses. But Jesus says our neighbors have claims on us. In society and in our families, in church and in marriage, at work and before our children we are called to give up living for ourselves and to live with Jesus. The ultimate test is not what we do, but who we are. Do we belong to those whom Jesus counts blessed? These are the children of God, those whom he knows. Jesus says, "Come to me!" He counts those blessed who remain open despite all they see in themselves and all they suffer from the world. If we are open and willing to play like children, if we know we are weak and yet can live without worry, if we have learned to lose ourselves and give ourselves away, then we are near to the God revealed in Jesus. Then we have turned away from the standards of the world—giving and taking, having and holding, wanting and possessing, ruling and serving. Then we can be called happy. We can learn to die and live with Jesus.

6.   Expectation and Fulfillment

What does the future hold?

The first thing Jesus is recorded to have said as he began his public ministry was, "The time is fulfilled, and the kingdom of God is at hand" (Mark 1:15). Christians live and receive life from this message. The world is God's good creation. But it will become his new creation when the old has passed away. For "the kingdom of God is at hand." No one can live without expectation, without some kind of hope. We think beyond the present, pondering the future and worrying about it before it arrives. For nothing ever remains as it is. Yet what do we expect from the future? Our raw materials are almost exhausted, science and technology have reached major limits, and the human race is on the verge of altering itself. We do not want to think about such things, so we close our windows to the outside world and concentrate on our little pleasures. At least we and our children will keep what we have. But then there is death. All of us must die. Even nations die, and in spite of all our technical progress our culture shows unmistakable signs of decay. Careful observers agree that the future can mean only catastrophe and decline. And yet Christians repeat Christ's message, "The kingdom of God is at hand."

What do we expect from life?

Death is already present in our lives. When we become ill and grow old, when we suffer loss, pain, and disappointment, then we have a premonition of death. Death comes uncomfortably closer every day. But our lives also have premonitions of resurrection. Leo Tolstoi told of a man who found his way back from a ruined life to one of fulfillment and meaning. Christians call this *conversion*. When we have had a conversion we begin to apprehend a little of what God has in store for us. This experience need not take hold of our lives violently, suddenly changing everything. We can know the breath of resurrection each day when we find more meaning in the world around us. All creation speaks the language of resurrection. We can detect it on a morning when a bird sings unexpectedly for the first time. Our lives lie before us. We never possess them.

They are promised to us. Our ultimate destiny is not settled. But that does not mean it is not already here. God carries us into a new life, however dark it may now seem to us. He will transform creation and crown our lives with glory. What do we expect from life? We expect God will fulfill his promise.

What is God's promise?

God's promise is that the ambiguities of our lives will be overcome. For God's glory and kingdom will appear among people in such a way that all will see and recognize it. God will conquer evil forever. The forces which plague us will be unmasked and destroyed. God will be all in all. Our human history will find its end. All our sorrows, cares, aims, and objectives will have their end. How do we know this? We know it from Jesus Christ, the very one who is the coming God. Jesus' disciples announced God's coming with certainty and carried his message into the world because they had experienced this future already present among them. For "the life was made manifest, and we saw it, and testify to it, and proclaim to you the eternal life which was with the Father and was made manifest to us" (1 John 1:2).

In Jesus the future is already present. The peace, love, and joy of God's kingdom can be experienced already in him. Thus his apostles could say that where faith is, there is the kingdom of God. There we experience the glory of Jesus' kingdom, the strength of his compassion, and the light of his hope. Where Jesus is present the sick are healed, the weary are lifted up, and prisoners are released. Jesus' power is still hidden today. That is why we call it a "miracle" when the incurably ill are healed, when the blind see, or when the lame walk. The glory of God is still hidden from our eyes, and "it does not yet appear what we shall be" (1 John 3:2).

How do we understand world history?

Human beings experience the progress of time. Language is the means by which we form concepts, establish laws, relate things to each other, and take the future into account. Because we are conscious of ourselves, evil is possible. We can challenge and obscure the lordship of God. Our egotism would remove God from his world.

But God cannot be removed. He works his salvation despite our opposition. And he offers it to all people. Thus both human evil and God's salvation develop side by side in human history. When Jesus proclaimed the acceptable year of the Lord (Luke 4:19) and the nearness of God's kingdom (Mark 1:15), the history of salvation reached its climax. But God's work of salvation is not only for the pious. God is involved in the history of all people. We are all bound up with the God who directs, comforts, heals, and sanctifies. Christians look forward to the fulfillment of the history of salvation, both for human beings and for the creation itself, which cries out for its redemption.

How do we learn to hope?

No one lives without anticipation of the future. But this can take the form of either hope or anxiety. Concern with the future breeds alarmists and astrologists. Clairvoyants have always had a good market. But no clairvoyant can communicate anything except the hopes and fears of our time. Christians live from the hope that God will someday be all in all. We need not know all the details beforehand. We need not think about where the present is leading, but we can look to the God who is always greater than what we see or experience. If we believe in Jesus and live with him, our present time gradually becomes more clear. God awaits us on the boundary of time. Every prayer is an expression of confidence that in the future God will bring light into our darkness. Prayer bears witness to God's faithfulness.

The Old Testament is a story of indestructible expectation. Whatever happened, God's promises would always be fulfilled. When God set the people of Israel free from slavery in Egypt he promised them a new land. He gave his people kings and prophets and promised his eternal lordship over all the nations from Mount Zion (Jerusalem). And at the same time he promised a Messiah who would redeem Israel and establish peace. We, too, can expect God to fulfill his promises. And that which is to come has already made its appearance.

One historical event is for Christians the most sure sign of God's promise: the resurrection of Christ. This event is at the heart of Christian faith. It is the turning point of time. The new has already begun. The church experiences the presence of the risen Christ. His Spirit is its life, foreseeing the future and proclaiming the return of the risen Lord. Christian hope therefore reaches into the new world, not as an extension of our present life (which could be hell), but as fully developed life, life with God and from God. In Christ the new is already here, grounded in his resurrection. And that past event becomes present for us as we experience Christ in our lives today.

What follows death?

Everyone wants to know what comes after death. Some believe in life after death, but is that merely wishful thinking? Few of us want everything to suddenly cease. It is part of our nature to long for eternity. What really happens in death? Death is the end of time for us. It sets a boundary. Materialists say everything ends with death because we consist only of the cells in our bodies. When our cells fail, that is the end of us. Idealists say death is only a bridge, because everything is spirit. The body is only a shell which the spirit casts off at death. Both explanations emasculate death. The Bible says death is God's judgment. It reveals the worth of what we have done. But the Bible also says Christ has conquered death forever. Death is a very serious matter, but Christ has overcome it. And because of Christ we will not only encounter God's judgment when we die, but we shall be raised with Christ and be with him at God's side.

Life after death is life with God. When our spirits have detected a tiny trace of God in our lives; when we have cried out for God as a child cries out for its mother, and been comforted by him; when we have contemplated God in ecstasy like the mystics; when adoration and praise have been wrung from our very selves—then we know just a little of the indescribable greatness of returning home to God. Love will find only love, and faith will be rewarded with sight. When we know the glory which awaits us, we are better able to live our lives now. As we sense God's power and mercy, we experience new freedom to give up our lives for the sake of others.

If we see how great God is, then we know in our hearts we cannot approach him on our own. Death makes that clear to us. Our striving, our goodness, our evil, and all that we are must undergo testing and judgment. But after death we will be the persons God intended us to be, reaching out our hands to the one who is both our Judge and our Redeemer. The seriousness with which the Bible speaks of judgment can make us ask whether some will find forgiveness and eternal life while others find eternal judgment. But we must remember that we are not the ones who will judge. It is easy to censure others. But God has the final word. We do not truly know how anyone stands before him. It is best that we ourselves cling to Christ and live as he intends.

The Bible offers many images of what death, judgment, and the resurrection of the dead will be like. The Revelation to John contains a particularly powerful image of these events:

> Then I saw a great white throne and him who sat upon it; from his presence earth and sky fled away, and no place was found for them. And I saw the dead, great and small, standing before the throne, and books were opened. Also another book was opened, which is the book of life. And the dead were judged by what was written in the books, by what they had done. And the sea gave up the dead in it, Death and Hades gave up the dead in them, and all were judged by what they had done. Then Death and Hades were thrown into the lake of fire. This is the second death, the lake of fire; and if any one's name was not found written in the book of life, he was thrown into the lake of fire.
>
> Then I saw a new heaven and a new earth; for the first heaven and the first earth had passed away, and the sea was no more. And I saw the holy city, new Jerusalem, coming down out of heaven from God, prepared as a bride adorned for her husband; and I heard a loud voice from the throne saying, "Behold, the dwelling of God is with men. He will dwell with them, and they shall be his people, and God himself will be with them; he will wipe away every tear from their eyes, and death shall be no more, neither shall there be mourning nor crying nor pain any more, for the former things have passed away" (Rev. 20:11—21:4).

Christians can rejoice in these images, even though no metaphor can adequately portray the form of the new world to come.

Where we have come

Death and life belong together. We die many deaths before our physical deaths. Every renunciation is a little death, a surrender of ourselves. Our lives become more clear to us when we see our goals. The world will have an end. That helps us to understand much of our suffering and sorrow. But when all visible things pass away,

God is the one who comes to us. The world must be understood in terms of God. We are discovering ever more clearly that the world is not a static existence, but a history and a process. Daily death and renewal are a parable of how the whole world moves into the future. We await the promise of a new heaven and a new earth. God has taught his people to hope. The new world will not be merely an extension or expansion of the present, but something quite literally new. And yet the new is already present in Christ. He is present in the experiences of Christians. The Christ who will come again gives daily evidence of his resurrection in every act of reconciliation among us, in every gift, in every experience of trust. But our existence must pass through death. In death we come to judgment. The judgment which we have experienced in life will be amplified to a destructive finality. It will be the demolition of our existence. At the same time, Christians persevere in the hope that God himself will meet us in our judgment, with Christ at his side. Our fate will be entirely in the hands of God, our Judge and Redeemer.

Summary

I experience

The world in which I live has its particular questions and laws, needs and claims. I face them every day, for they cannot be ignored. They lie obtrusively in my path. They easily crowd out my deepest questions.

I experience a constant contradiction between what I want to do and what I am able to do. Like others, I hunger and thirst for righteousness. I want everyone to receive their due; no one should be devalued; I wish no one would speak words that contradict their actions.

The contradiction between what I want and what I do alienates me from myself, from others, and from God.

I question

What is God's law for our world?
How can I live according to God's law?
What does the good news of Jesus have to do with God's law?

How can the Ten Commandments speak to today's questions?
How is our destiny fulfilled?
Where is world history leading?

I believe

The gospel of Jesus Christ explains my history to me. Jesus seeks me in my world. He wants me to be his disciple. He wants to liberate the world from its imprisonment.

Jesus is more than my life and my example. He promises and gives me salvation. He has not only explained the law of God by which I am to live, but he has lived it. Because he lives with me, now I too can live.

No one has explained the law of God more clearly than Jesus. But if he is right in saying that God demands my absolute love, purity, truthfulness, and fidelity, then I am lost. Then I must go away in sorrow like the rich young ruler of Luke 18. For Jesus reveals my inner self and shows that I am not as God wants me to be.

But now Jesus stands in my place and I in his. He has fulfilled God's will for me. He has taken on himself the judgment which I deserve. The good news therefore must be heard above the sound of God's demands of me; for what God requires of me has already been accomplished by Jesus. He has opened the way to God for me. He has set me free. My salvation and future no longer depend on my fulfilling the law's impossible demands. I am oppressed no longer. I may look at Jesus with freedom and ask, "How would you have me live?"

Jesus shows me the heart of God. God requires love from me. And loving God with my whole heart means to love my neighbors who are in need.

I believe God is the one and only God. He wants my whole love and fidelity. He lays claim to my time, my work, my play, my rest, my celebration, and my worship.

I believe I am to begin in my own community. I am to seek out the old, the sick, the crippled, the weary, and the poor. I am to show love in my political and commercial life. I am to care for my parents and my marriage partner.

I believe Jesus will judge me by one standard: love. The smallest thing done in love is more blessed than the greatest work done in pride or for myself. But to be able to love I must be united with Jesus. I must become like a child, who contributes nothing but receives all.

I believe that in company with Jesus I find peace, because he takes my sorrow on himself. I learn to bear burdens because he carries me. I can mature as I become old and weak because he takes me under his protection. I can play and celebrate God's creation, even though the world is full of unrest. I can die peacefully because God has conquered death.

I believe my life and the life of the whole world will be completed one day, as in the biblical image of a new heaven and a new earth. I can live by faith, because Christ has secured my salvation. I can live by love, because Christ loves me to the end. And I can live by hope, because Christ gives me a future.

6

THE GOAL
OF OUR CALLING

God Seeks Us:

The Church and
the Consummation
of the World

1.   The Nature of Christ's Church

What is the church?

What is the church? A large building with a steeple? A room with a cross, altar, lectern, font, and pulpit? A place with an organ, vestments, hymns, readings, prayers, and a sermon? An office with records, staff, and meetings? An institution with children's homes, nursing homes, hospitals, and mission fields? These are what most people think of when we say the word *church*. They see it as something with a prevailing color (black), a prevailing mood (gloomy), and a prevailing attitude (strict).

All that we have listed—buildings and their furnishings, administration and institutions, organization and history—all this and much more is related to the church. But none of these can be called the church itself. The church is people who belong to Jesus Christ. The New Testament describes the church with the metaphor of a body: "Now you are the body of Christ and individually members of it" (1 Cor. 12:27). The head of the church is Jesus. The body is the people, who are directed by the head. There is a unity between Jesus and his church.

What are the boundaries of the church?

All those who have been baptized into Christ belong to the church. People leave the church for a variety of reasons. They may dislike its demands or their minister's face. But when people leave the institutional church, only God knows whether they have left his people. Others may be actively involved with the church, attending regularly for years. But if their hearts are unrelated to Christ and they live apart from him, they are Christian in name only. Whether these, too, belong to the true church only God knows. The boundaries of the church are not to be found at the point where the institutional church draws them. The church is both much larger and much smaller than that.

Almost one third of the world's population is numbered as Christian. But do they all belong to the church of Christ? And does no one else belong to Christ? Statistics can tell us how many people have been baptized into Jesus' name. But we cannot grasp the true church by counting. The church is not a club. People seek Jesus and experience his presence. They find others who feel sought out and called by Christ. In gathering together they sense the break-down of the walls between them. They experience an understanding without words, created through Christ's word. This gathering is the church, the communion of saints. Such people belong to God, even when they know very little about him. They hear the word of Christ and are his possession.

Is the church visible or invisible?

The church is both visible and invisible. It preaches an invisible kingdom of God in the hearts of people which seeks a visible home in the world. It wants to show God's will to all people. The invisible church is housed in the visible. But God is much greater than the visible church. Christ finds his disciples everywhere. His Spirit blows where it wills. In the Nicene Creed Christians confess, "We believe in one holy catholic and apostolic church." In spite of all its visible divisions, the church is one. It is the communion of saints and there-fore holy, or set apart for God. And it is catholic or universal, be-cause the people of God span the whole world. Christ's church sur-passes the narrowness of nations and cultures, ages and life-styles, ideologies and religions. The Spirit of Christ cannot be confined to one denomination, one locale, one land, or one confession. And the kingdom of God binds Christians together in family love. All are to bear witness to this love in common works, service, gatherings, and celebrations.

Can one be a Christian without the church?

Many people are offended by the church and ask, "Why do I need it anyway? Can't I live with Jesus by myself?" Some live in large cities and find it difficult to make contact with a congregation. Some do not find a sense of community in the church. The church may seem middle-class and old-fashioned. Its worship may seem dead and a hundred years out of date. Or the church may seem so pro-gressive that we no longer feel at home in it. Changes make us uncomfortable. We may look to our jobs, families, and friends in-stead. Isn't rest what we really need on Sundays? If God is so great, why can't the woods and the beaches be our places of worship? But it is idle and boring to list everything that should be changed in the church today. Every Christian should rather work to improve it. The church gathers in many places and takes diverse shapes and forms. There are many possibilities for involvement. Have we seriously explored them?

What is the church's source?

The church of Christ had its origin in God, its ground in Christ, and its beginning in history. It is an expression of the Word of God, who is active in time. God speaks to us in Jesus Christ. The church's task is to preach him as God's Word. Insofar as its preaching is faithful, the church itself becomes the Word of God. Christ, the head, gives life to the church, the body, through his Spirit and power, his word and sacraments. His church is to listen to him, receive him, and obey his word. When the church is faithful it preaches neither human wisdom nor love in general, but rather the one who is among us, the one who loves us through all eternity. Like all human language, the language of the church changes. But if the church is faithful to Christ its language will always be the language of Christ. He speaks through the church. The church leads people to salvation in his name. In his name it accompanies individuals through sorrow and joy. The church reminds us that we are not our own, but belong to Christ. Certainly the church is not always faithful to its task. Luther called the Holy Spirit a heavy rain, and we must often live through times of drought. We remain dependent on the rain. Like the world itself, which was not created once and for all, the church must be renewed each day by the Spirit.

Why must the church struggle and suffer?

When we become angry and dissatisfied with the church, we come to know some of the church's own suffering. Medieval people imagined Christ would exercise lordship over the world through his church and through the emperor. That image of God's kingdom disappeared long ago. We can more aptly compare the church to the nomadic people of Israel. They were led through the wilderness without knowing where their food and water would come from. The church lives from hand to mouth. It must guard against foes both outside and inside. It suffers from its weakness and its fruitless witness to the one who is the faithful witness (Rev. 1:5). When we are offended by the church we share in the church's own pain. The church is not yet "without spot or wrinkle" (Eph. 5:27). It suffers with Jesus, who loved the world and yet was cast out and rejected by the world. The church is God's suffering servant. It follows Christ. Those who want it to be strict and intolerant where Christ is forgiving and kind, to sacrifice the truth for expediency and evade suffering, are not faithful to Christ. Jesus suffers not only at the hands of those who do not believe in him, but also at the hands of those who do. The church is not a human creation. It belongs to God and is his suffering servant in the world.

Where we have come

The church is the community of those Christ has brought to faith, who seek him because he has sought them, who want to live with him and for him. Only God knows the church's boundaries. The church is both visible and invisible. It lives in the world, yet must not resemble the world. It must work for the world, yet never be at home in the world. It gives home and shelter to those who believe, yet cannot be safe and secure. That which it has does not belong to it, and that which it gives it has first received. It is the means by which Christ comes to people, but is not itself the goal. God's purpose is the redemption of the world, not the glorification of the church. Christ comes by way of the church. He speaks his word through the church. The church is to serve this word. As Christ himself was a servant, so he would have his disciples be servants of God (Luke 22:26-27). The church suffers not only from the world's hostility to Jesus' message, but from its own imperfections. It must fight not only against enemies outside it but against its own unbelief and meager faith. The church is the community of those who hope in Christ and in the certainty of his coming again.

2. The Origin of Christ's Church

Did Jesus establish the church?

Christian faith lives in the hope of change—change in human hearts and in the world. The ground of this hope is Christ. He

promised his disciples he would be with them until the end of the
world, and they experienced the truth of his promise. But Jesus did
not establish the church during his earthly life. Neither did he pro-
pound a system of doctrine. He himself was spirit, life, and meaning.
The church is present when faith in Christ begins. And it lives by
the ever-new experience of his presence.

Easter marks the beginning of the church. Easter means Christ is
not dead, but alive. Pentecost propelled the church into the world.
Pentecost means Christ lives among us by his Spirit. Jesus continues
to live in his church. But he does not live on in the same way
Shakespeare lives on among English-speaking people. We are talking
about more than a mere memory of Jesus, more than a recognition
of his greatness. Our language is inadequate to express this new
reality. We must use three different statements to express it: (1) God
the Father sent his Word into the world to make his will and nature
known. (2) "The word became flesh and dwelt among us, full of
grace and truth" (John 1:14). This is Jesus, God the Son. (3) And
through God the Holy Spirit Christ continues to live in his church
and speak to us.

On what is the church founded?

Every house needs a foundation on which it can safely rest. On
what does the church rest? It is called "holy," and Christians call
themselves "the saints." This does not mean they are superior, but
simply that they are in a relationship with God. Every Christian is
a saint. The early church also used this term for its martyrs, those
who witnessed to the Lord with their blood. The church is catholic
or universal, because there is only one body of Christ throughout
the world. It is apostolic because its foundation and source of unity
is the gospel which the apostles preached. This is the meaning of
Jesus' famous words to Simon, the leader and spokesman of the
apostles: "You are Peter, and on this rock I will build my church"
(Matt. 16:18). The New Testament has been collected and preserved by the church as the basic written form of the apostolic
gospel. And the church has repeatedly discovered how important it
is to possess the New Testament witness. "For no other foundation
can any one lay than that which is laid, which is Jesus Christ" (1 Cor.

3:11). The apostles built on this ground. Therefore only that which is constructed on the same ground can be called "apostolic." There will always be those who want to lay other foundations. Some think the Christian faith would stand more firmly if it emphasized human wisdom. Others want to promote the faith through secular values, influence, or power. But Jesus Christ has always been the church's one foundation.

Why is the Old Testament important for the church?

Both Jesus and his first disciples were Jews. They lived in the traditions of Israel. Their Scriptures were the Hebrew Scriptures: the Law (the five "books of Moses"), the Prophets, and the Writings. Both the Law and the Prophets became part of the Christian Old Testament, together with many of the Writings, such as the Psalms. Jesus died with the words of Psalm 22 on his lips. His disciples belonged to synagogues. They visited the temple in Jerusalem, and there Peter and John were arrested. The Christian church did become separate from Judaism, but the split was slow and painful. The early Christian communities were so thoroughly Jewish that Gentiles were admitted only after long and heated arguments.

Despite the church's eventual separation from Judaism, Christians retained the Hebrew Scriptures. They believed these could be understood in light of Christ. Did they not speak of Jesus when they foretold the coming of God's Messiah? Was it not possible to see Christ in the old images, to remove the veil which lay over the time-honored stories? Had not Jesus called himself the Good Shepherd? How many shepherds there are to be found in the Old Testament! Had not Jesus called himself the bread from heaven? In their wilderness wanderings the people of Israel had received bread from heaven! Had not the Lord suffered and cried out in his pain like a psalmist? Was he not a king like David and a prince of peace like Solomon? Christians saw the meaning of the Hebrew Scriptures in Jesus. Their ancestors had spoken of him without knowing his name. And now he would lead his people home.

The church of Christ could neither forget its Jewish origins nor give up hope in a future reconciliation. It gave the Old Testament an honored place, heard its message, sang its songs, and prayed its prayers. It still does the same. For the God of Israel is different from the gods of philosophers. He is active, involved and suffering, angry and loving. He is neither an idea nor an ideal of the human mind. History must be told from the point of view of his saving acts. He is the Creator and the Redeemer. We experience him in what he does for us and with us. The church has come to know this God through his people Israel, and that is something it must never forget.

How did the New Testament originate?

The Christian church grew out of the people of Israel. At first it was composed of Jews who saw Jesus of Nazareth as the long-expected Messiah. But Christians soon realized that Jesus' life and death called for new ways of thinking, speaking, and acting. To the Hebrew Scriptures were added new writings stemming from God's new covenant with human beings, his "new testament." The New Testament has come down to us as a collection of 27 books. It includes the four Gospels, the book of Acts, 21 letters by the apostles or their disciples, and the book of Revelation.

Many of the apostles' letters are older than the completed Gospels. The oldest part of the New Testament is found among the letters of the apostle Paul, probably his two letters to the Thessalonian Christians (dating from about A.D. 51). Paul was a Jewish theologian who had not been a disciple of Jesus but was overwhelmed by an appearance of the risen Lord. He became the most important missionary to the Gentiles. Paul explained the Christian faith with great clarity. His letters also preserve some of the oral traditions of the early church, as in 1 Cor. 15:3-5 and Phil. 2:5-11. Long before the written Gospels there were prayers, hymns, and other expressions of the gospel in short, memorable form. These helped communicate Christ's message during the church's early years. Only gradually were stories about Jesus circulated, written down, collected, and given new shape in the Gospels. Not until the fourth century were all the writings in our New Testament universally accepted as authoritative Scripture. Therefore the Christian church existed before the New Testament, although Christ's revelation and message created the church and was from the beginning expressed in its life, preaching, and worship.

What did the early church believe?

People often say the church today is not what Jesus intended it to be, that the Christ of the church is not the same as Jesus of Nazareth, or that Christianity was made up by Paul or the apostles. But long before the books which constitute the New Testament were written, the Christian church had spread to many parts of the Roman Empire. What was the good news that stood at the heart of the church's early mission and worship? Modern investigation and research has identified several core elements in early Christian proclamation which were present from the very beginning: (1) Jesus died, was buried, and rose from the dead; (2) When God raised Jesus up it was for our salvation; (3) In Christ is fulfilled the hope of the people of Israel. Shortly after Jesus' death the church stood before the world with this confession, and these three elements are still at the center of its preaching. The salvation of human beings is bound up with the unique historical events recorded by the evangelists. Again and again Christians have thought through the meaning of those events. But the core of their message has remained the same from the first Pentecost to this very day.

How does the church live?

The Christian faith is related to the Scriptures. It stems from the event we call Easter, and constantly turns back to that event. But as God was not only there before creation but *in* creation and *with* creation, so Christ was not only present before the church existed but also accompanies it. His presence is experienced by the church, and must be understood in light of the witness of the disciples and apostles. The Bible is both a source of our faith in Christ and a standard for judging our experiences of Christ. For that reason the church reads and interprets the Bible in its worship. Theologians dig deeply into it, seeking to translate its message into terms meaningful today. As you read the Bible in faith you will learn that its Word is fresh and alive even though its words are from ancient languages and times. All that the church does today must be measured by the Bible. How we act toward the rich and poor, toward those near us and those far away, how we worship, educate our children, care for the dying, help the distressed, and comfort the sad—all this must be judged by the Bible. But we must not interpret it literally, failing to overlook the differences between its context and our own. We must interpret its texts with freedom, applying them faithfully to our situation. Whenever Christians engage in this task they will discover the presence and authority of the risen Lord who remains the same through all generations.

Where we have come

The Christian church reaches out into the future because it looks back to a Jew, Jesus of Nazareth, who was born, suffered and died on a cross, and was raised from the dead by God. The church began with the faith of the disciples, and lives in continuity with the faith of the apostles. It is the communion of saints, those called by God and given the task of proclaiming their faith in Jesus. The source of the church's witness is the Old and New Testaments. In the Old Testament we read that God entered history at creation and awakened hope of redemption in his people Israel. The New Testament tells us this hope has been fulfilled in Jesus of Nazareth. In his life, death, and resurrection his disciples saw the hand of God at work, loving and rescuing his world. In the Bible Christians find their faith in Jesus nourished, grounded, and explained. The Bible is the normative witness for Christian faith and life.

3. The History of Christ's Church

Can we look honestly at the church's history?

It has become fashionable to look only critically at the history of the church. This is unfair. One can also discover many people who have followed their Lord and suffered for it. But we must indeed see the other side. The church is not the kingdom of God. God's kingdom is present in the church, but in a hidden way. Christ will continue to suffer in the world until the very end. His name will be misused, his mission betrayed, and his love abused even in the church. The church has built cathedrals, castles, and palaces to honor Christ, but these have often imprisoned him. The church has been intolerant in the name of its tolerant, suffering Lord. The church has cruelly persecuted others, particularly Jewish people. The cross has been carried before advancing armies. Christians have tried to promote the gospel through human strength and world rule. They have punished sin with fire and the sword. They have often forgotten that the line between guilt and innocence runs right through each human heart. They have forgotten that Jesus gladly associated with sinners.

The two sides to church history are thoroughly intertwined. There is a great history of faith—of love, obedience, and suffering. And there is a history of unfaithfulness—greed, wealth, corruption, political influence, and military might. History should be neither touched up nor revised. The New Testament itself tells us that the saints who constitute the church are also sinners. Yet there is still much to love in the church. For the church of sinners is also the church of saints and therefore a holy church. In our disappointment we sometimes forget its moments of faithfulness. But when we judge others we also condemn ourselves (Rom. 2:1). Jesus does not want us to ignore the weaknesses of the church. But we betray him when we stop loving because of the sins and weaknesses of others.

Jesus knows human beings. He chose Peter to be chief of the disciples and yet knew he would betray him three times (Matt. 26:34). Even in the worst periods of church history some Christians have exercised faithfulness to their Lord. Many have suffered and made great sacrifices for others. And there is hope for the church so long as it continues to proclaim the one who came to seek a home with the poor, the humble, and with sinners.

What about the Middle Ages?

The history of the church has included constant demands for reform. This was true of the first centuries and is still true today. It was also true of the Middle Ages. During its first three hundred years the church was often persecuted. Some of the Roman persecutions were more severe than others, and there were long periods of peace. But the experience of Christians as a minority in the Roman Empire showed clearly that to believe and follow Jesus can be costly. Many Christians laid down their lives in Roman arenas and on Roman crosses.

With the conversion of the Emperor Constantine came open

recognition of Christianity. This was the beginning of the ecumenical councils, of increasing organization and consolidation of the church. Responding to heresy and philosophical movements, Christians formulated their faith in great detail. The church became tied to the state and imitated its organization. A body of church law was developed. Many were disturbed by these changes, fearing that Christ's radical demand for repentance and discipleship would be obscured. One result of this concern was the development of monasticism.

After the disintegration of the Roman Empire the church stood as the only significant source of social unity. It attempted to preserve Roman culture and extend its own influence. The church's religious orders began the immense task of converting the peoples of Europe. Authority became centered in the Roman papacy. Only after several centuries did the church's long labors bring great fruit. But when Europe finally emerged from its "dark ages," cathedrals and monasteries grew up everywhere and great systems of scholastic theology were developed.

Although the Middle Ages were a time of great faith, they were also a time of great contradictions. The church became wealthy and powerful, and it aspired to be both political and spiritual ruler of the world. Cries for reform came from many quarters. Francis of Assisi founded an order of mendicant friars which greatly influenced the common people. Others followed his lead. But eventually even these orders, which were based on the ideal of poverty, became wealthy. Bernard of Clairvaux symbolized the contradictions of the Middle Ages. His sincere faith and piety made him universally loved and respected. Though he held no great office, his sheer spiritual influence made him one of the most powerful persons of his day. And yet Bernard is also known as one of the great supporters of the Crusades, a ruthless and bloody chapter in the history of the church.

What was the Reformation?

Sometimes we think of the medieval church as a monolithic, closed institution. But the closer we look the more clearly we see how many different streams flowed through it. Most of the movements for reform, such as religious orders, were encouraged or tolerated. But there were also groups like the Albigensians, Waldensians, and Hussites which sought a return to New Testament models of the church. These groups were suppressed with terrible cruelty. When the monk Martin Luther protested certain church practices which seemed to contradict the gospel, he heard echoes all over Europe. What began as a modest theological discussion turned into a comprehensive reform. Though Luther and his followers had no intention of establishing a separate church, they failed in their efforts to stay within the Roman Catholic Church. In the 11th century the church had been split by differences between the West and the East. Now in the 16th century the western church was torn asunder. Christ's one church became increasingly divided into different groups with different confessions of faith.

What did the Reformers want? They wanted the gospel of Jesus Christ to be clearly heard in his church. Only Jesus can answer our most basic questions: Where do we stand? From where have we come? What oppresses us? Who rescues us? How should we live? To what are we called? God's word comes to us by the Spirit through the Scriptures. We do not obtain salvation from ourselves, but from God through Christ. Christ comes to the world through his word, his sacraments, and his church. We can only explain our lives through his cross. God wants to become known in the crucified Christ. He comes near to us in his suffering. We cannot fulfill the whole will of God, but Christ has fulfilled it. He has suffered for us. He stands in our place. He justifies us before God. All this is clearly written in the Bible. The Reformers reminded us of that.

It must be admitted that the Reformation had its dark side. It led to great strife and ultimately to the Thirty Years War (1618-1648). But in spite of all the intolerance, blindness, and confusion of that time, people were searching for the truth. When the smoke had cleared, the Roman Catholic Church remained under the Pope but had also carried out extensive reforms. And the churches of the Reformation had established their own confessing tradition, translating the Bible, liturgies, hymnbooks, sermons, and prayers into the language of everyday people.

What do we learn from recent church history?

New questions were posed for the church by the 18th-century Enlightenment. The Enlightenment saw human beings as the center

of all things, rejected religion, emphasized human reason and goodness, and replaced the God of the Bible with an impersonal creator.
It was said that people could be improved through education and
evil overcome by reason. The biblical view of human beings is not
so optimistic. But the Enlightenment challenged Christians to think
more clearly about the world, the Bible, and church tradition. The
history of modern interpretation of the Bible has demonstrated how
much can be learned from the Scriptures through disciplined
examination.

While the church reacted against the Enlightenment, it was also
heavily influenced by it. One result of this influence was the movement known as Pietism. The Pietists rejected the Enlightenment's
emphasis on human reason. In place of a critical reading of the Bible
they called for obedience to it; in place of compromise with the
world they called for nurture of the church; in place of education
they called for repentance and conversion. The Pietists have helped
to keep the church from forgetting the moral and personal nature of
the gospel.

In the 20th century we have seen the gradual emergence of the
charismatic movement. For a long time it was limited to Pentecostal
church bodies, but now is active among major denominations. Char-
ismatics seek a renewed experience of the gifts of the Spirit (*charis-
mata* in Greek). For some, the most important of the Spirit's gifts
are healing and speaking in tongues. Others understand the gifts of
the Spirit in the broad sense outlined by the apostle Paul in 1 Corinthians 12-14.

What are some lessons from church history?

How is the church to be distinguished from other groups? How
does it relate to the structures of the world? Every generation of
Christians must ask these questions. During its history the church
has experienced a variety of relationships with the state, and has
learned some lessons. Where it has humbled itself before the state
and become dependent on it, the truth has suffered. And where it has
developed its own political power structures, love has suffered.
When the church conforms to the state it fails to witness to God's
rule. And when it tries to gain worldly power it betrays its Lord,

who chose the way of suffering and said, "My kingship is not of this world" (John 18:36).

Today the church is experiencing a third kind of relationship with the state. In many places it is separate from the state, but it cannot renounce its role as an advocate for those who have no voice: the poor, the oppressed, the sick, the handicapped, prisoners, and outcasts. The church must concern itself with the welfare of families and workers. It must demand that world powers reconcile their differences and work toward a future with equal rights for all. The church itself must not exercise political power, but neither can it be silent. To be silent would be to betray the God who wants the world to be saved.

The church must also forever face the question of its own structure. The church is a social and political entity. Though Christians everywhere confess the same Lord, they are different from each other. They have different tasks and often speak different languages. The church will always have a structure. But that structure must reflect the gospel. It cannot be a class society, with superior and inferior members. It must be a community of equals in which varieties of gifts and experiences are recognized.

How many churches are there?

The New Testament speaks both of churches at Rome and Jerusalem and of the one church of Jesus Christ. The Greek word used for *church* can also be translated "congregation." There are many congregations, but each in its separate place is part of the one congregation of Christ. Unity is given by the fact that Christ is the head of the church (Eph. 1:22). And this unity remains only so long as he is the head. Today Christians of different denominations are increasingly aware of their basic unity in the faith given by the apostles. They are striving for a more unified witness to Christ in our conflict-ridden world. Since the middle of the 19th century an ecumenical movement has developed, first among young people, then among missionary societies and their supporting churches, and finally in various confessional federations and the establishment of the World Council of Churches in 1948. The Second Vatican Council (1962-1965) has brought many changes to the Roman Catholic Church, including an increased willingness to seek reconciliation

with Orthodox and Protestant church bodies. The ecumenical movement seeks to express the unity which Christ has already given to
his church. No one believes there could or should be uniformity in
organization, ritual, theology, or practice. The churches are learning
to rejoice in the richness of each other's traditions. But Christ's one
church suffers from the fact that its unity in diversity cannot be more
adequately expressed. Two major goals which are still unachieved
are a mutual recognition of ministries and a common celebration of
the Lord's Supper. Christians are members of local congregations,
but there is only one church of Christ in the world. To that church
every Christian is bound.

Where we have come

Jesus promised to remain with his church to the end of the world.
Generations of Christians have learned to proclaim the gospel of
Jesus Christ in new ways appropriate to their own times and places.
But sometimes the gospel has been obscured to the point where the
living Christ is only a memory. The image of the institutional church
often covers up the quiet witness of Jesus' true disciples. But their
witness is nevertheless always present, and the gospel has been preserved down to our own day. The church has gone through times of
apostasy and betrayal. We can be angry about that. But even in its
darkest days it has seen attempts at renewal. The Reformation
brought many changes and expressed the gospel with renewed
clarity. Today the ecumenical movement has developed out of the
desire to bring the abundant resources of Christ's church to the task
of proclaiming the message of Jesus to our time. Out of the diversity
of confessions and worship are emerging new expressions of the
unity of Christ's one church.

4.   The Mission of Christ's Church

How does the church follow Christ?

Christ intends his church to follow him by engaging in witness,
worship, and service. The Greek words used in the New Testament
for these are *martyria, leiturgia,* and *diakonia.* The church listens

to its Lord and confesses what it has heard in word and deed. We call this *martyria*. Christians remember their Lord in private prayer and common worship. We call this *leiturgia*. And the church's love is built up through service to people. We call this *diakonia*.

Christians can witness to Jesus in many ways. They can listen carefully to him, read the Bible, and give attention to the proclaimed word. They can pray, confess, and worship together. Bearing witness to Christ is not reserved to a few educated individuals specially appointed for that task. Every Christian is called to make the faith known to others. Yet Christians will be aided in this task by trained people who can help them understand Christ better and witness to him more clearly. Every person we meet is someone before whom we can glorify Christ, through both our words and actions. The church must always proclaim its faith before the world: " 'What I tell you in the dark, utter in the light; and what you hear whispered, proclaim upon the housetops' " (Matt. 10:27).

The best-known form of Christian proclamation is a sermon, given by a minister in a worship service. Sermons may appear old-fashioned, but there is a purpose to them. They are to be based on the Bible. And this usually means not on any text a preacher happens to be drawn to, but on particular *pericopes*, texts the church has chosen from the Bible for different Sundays during the church year. In this way the whole church guides its preachers in their task, just as preachers guide their people in theirs. True freedom in proclamation is found only through guidance and limitation. Faithfulness to pericope texts can prevent preachers from becoming slaves to their own idiosyncrasies. But at the same time preaching requires the involvement of a preacher's whole personality.

The New Testament provides us many examples of preaching the gospel—of declaring the great works of God in the past and present. The proclamation of Christ's love and faithfulness can awaken, comfort, and enlighten. It can bring people to faith. The apostle Paul said faith comes through hearing the gospel (Rom. 10:14-17). Preaching is therefore an immense task. Who is capable of it? Today the church suffers from a multitude of words that are lost in the void. There is a scarcity of the powerful word of the Lord. But God has also appointed prophets in our midst—men and women to whom he has given the ability to interpret his word for our day. By the power of the Spirit God himself can speak to us through such preachers.

How does the church confess Christ?

The New Testament sense of witness includes both the witness we give and the witness we are. The danger of Protestant Christianity is always to understand faith simply as a matter of the intellect. But we commit ourselves to Christ not only with our minds, but with all we have and are. The Christian church does not gather around the memory of an ancient wise man with good ideas. It gathers around the bloodstained Jesus. He himself was the Word which he spoke. The early church was built on the graves of its martyrs, and for some time in Rome it worshiped near their tombs. Clever words can achieve much, but far more powerful are the words which are united to deeds. We will never be able to forget those who witnessed to Christ in Hitler's death camps.

The apostle John wrote a mysterious sentence: "There are three witnesses, the Spirit, the water, and the blood" (1 John 5:8). This means we are given God's Spirit, we die through the waters of Baptism, and we also suffer. The Word of God makes claims on us. The church always needs to be led beyond its verbalized faith and theological insight to actual confession of Christ before the world. Some people perceive things more clearly than others, but all are called to confess Christ in their lives. And wherever we are challenged for our faith and suffer for it, we know Christ himself stands behind us. "So every one who acknowledges me before men, I also will acknowledge before my Father who is in heaven; but whoever denies me before men, I also will deny before my Father who is in heaven" (Matt. 10:32-33).

How does the church remember Christ?

The second task of the church is active remembrance. The Greek word *leiturgia* means rendering service, and in the New Testament it means rendering service to God. We are to meditate on God and remember what he has done for us in Christ. Through the liturgy of the church we speak to God. Liturgy is prayer, and we cannot trust in God without prayer. But what is prayer? And how shall we pray? When people get together they speak with each other. God speaks to us in his Word. We hear him and answer him. Prayer is speaking to God through Jesus. We thank and praise him for his gifts, and we ask him for what we need.

You can learn to live a life of prayer from Jesus, who took time regularly for prayer. First you must be still. Meditation and contemplation—or concentration and reflection—are very old ways of becoming still. But be careful that your prayer does not turn into a conversation with yourself! You need to become still and at the same time hear what God says to you in that stillness. You may call God "Father," for he has given us that right through Jesus. He has promised to hear. At first you may think you are speaking into the void. You should therefore ask him to speak to you. Jesus promises that you will hear him. There are many styles of prayer. The Psalms of the Old Testament are patterns which Jesus and many others have used. But don't imagine that you can master prayer as you would master a language. You must rather let yourself be mastered. Prayer requires a giving up of ourselves to God. The apostle Paul urged the Thessalonian Christians to "pray constantly" (1 Thess. 5:17). At the same time he confessed, "we do not know how to pray as we ought" (Rom. 8:26). The Spirit must teach us how to pray.

How does the church celebrate Christ?

Prayer is at the heart of all piety. When you gather together to pray with your family, or even if you simply pray with a friend, you are part of a congregation. And the most important liturgical activity of the church as a public, gathered assembly is also prayer. In worship the church hears the read and preached Word of God; it responds to God in confessions and prayers; it celebrates his saving presence in the sacraments. In listening and responding, in prayer and participation the church becomes a community of love with Christ at its head. It confesses its guilt and receives forgiveness. It plays and sings and praises the glory of God and his works. It prays for its suffering members, for the poor, the distressed, and the persecuted. It allows itself to be sent into all the world.

The celebrations of the church follow the church year. On Sunday, the first day of the week, it celebrates the Lord's resurrection. During the course of the year it celebrates various feasts: Advent, a time of waiting for the Lord's coming; Christmas, the feast of his birth; Epiphany, his appearance in the world; Lent, a time of repentance and meditation on Christ's suffering; Palm Sunday, Jesus' entry into Jerusalem; Good Friday, the day of his death; Easter, the highest of all Christian festivals, the day of Christ's resurrection from the dead; Ascension, the day of his return to God; Pentecost, the celebration of the Holy Spirit and the birthday of the church; as well as other festivals.

The church's worship retains the traditional elements of hearing and responding, praise and petition, confession and sacramental celebration. But the church also has the freedom of the Spirit to fill up the old forms in new ways. While details change, the basic outline of the celebration of the Lord's Supper is much the same as it was in the early church. It is a meal in which Christians gather to celebrate their Lord in the presence of God. It often begins with the confession of sins. A greeting follows. A hymn is sung. Christ is acknowledged in the words of the *Kyrie,* "Lord have mercy on us." God is praised, thanked, and told of the community's needs. His Word is heard through Scripture texts and preaching. He is thanked with gifts for the poor and for his house. Prayers are offered for those who suffer, and his meal is shared. In that meal Christians encounter Christ and proclaim his death and resurrection. The congregation leaves with a blessing. The church's celebration of the Lord's Supper is an assurance of its union with Christ at the deepest level.

How does the church serve Christ?

The early Christians called the third task of the church the service of love, or *diakonia.* The church itself is a community of love. Jesus said, "A new commandment I give to you, that you love one another; even as I have loved you, that you also love one another. By this all men will know that you are my disciples, if you have love for one another" (John 13:34-35). People have a good sense of smell for Christians who betray their name through lack of love, and for churches which are cold and uncaring. Many leave the traditional churches to form their own communities. Others remain, but form little pious groups, searching for a more intimate spirit, human friendship, and a willingness to help each other.

People long to see faith active in love. Paul wrote, "If one member suffers, all suffer together; if one member is honored, all rejoice together" (1 Cor. 12:26). And of the first years of the church in Jerusalem it was said, "Now the company of those who believed were of one heart and soul, and no one said that any of the things which he possessed was his own, but they had everything in common" (Acts 4:32). The Word of God may be correctly taught, and worship may be conducted beautifully, but these are of little use to a church if there is no love (1 Corinthians 13; Rev. 2:2-4). Are there sick or suffering people in your congregation who are not being visited? Are there poor people nearby who are not being cared for? Are you expecting paid specialists to love them for you?

How does the church serve the world?

The apostle Paul said, "So then, as we have opportunity, let us do good to all men, and especially to those who are of the household of faith" (Gal. 6:10). The community of love within the church is the foundation of love for those outside the church. The goal of Christian life is to learn love. No one can say faith is more important than love, or love is more important than faith. The one is inseparably united to the other. Neither can stand alone. We do not have faith if we do not care for our neighbors, and our love is incomplete if we cannot embrace our neighbors in faith. Who are our neighbors? They are the shut-in and the shut-out, the poor, the oppressed, the imprisoned, the injured, the wounded, the neurotic and faithless— all those for whom Christ died. From the earliest days of the church Christian service has cared for such as these. Some say we accomplish nothing by satisfying one person's hunger if we ignore the structures that produce hunger. "Why help only one? It is better to change society." The church must respond, "We can try to change the structures of society, but we cannot ignore those in need today." Help is needed now. And to help individuals does not rule out striving to alter the whole. The church can never stop helping those who need help. For faith is always active in love.

Where we have come

The Christian church has three tasks in the world: witness, worship, and service. It learns of Christ through proclamation, Bible study, instruction, reflection, listening, and pastoral care. It confesses Christ in word and deed, speaking of him in new ways in different times and places. The church has had many martyrs—those who have stood by their confession of Christ even in death. They are the truest of witnesses. Christians are to lead lives of prayer. God wants to speak with us every day. Faith seeks not the mechanical repetition of platitudes but God's nearness in our own suffering and joy. The church's liturgy is public praise of God. In liturgy it expresses its faith every Sunday and on various festivals during the year. God speaks to his people in their worship, and they respond with thanks, praise, and celebration. The bonds of love hold the church together and bind it to the poor and suffering of the world. And loving service to others is the plumbline by which Christ will measure his church. The church cannot relinquish any of these tasks. And it must never give up its feedom to proclaim, confess, pray, worship, love, and serve.

5. The Life of Christ's Church

How is the church organized?

If we look at different Christian denominations we find a bewildering variety of structures, orders, and forms. Even in the New Testament different forms can be seen. Today's structures have developed through history. At the same time we cannot call any church order good simply because it has tradition behind it. The church's standard is always Jesus. As he served his disciples, so Christians must serve each other: "He who is greatest among you shall be your servant" (Matt. 23:11). All church order must be judged by this standard. In the church there cannot be masters and slaves, those who serve and those who are served.

Today various traditions are increasingly learning from each other. Strengths and weaknesses of different structures are being noted. The Roman Catholic Church has developed a form of church order that is both monarchical and synodical. The Orthodox churches, which were once almost totally governed by regional episcopal synods, have been striving to develop a more unified structure. Among Protestants various New Testament forms of church government live side by side: episcopal forms, presbyterian forms, and free movements.

Every form of church order must be measured to see whether it helps or hinders the church's task as a community of love and proclamation in Christ. Every denomination requires some kind of authoritative ministry, a ministry that is within the church and for the church in its mission. Where there is no ministry, there is no church. The Reformers knew this as clearly as the medieval church. But they also knew something else which the church must be continually reminded of: having an office of ministry is no guarantee that those who hold the office will be guided by the Spirit. Every ministry in the church must be tested by two yardsticks, one external and one internal. A ministry must first of all be bound up with the tradition of the whole church. This happens formally in the ordination of ministers and the dedication of elders and presbyters. But a ministry must also reflect the inner authority of the Spirit. Throughout its history the church has rightly rejected the arbitrary authority claimed by persons apart from the church's approval. We must distinguish between the spirits. But there is also the constant danger that an official or approved ministry will act independently of Christ's Spirit. When this happens, church order is reduced to an empty shell. For Christ is the head of the church, and he governs through his Spirit.

What are the church's offices and gifts?

We have already spoken of an essential office in the church, namely the ministry of guidance. But this task cannot be understood apart from preaching, administration of the sacraments, pastoral care, and supervision of a congregation's work. Proclaiming the gospel is therefore the central task of ministry, to which giving direction is subordinate. But we must discard the idea that there is only one person in each congregation with the task of proclamation. The Reformation emphasized the biblical truth that every Christian is called to proclaim the gospel in word and deed. This is what is meant by the phrase, "the priesthood of all believers."

The apostle Paul taught his churches to think about the riches of the gifts God had given them: "each has his own special gift from God" (1 Cor. 7:7). He called these "spiritual gifts." Some are preachers, some heal the sick, some sing, some understand how to deal with children, and some have the gift of ministering to the sick and the dying. Some can organize, some can manage money, some can glorify God through the arts, some can bear witness to Christ through mission work. Some have the gift of patience—they can stay with a troubled person and wrestle for their soul. Some have the gift of selfless hospitality, and adopt children or take handicapped persons into their home. A Christian church, which lives with Jesus, experiences many wonderful gifts, and God knows that in every age new gifts are needed. They are the mark of a living church. Every Christian has an office of proclamation, and is given gifts to share with others. It is a terrible misunderstanding of the church to imagine that the need for an official ministry precludes the ministries of all God's people. And it is a misunderstanding of worship when a minister says and does everything—as though the church belonged to him or her. Corporate worship is the work of the entire Christian community.

Who can forgive sins?

We often hear it said that only God can forgive sins. People were shocked when Jesus claimed that right. His central work was to take away human sin and make us right before God. And he has passed his authority on to his church. The apostles were promised that God would speak through them. Therefore their words of forgiveness were not empty: "If you forgive the sins of any, they are forgiven; if you retain the sins of any, they are retained" (John 20:23). Forgiveness is the continuing promise of the Christian church. The church is not a gathering of the free, but of the freed. In the life of the church forgiveness takes place in many ways. Worship can be understood as corporate forgiveness. Forgiveness is also the heart of pastoral care, which sees human beings as responsible before God. We are answerable for ourselves and what we do. But there is no guilt that cannot be forgiven. Jesus spoke of the possibility of sin being "retained." What he meant was that obstinacy, refusal to confess, and unwillingness to change could keep people from receiving forgiveness. Paul said the church is called to "the ministry of reconciliation" (2 Cor. 5:18). Ministers forgive sins in the name of God. It is to them that Christians look for the formal words of absolution and liberation. Yet every Christian is to forgive the sins of others, even as Jesus taught: "Forgive us our sins as we forgive those who sin against us."

What are sacraments?

The church lives by the language of the gospel. But words do not exhaust the richness of language. Things can also speak to us: a wedding ring, or an oil lamp which belonged to our grandparents. Actions and gestures can speak as well: a clenched fist, a handshake, a pat on the shoulder. The church has many actions that speak, including the sign of the cross, the lifting of a minister's hands in prayer or in blessing, and a hand upon the sorrowing or the dying. In Protestant churches two ritual actions are called "sacraments": Baptism and Holy Communion. The word *sacrament* does not occur in the Bible, and there have been many disputes over the meaning and number of the church's sacraments. The healing of the sick in Jesus' name could also be called a sacrament, and Luther wondered whether repentance and forgiveness were not sacraments.

In Holy Communion bread and wine are distributed and received in the tradition of Christ's Last Supper with his disciples: "The Lord Jesus on the night when he was betrayed took bread, and when he had given thanks, he broke it, and said, 'This is my body which is for you. Do this in remembrance of me.' In the same way also the cup, after supper, saying, 'This cup is the new covenant in my blood. Do this, as often as you drink it, in remembrance of me'" (1 Cor. 11:23-25). With these words Jesus imparts to us his life and himself. Holy Communion is a meal of grace. It reminds us of Christ's death for us and tells us that only through him, through his very body and blood, can we live with God in eternity. Holy Communion is also a memorial. As we remember the Lord at his table we are united with him, with his first disciples, with Christians through the centuries, and with those everywhere who celebrate his meal. Holy Communion is a meal of forgiveness, peace, and friendship. It combines words and actions. The spoken word proclaims our riches in Christ, and the actions give us a foretaste of God's kingdom.

What does it mean to be baptized?

In the Christian church life begins with Baptism. The church is the assembly of the baptized, and only those who have been baptized share in the Lord's Supper. Young children are usually brought to be baptized by their parents and godparents, who confess their faith and promise to raise them in the church. Baptism is done in the name of the Father, the Son, and the Holy Spirit, and involves either immersion in water or sprinkling with water.

In Baptism we already experience that which is being fulfilled in us step by step and day by day. We were dead in sins but have been made alive with God; we were blind and ignorant but now know the truth; we were alone and helpless and are now part of a community of faith. Martin Luther recommended that Christians constantly remind themselves of their baptisms. We should "creep back" to Baptism each day. In Baptism God encompasses us with water and his word. How powerful are a few words and a little water when God chooses to use them! When we say "in the name of the Father" we know God gives us eternal life. When we say "in the name of the Son" we know God washes away our sins. When we say "in the name of the Holy Spirit" we know God lives in us and in the church.

Some church bodies do not baptize infants. They remind us that we must not unquestioningly accept the practice of infant baptism. We can learn from the 16th-century Anabaptists, who knew that even if small children were baptized in the time of the New Testament, this was by no means the rule. Faith and baptism do belong together. But when does someone believe sincerely enough to be baptized? Luther defended infant Baptism because it is a magnificent sign of God's pure grace. God freely gives us new life. Even faith is not our work, but his gracious gift. People sometimes say the church should not think of children as needing sins washed away in Baptism. But we should remember what we have said about sin and original sin. God is concerned primarily about who we are. Our actions spring from our wills; our deeds grow from our desires. And it is our wills and our desires which God renews in Baptism.

Where is the church sent?

The book of Exodus depicts the people of Israel as being freed by God from slavery in Egypt and then wandering through the wilderness. The church is also God's wandering people. The church, like faith itself, is in a process of becoming. To be a part of the church means to be active, to serve people. Baptized children need to be instructed, adolescents need guidance, the aged must be visited, and the sick must be comforted. And what happens in the church must be expressed outside as well. The church grew because Jesus' followers were sent out into the world. And Jesus gave them authority to say and do what he himself had done (Mark 6:7). People need to know who Jesus is and what he has done for us. As God sent Jesus to us, so Jesus sends us to others. All of the church's teachings, confessions, and prayers must lead it into the world. At the close of every worship service congregations are sent out. This is the root meaning of the term *mass*—"to send out." The church is the "city set on a hill" of the Sermon on the Mount, which should be seen by all, and the "light of the world" which should give its light to all (Matt. 5:14-16). The Spirit teaches Christians to worship in the stillness of their rooms and congregations, and then it drives them out. And it is not for the sake of the church that Christ prayed for its unity, but that "the world may believe" (John 17:20-21).

Where we have come

The church receives its life from the Holy Spirit. Structures will always be needed. But Jesus questions every structure. Does it reflect his Spirit and love? The church needs a particular ministry to gather and guide it, to proclaim the gospel, administer the sacraments, and make disciples. Sin still exists in the church. But we can love the church in spite of its faults, for it is the place where Jesus is found—where his name is invoked and his love is proclaimed. In spite of all the differences between church orders, each attempts to help Christians fulfill Christ's command and serve others. The New Testament sees varieties of gifts and ministries as expressions of the church's spiritual life. Every Christian needs to take his or her own priesthood seriously: to bear witness to Christ in word and deed, to forgive sins and heal wounds. In Baptism God brings us from death to life, from sin to grace. As the church gathers in worship the will of Christ for today is made known. In Holy Communion Christ comes to us and reveals the wounds by which we are redeemed. The church cannot be content just to do good, but must proclaim Christ. And it does not proclaim Christ if it does not serve others as he did.

6. The Completion of the World

Why are we bound to a community?

We can only be Christians together with other Christians. This is hard for our church-weary generation to understand. But it is also remarkable that a generation so attracted by utopian dreams, collectivism, and communes should rebel against responsibility to a community. If we are Christians, we belong to the Christian church. We are bound to the destiny of God's people and share in the destiny of humanity. In Baptism God has called us by name. We have been justified by Christ and will become holy, saved, and perfected. God wants to lead all people to faith and to give salvation to all. It is his church which represents Christ when we become weak and brings us back when we have left him. Each of us will appear alone with Christ before God's judgment seat. But we will not be alone in God's eternal kingdom. Eternal loneliness would be hell; heaven is a loving community. We will join the "heavenly hosts," the perfected church that will rise out of today's poor, sinful, and suffering church just as our new bodies will rise out of our present broken bodies.

Is the church God's sacrament to the world?

The church is not an end in itself. It is God's instrument for dealing with the nations. The church can forget this fact and glorify itself, as its history amply illustrates. But the Bible says judgment will begin at the house of God (1 Peter 4:17). Because the Lord gives himself totally to the church, he also totally claims it. The church of Christ betrays itself when it looks to its own future and not to the future of the human race. Such signs of resurrection as conversion, love, liberation, unity, and service are given to the church as a sign of the world's own redemption. God's aim is not the triumph of the church but the redemption of all creation. The church is to serve the world and announce to it the good news of

God's salvation. Through the gifts of the Spirit the church itself becomes a sacrament to the world. The existence of the church is a sign that the world will not remain as we now experience it. And only to the degree that the church loses itself on behalf of the world does it truly bear witness to Christ, who will be all in all.

What will it mean to be in Christ?

The world was created "in Christ," and moves toward its fulfillment in Christ. Paul said, "for in him all things were created" (Col. 1:16). In the same letter he said, "For you have died, and your life is hid with Christ in God. When Christ who is our life appears, then you also will appear with him in glory" (Col. 3:3-4). That which is to come is greater than what now is. We can only surmise what we will see from the signs God has given us. The Christian faith is different from all ideologies, all philosophies. It focuses on the message Jesus proclaimed when he began his ministry: "God is coming!" The one who is eternity itself is on his way to us. Christians see God in Christ. However unsearchable God may seem, we know him in the unending love of Christ. It is Jesus Christ who comes when God comes to us. That is why our future is in Christ. Today his love in the church and the world is limited and hidden by evil. But he will one day embrace all existence. He who was in the beginning will be all in all. And we will be like him, with him, and in him. We will appear before God as his saints, the creatures he created in goodness whom he calls to himself.

What is the new Jerusalem?

God wants to lead his world back home. Many of our contemporaries see catastrophe almost upon us. Did not Christ himself believe in the nearness of the end and describe the signs which would foretell it? But no matter how close the end may be, we know that God's way with his world is goodness and love, faithfulness and glory. One biblical tradition saw God's future for the world in the image of a new or heavenly Jerusalem. Jerusalem, the city on a hill, will be a place of refuge, a free and open city for all. Its bejeweled gates will open to draw in the nations and gather them on its mountain.

There they will see the glory of the Lord appear on earth (Isaiah 60). According to this vision, Jerusalem will no longer be just the city of Judah, but God's city for all people. Today the church is God's sign in the world, but at the end of time there will no longer be need for such a sign. God will reveal himself. And the church itself will be the new Jerusalem, God's glorious house on Zion's hill. And Christ himself will be the temple of the Lord (Matt. 26:61).

Why do we celebrate Pentecost?

The Christian church arose out of Christ's Spirit. During one of the encounters the disciples had with the risen Lord he breathed on them and said, "Receive the Holy Spirit" (John 20:22). The book of Acts tells us that on the day of Pentecost, 50 days after Christ's resurrection, the Spirit of Jesus powerfully visited the disciples. He inspired them to proclaim to the many pilgrims in Jerusalem what God had done in Christ. They were able to speak in the languages of these people even though they had never learned them (Acts 2). Just as God had once punished the human race for its pride by confusing its language, so now the Spirit overcame this diversity. The unity of the human race was reestablished in the unity of the church. That which divided was removed and reconciled in Christ. The church is a continuing expression of Christ's reconciling Spirit. It lives and prays by the Spirit. We can never grasp God's Spirit. He is as free as the freedom he gives. The kingdom of God into which Christ's Spirit leads us is here but not yet fulfilled. We have received the promise and its signs, but only the beginnings of the substance. On Pentecost the church celebrates the power of God's Spirit, which created the world and created the church. And it prays that the Spirit will give it greater power to proclaim what God has done in Jesus Christ.

What does the Spirit say to us?

We have arrived at the place where we began. We began with the spirit which created the world. And we finished with the Spirit who creates Christ's church. They are the same. The Spirit which was with Jesus is the Spirit which is the root of our existence and our future. This is the Spirit which brooded over the waters before the world had yet come into being, the one who will not let us be destroyed when we die. This Spirit is God. He breaks into our lives, changing and renewing us. He is our life.

The God who created us together with the animals, stars, and all the world is with us. This is a God we can trust. In Christ he sought out the sick and the outcast, stilled the storm, conquered sin, and drew sinners to himself. And he is alive today in his church. Christ is with us to the end of the age. But he is not ours to control. He is not at our disposal. Rather we are at *his* disposal. He fills us with his love and draws us forth like a strong wind. Until Christ becomes all in all we hang over the edge of the abyss, unable to hold on by ourselves, plagued by our consciences and shamed by our sin. But when we fall, Christ picks us up. "It is no longer I who live, but Christ who lives in me; and the life I now live in the flesh I live by faith in the Son of God, who loved me and gave himself for me" (Gal. 2:20).

Life with Jesus is sometimes like a great rest, like breathing fragrant air. But all that he says, demands, proclaims, and foretells has an inescapable urgency. The glory of God waits at the door! God is coming! God has chosen us, and makes us part of his church. One day he will free us from our bonds. He will redeem all his creatures, and gather the nations to himself. For the whole world belongs to him.

Where we have come

The destiny of every Christian is bound up with the destiny of the church. And the destiny of the church is bound up with the destiny of the human race. The struggling and suffering church we know today will one day be fulfilled as the bride of Christ. And the church is a sign of the coming redemption of the whole world. We move toward God and toward his judgment. But the God we will meet is the one who created the world in love and daily renews it in Christ. At Pentecost we celebrate the Spirit of Christ in the church. In him the human race is once again united. Christ is the church's peace, but at the same time he gives it no rest. His claim is as urgent as the certainty that the last day stands at the door. The Spirit of Christ, the life of the world, drives the church on toward its goal. And Christ himself *is* the goal. With him and through him and in him we will appear in glory (Col. 3:4).

Summary

I experience

I experience my loneliness. Every day others pass by me. Children and friends leave me. Even when I am with others I often feel terribly alone.

I find I am not satisfied by the answers I hear to my questions. I long for people who truly believe, who can show me the meaning of faith.

I am dissatisfied with others. Nowhere do I find a true sense of community and a willingness to help each other.

I have experienced the warmth of small groups and the coldness of large gatherings. I am offended by the lukewarm kind of friendship in many churches. I feel uncomfortable when people gather without unity and without love.

I see that it becomes more difficult to build relationships in large groups. I long for a community in which there is true sincerity of faith and love for one another.

I question

Can I remain alone?
Where is the true church?
Who should lead the church?
How do I fit into the church?
Is the sinful church still my church?
What is the church's origin?
Where is the church going?
What does the church mean for the world?
What will be the end of the church?

I believe

I believe in the communion of saints, those who are called and saved by God. God's saints belong to him and long for salvation from the sin and uncertainty of this world.

I believe Jesus instituted no religion. Rather he himself is the meaning of Christian faith, the head and life of the church.

I believe in the holy, catholic, and apostolic church. It is one because it has only one head, Christ, and only one body, his disciples. It is holy because God has called it out of the world. It is catholic or universal because there is only one church in all the nations. It is apostolic because its enduring, immovable foundation is the witness of Jesus' apostles and first disciples.

I believe the boundaries of the church are not the same as the limits set by the institutional church. There are members whom the church does not see, and it counts some as members who do not truly belong to it.

I believe the invisible church of God's saints has its visible form in the churches of the world, in their preaching, sacraments, confessions, worship, ministries, and deeds of love.

I believe I share in the church by hearing and believing, through Baptism and Holy Communion. By his word and sacraments Jesus is made known from one generation to another.

I believe in the church as a community of love despite all its selfishness, in its unity in the Spirit despite all its divisions, and in the responsibility of Christians to bear each other's burdens.

I believe Christ bears with his church through all its sin, poverty, and betrayal because of his promises. But I believe he is free to remove his Spirit if he wills. Christ is not the prisoner of his church.

I believe God will use the church as his instrument to lead the world to fulfillment and to hasten its growth and healing.

I believe in the priesthood of all believers, because the church is a place of mutual forgiveness and renewal. I believe the church is called to use its gifts, imagination, and skills to proclaim the gospel anew to each generation. I believe it needs a teaching office to maintain continuity with the scriptural tradition.

I believe the Spirit urges the church not to live for itself but to sacrifice itself for the world.

I believe the church of Christ will one day find fulfillment together with the world it serves. I believe that Christ, the one in whom the world was created, will one day be all in all.

I believe in the glory of the future world.

I believe that the church of Christ in all its brokenness, as we see it today, bears the stamp of this glory already on its body, and that the Christ who is to come is already in its midst when it hears, confesses, and celebrates the gospel of his good news and authenticates it by its love. That is what I believe. Amen.

WHAT UNITES US

**What the Spirit
Says to the Church:**

Voices of Christian Witnesses

The church of Christ is more than just this generation of Chris-
tians; it also embraces a great "cloud of witnesses" from the past
(Heb. 12:1). Each generation of witnesses has given testimony to
its faith in response to the questions of its own time, providing us
with a rich history of Christ's self-revelation to his church. In this
final section a number of readings from this heritage have been
assembled. First in order are readings from the Bible, that book by
which all other witnesses are judged. Second are samples of a variety
of corporate confessions and statements, including documents of the
modern ecumenical movement. Finally there are selections from the
writings of individual Christians whose works have been especially
influential. The readings found here are only a small bucketful drawn
from the vast ocean of Christian history. Every individual name
stands for countless others who have contributed to our understand-
ing of Christ's will for his church.

The Ten Commandments

And God spoke all these words, saying,

"I am the Lord your God, who brought you out of the land of
Egypt, out of the house of bondage.

"You shall have no other gods before me.

"You shall not make for yourself a graven image, or any likeness
of anything that is in heaven above, or that is in the earth beneath,
or that is in the water under the earth; you shall not bow down to
them or serve them; for I the Lord your God am a jealous God,
visiting the iniquity of the fathers upon the children to the third and
the fourth generation of those who hate me, but showing steadfast
love to thousands of those who love me and keep my commandments.

"You shall not take the name of the Lord your God in vain; for
the Lord will not hold him guiltless who takes his name in vain.

"Remember the sabbath day, to keep it holy. Six days you shall
labor, and do all your work; but the seventh day is a sabbath to the
Lord your God; in it you shall not do any work, you, or your son, or
your daughter, your manservant, or your maidservant, or your cattle,
or the sojourner who is within your gates; for in six days the Lord
made heaven and earth, the sea, and all that is in them, and rested
the seventh day; therefore the Lord blessed the sabbath day and
hallowed it.

"Honor your father and your mother, that your days may be long in the land which the Lord your God gives you.

"You shall not kill.

"You shall not commit adultery.

"You shall not steal.

"You shall not bear false witness against your neighbor.

"You shall not covet your neighbor's house; you shall not covet your neighbor's wife, or his manservant, or his maidservant, or his ox, or his ass, or anything that is your neighbor's" (Exod. 20:1-17).

The Shema

Hear, O Israel: The Lord our God is one Lord; and you shall love the Lord your God with all your heart, and with all your soul, and with all your might. And these words which I command you this day shall be upon your heart; and you shall teach them diligently to your children, and shall talk of them when you sit in your house, and when you walk by the way, and when you lie down, and when you rise. And you shall bind them as a sign upon your hand, and they shall be as frontlets between your eyes. And you shall write them on the doorposts of your house and on your gates (Deut. 6:4-9).

The Lord's Prayer

Our Father in heaven,
hallowed be your Name,
your kingdom come,
your will be done,
on earth as in heaven.
Give us today our daily bread.
Forgive us our sins
as we forgive those who sin against us.
Save us from the time of trial
and deliver us from evil.
For the kingdom, the power, and the glory are yours
now and for ever.

The Beatitudes

Blessed are the poor in spirit, for theirs is the kingdom of heaven.
Blessed are those who mourn, for they shall be comforted.

Blessed are the meek, for they shall inherit the earth.

Blessed are those who hunger and thirst for righteousness, for they shall be satisfied.

Blessed are the merciful, for they shall obtain mercy.

Blessed are the pure in heart, for they shall see God.

Blessed are the peacemakers, for they shall be called sons of God.

Blessed are those who are persecuted for righteousness' sake, for theirs is the kingdom of heaven.

Blessed are you when men revile you and persecute you and utter all kinds of evil against you falsely on my account. Rejoice and be glad, for your reward is great in heaven, for so men persecuted the prophets who were before you (Matt. 5:3-12).

The Greatest Commandment

You shall love the Lord your God with all your heart, and with all your soul, and with all your mind. This is the greatest and first commandment. And a second is like it, You shall love your neighbor as yourself. On these two commandments depend all the law and the prophets (Matt. 22:37-40).

The Prayer for Unity

I do not pray for these only, but also for those who believe in me through their word, that they may all be one; even as thou, Father, art in me, and I in thee, that they also may be in us, so that the world may believe that thou hast sent me. The glory which thou hast given me I have given to them, that they may be one even as we are one, I in them and thou in me, that they may become perfectly one, so that the world may know that thou hast sent me and hast loved them even as thou hast loved me (John 17:20-23).

The Great Commission

All authority in heaven and on earth has been given to me. Go therefore and make disciples of all nations, baptizing them in the name of the Father and of the Son and of the Holy Spirit, teaching them to observe all that I have commanded you; and lo, I am with you always, to the close of the age (Matt. 28:18-20).

Testimony to the Resurrection

For I delivered to you as of first importance what I also received, that Christ died for our sins in accordance with the Scriptures, that he was buried, that he was raised on the third day in accordance with the Scriptures, and that he appeared to Cephas, then to the twelve. Then he appeared to more than five hundred brethren at one time, most of whom are still alive, though some have fallen asleep. Then he appeared to James, then to all the apostles. Last of all, as to one untimely born, he appeared also to me (1 Cor. 15:3-8).

The Words of Institution

For I received from the Lord what I also delivered to you, that the Lord Jesus on the night when he was betrayed took bread, and when he had given thanks, he broke it, and said, "This is my body which is for you. Do this in remembrance of me." In the same way also the cup, after supper, saying, "This cup is the new covenant in my blood. Do this, as often as you drink it, in remembrance of me." For as often as you eat this bread and drink the cup, you proclaim the Lord's death until he comes (1 Cor. 11:23-25).

The Apostles' Creed

I believe in God, the Father almighty,
   creator of heaven and earth.
I believe in Jesus Christ, his only Son, our Lord.
   He was conceived by the power of the Holy Spirit
   and born of the Virgin Mary.
   He suffered under Pontius Pilate,
   was crucified, died, and was buried.
   He descended into hell.
   On the third day he rose again.
   He ascended into heaven,
   and is seated at the right hand of the Father.
   He will come again to judge the living and the dead.
I believe in the holy Spirit,
   the holy catholic Church,
   the communion of saints,

the forgiveness of sins,
the resurrection of the body,
and the life everlasting. Amen.

The Nicene Creed

We believe in one God,
   the Father, the Almighty,
   maker of heaven and earth,
   of all that is, seen and unseen.
We believe in one Lord, Jesus Christ,
   the only Son of God,
   eternally begotten of the Father,
   God from God, Light from Light,
   true God from true God,
   begotten, not made,
   of one Being with the Father.
   Through him all things were made.
   For us and for our salvation
   he came down from heaven:
   by the power of the Holy Spirit
   he became incarnate from the Virgin Mary, and was made man.
   For our sake he was crucified under Pontius Pilate;
   He suffered death and was buried.
   On the third day he rose again
   in accordance with the Scriptures;
   he ascended into heaven
   and is seated at the right hand of the Father.
   He will come again in glory to judge the living and the dead,
   and his kingdom will have no end.
We believe in the Holy Spirit, the Lord, the giver of life,
   who proceeds from the Father and the Son.
   With the Father and the Son he is worshiped and glorified.
   He has spoken through the Prophets.
   We believe in one holy catholic and apostolic Church.
   We acknowledge one baptism for the forgiveness of sins.
   We look for the resurrection of the dead,
   and the life of the world to come. Amen.

Luther's Small Catechism
The Sacrament of Holy Baptism

What gifts or benefits does Baptism bestow?

Answer: It effects forgiveness of sins, delivers from death and the devil, and grants eternal salvation to all who believe, as the Word and promise of God declare. . . .

How can water produce such great effects?

Answer: It is not the water that produces these effects, but the Word of God connected with the water, and our faith which relies on the Word of God connected with the water. For without the Word of God the water is merely water and no Baptism. But when connected with the Word of God it is a Baptism, that is, a gracious water of life and a washing of regeneration in the Holy Spirit. . . .

The Sacrament of the Altar

What is the benefit of such eating and drinking?

Answer: We are told in the words "for you" and "for the forgiveness of sins." By these words the forgiveness of sins, life, and salvation are given to us in the sacrament, for where there is forgiveness of sins, there are also life and salvation.

How can bodily eating and drinking produce such great effects?

Answer: The eating and drinking do not in themselves produce them, but the words "for you" and "for the forgiveness of sins." These words, when accompanied by the bodily eating and drinking, are the chief thing in the sacrament, and he who believes these words has what they say and declare: the forgiveness of sins (*The Book of Concord*, Fortress, 1959, pp. 348-349, 352).

The Augsburg Confession
Article IV

It is also taught among us that we cannot obtain forgiveness of sin and righteousness before God by our own merits, works, or satisfactions, but that we receive forgiveness of sin and become righteous before God by grace, for Christ's sake, through faith, when we believe that Christ suffered for us and that for his sake our sin is forgiven and righteousness and eternal life are given to us. For God will regard and reckon this faith as righteousness, as Paul says in Romans 3:21-26 and 4:5.

Article V

To obtain such faith God instituted the office of the ministry, that is, provided the Gospel and the sacraments. Through these, as through means, he gives the Holy Spirit, who works faith, when and where he pleases, in those who hear the Gospel. And the Gospel teaches that we have a gracious God, not by our own merits but by the merit of Christ, when we believe this.

Condemned are the Anabaptists and others who teach that the Holy Spirit comes to us through our own preparations, thoughts, and works without the external word of the Gospel.

Article VI

It is also taught among us that such faith should produce good fruits and good works and that we must do all such good works as God has commanded, but we should do them for God's sake and not place our trust in them as if thereby to merit favor before God. For we receive forgiveness of sin and righteousness through faith in Christ, as Christ himself says, "So you also, when you have done all that is commanded you, say, 'We are unworthy servants'" (Luke 17:10). The Fathers also teach thus, for Ambrose says, "It is ordained of God that whoever believes in Christ shall be saved, and he shall have forgiveness of sins, not through works but through faith alone, without merit."

Article VII

It is also taught among us that one holy Christian church will be and remain forever. This is the assembly of all believers among whom the Gospel is preached in its purity and the holy sacraments are administered according to the Gospel. For it is sufficient for the true unity of the Christian church that the Gospel be preached in conformity with a pure understanding of it and that the sacraments be administered in accordance with the divine Word. It is not necessary for the true unity of the Christian church that ceremonies, instituted by men, should be observed uniformly in all places. It is as Paul says in Eph. 4:4-5, "There is one body and one Spirit, just as you were called to the one hope that belongs to your call, one Lord, one faith, one baptism" (*The Book of Concord,* pp. 30-32).

The Heidelberg Catechism

Q. 1. What is your only comfort, in life and in death?

A. That I belong—body and soul, in life and in death—not to myself but to my faithful Savior, Jesus Christ, who at the cost of his own blood has fully paid for all my sins and has completely freed me from the dominion of the devil; that he protects me so well that without the will of my Father in heaven not a hair can fall from my head; indeed, that everything must fit his purpose for my salvation. Therefore, by his Holy Spirit, he also assures me of eternal life, and makes me wholeheartedly willing and ready from now on to live for him.

Q. 55. What do you understand by "the communion of saints"?

A. First, that believers one and all, as partakers of the Lord Christ, and all his treasures and gifts, shall share in one fellowship. Second, that each one ought to know that he is obliged to use his gifts freely and with joy for the benefit and welfare of other members.

Q. 86. Since we are redeemed from our sin and its wretched consequences by grace through Christ without any merit of our own, why must we do good works?

A. Because just as Christ has redeemed us with his blood he also renews us through his Holy Spirit according to his own image, so that with our whole life we may show ourselves grateful to God for his goodness and that he may be glorified through us; and further, so that we ourselves may be assured of our faith by its fruits and by our reverent behavior may win our neighbors to Christ (*Reformed Confessions of the 16th Century,* Westminster, 1966, pp. 305, 314-315, 322).

The Thirty-Nine Articles of the Church of England

1. Of Faith in the Holy Trinity

There is but one living and true God, everlasting, without body, parts, or passions; of infinite power, wisdom, and goodness; the

Maker, and Preserver of all things both visible and invisible. And in unity of this Godhead there be three Persons, of one substance, power, and eternity; the Father, the Son, and the Holy Ghost.

7. Of the Old Testament

The Old Testament is not contrary to the New: for both in the Old and New Testament everlasting life is offered to Mankind by Christ, who is the only Mediator between God and Man, being both God and Man. Wherefore they are not to be heard, which feign that the old Fathers did look only for transitory promises. Although the Law given from God by Moses, as touching Ceremonies and Rites, do not bind Christian men, nor the Civil precepts thereof ought of necessity to be received in any commonwealth; yet notwithstanding, no Christian man whatsoever is free from the obedience of the Commandments which are called Moral.

12. Of Good Works

Albeit that Good Works, which are the fruits of Faith, and follow after Justification, cannot put away our sins, and endure the severity of God's Judgment; yet are they pleasing and acceptable to God in Christ, and do spring out necessarily of a true and lively Faith; insomuch that by them a lively Faith may be as evidently known as a tree discerned by the fruit.

19. Of the Church

The visible Church of Christ is a congregation of faithful men, in which the pure Word of God is preached, and the Sacraments be duly ministered according to Christ's ordinance in all those things that of necessity are requisite to the same. . . .

27. Of Baptism

Baptism is not only a sign of profession, and mark of difference, whereby Christian men are discerned from others that be not christened, but it is also a sign of Regeneration or new Birth, whereby, as by an instrument, they that receive Baptism rightly are grafted into the Church; the promises of forgiveness of sin, and of our adoption to be the sons of God by the Holy Ghost, are visibly signed and sealed; Faith is confirmed, and Grace increased by virtue of prayer unto God. The Baptism of young Children is in any wise to be retained in the Church, as most agreeable with the institution of Christ.

28. Of the Lord's Supper

The Supper of the Lord is not only a sign of the love that Christians ought to have among themselves one to another; but rather is a Sacrament of our Redemption by Christ's death: insomuch that to such as rightly, worthily, and with faith, receive the same, the Bread which we break is a partaking of the Body of Christ; and likewise the Cup of Blessing is a partaking of the Blood of Christ.

The Second Vatican Council

The People of God

9. At all times and among every people, God has given welcome to whosoever fears Him and does what is right (cf. Acts 10:35). It has pleased God, however, to make men holy and save them not merely as individuals without any mutual bonds, but by making them into a single people, a people which acknowledges Him in truth and serves Him in holiness. He therefore chose the race of Israel as a people unto Himself. With it He set up a covenant. Step by step He taught this people by manifesting in its history both Himself and the decree of His will, and by making it holy unto Himself. All these things, however, were done by way of preparation and as a figure of that new and perfect covenant which was to be ratified in Christ, and of that more luminous revelation which was to be given through God's very Word made flesh. . . .

Catholic Principles on Ecumenism

4. Today, in many parts of the world, under the inspiring grace of the Holy Spirit, multiple efforts are being expended through

prayer, word, and action to attain that fullness of unity which Jesus Christ desires. This sacred Synod, therefore, exhorts all the Catholic faithful to recognize the signs of the times and to participate skillfully in the work of ecumenism . . . (*The Documents of Vatican II*, Herder and Herder, 1966, pp. 24-25).

The Paris Basis of the YMCA (1855)

The Young Men's Christian Associations seek to unite those young men who, regarding Jesus Christ as their God and Saviour according to the Holy Scriptures, desire to be His disciples in their doctrine and in their life, and to associate their efforts for the extension of His Kingdom amongst young men (*Conference Report*, Paris, 1855, English edition, p. 23).

Faith and Order Conference, Lausanne (1927)

We members of the Conference on Faith and Order, coming from all parts of the world in the interest of Christian unity, have with deep gratitude to God found ourselves united in common prayer, in God our heavenly Father and His Son Jesus Christ, our Saviour, in the fellowship of the Holy Spirit.

Notwithstanding the differences in doctrine among us, we are united in a common Christian Faith which is proclaimed in the Holy Scriptures and is witnessed to and safeguarded in the Ecumenical Creed, commonly called the Nicene, and in the Apostles' Creed, which Faith is continuously confirmed in the spiritual experience of the Church of Christ.

We believe that the Holy Spirit in leading the Church into all truth may enable it, while firmly adhering to the witness of these Creeds (our common heritage from the ancient Church), to express the truths of revelation in such other forms as new problems may from time to time demand.

Finally, we desire to leave on record our solemn and unanimous testimony that no external and written standards can suffice without an inward and personal experience of union with God in Christ (Report of Section IV, "The Church's Common Confession of Faith." From *Faith and Order*, Doubleday, 1928, pp. 466-467).

First Assembly,
World Council of Churches,
Amsterdam (1948)

We bless God our Father, and our Lord Jesus Christ Who gathers together in one the children of God that are scattered abroad. He has brought us here together at Amsterdam. We are one in acknowledging Him as our God and Saviour. We are divided from one another not only in matters of faith, order and tradition, but also by pride of nation, class and race. But Christ has made us His own, and He is not divided. In seeking Him we find one another. Here at Amsterdam we have committed ourselves afresh to Him, and have covenanted with one another in constituting this World Council of Churches. We intend to stay together. We call upon Christian congregations everywhere to endorse and fulfill this covenant in their relations one with another. In thankfulness to God we commit the future to Him.

. . . there is a word of God for our world. It is that the world is in the hands of the living God, Whose will for it is wholly good; that in Christ Jesus, His incarnate Word, Who lived and died and rose from the dead, God has broken the power of evil once for all, and opened for everyone the gate into freedom and joy in the Holy Spirit; that the final judgment on all human history and on every human deed is the judgment of the merciful Christ; and that the end of history will be triumph of His Kingdom, where alone we shall understand how much God has loved the world. This is God's unchanging word to the world. Millions of our fellow-men have never heard of it. As we are met here from many lands, we pray God to stir up His whole Church to make this Gospel known to the whole world, and to call on all men to believe in Christ, to live in His love and to hope for His coming (*Findings and Decisions, First Assembly of the World Council of Churches,* World Council of Churches, 1948, pp. 8-9).

Commission on Faith and Order,
World Council of Churches, Accra (1974)

The Church is called to be a visible sign of the presence of Christ, who is both hidden and revealed to faith, reconciling and healing human alienation in the worshiping community. The Church's calling to be such a sign includes struggle and conflict for the sake of the just interdependence of mankind.

There is here an enduring tension which will not be resolved until the promise is fulfilled of a new heaven and a new earth. Until that day we have to accept the fact that we do not fully know how to embody in the life of the nations and communities of our time the unity which God wills. There is only one foundation for human unity—the new Man, Jesus Christ. But what we build on that foundation will be tested by fire, and may not pass the test.

We must resolutely refuse any too easy forms of unity, or any misuse of the "sign," that conceal a deeper disunity. At the same time, we may believe in and give witness to our unity in Christ, even with those from whom we may, for his sake, have to part. This means to be prepared to be a "fellowship in darkness"—dependent on the guidance of the Holy Spirit for the form which our fellowship should seek and take; and a "unity in tension"—dependent on the Spirit for the strength to reconcile within the one body of the Church all whom the forces of disunity would otherwise continue to drive apart. For there is no "fellowship in darkness" without some sign of the reconciling judgment and love of Christ ("Towards Unity in Tension." From *Uniting in Hope: Reports and Documents from the Meeting of the Faith and Order Commission, Accra, 1974,* World Council of Churches, 1975, pp. 93-94).

Clement of Rome (c. A.D. 94)

Let us look at the marvellous sign which takes place in the East, in the district of Arabia. There is a bird called the phoenix. It is the only one of its kind, and it lives for five hundred years. And when it reaches the time of its dissolution, the time for it to die, it makes for itself a coffin of incense and myrrh and other spices, which when the time is up it enters and dies. But with the decay of its flesh a worm is produced, which is nourished from the moisture of the dead creature and grows wings. Then, when it has grown into a fine specimen, it takes up the coffin in which are the bones of its progenitor and flies with them from Arabia to Egypt, to the city called Heliopolis. And in the day-time, in view of all, it flies to the altar of the Sun and lays them on it, and then sets off back again. The priests then examine the records, and find that it has come after an interval of exactly five hundred years. Do we then think it a great marvel if the Creator of the universe is to effect the resurrection of those who served him in holiness with the confidence of a good faith, seeing that he shows us the magnificence of his promise even by a bird? (*First Epistle to the Corinthians,* xxv-xxvi. From *The Early Christian Fathers,* Oxford, 1956, p. 37).

Augustine (354-430)

28. Now when deep reflection had drawn up out of the secret depths of my soul all my misery and had heaped it up before the sight of my heart, there arose a mighty storm, accompanied by a mighty rain of tears. That I might give way fully to my tears and lamentations, I stole away from Alypius, for it seemed to me that solitude was more appropriate for the business of weeping. I went far enough away that I could feel that even his presence was no restraint upon me. This was the way I felt at the time, and he realized it. I suppose I had said something before I started up and he noticed that the sound of my voice was choked with weeping. And so he stayed alone, where we had been sitting together, greatly astonished. I flung myself down under a fig tree—how I know not—and gave free course to my tears. The streams of my eyes gushed out an acceptable sacrifice to thee. And, not indeed in these words, but to this effect, I cried to thee: "And thou, O Lord, how long? How long, O Lord? Wilt thou be angry forever? Oh, remember not against us our former iniquities." For I felt that I was still enthralled by them. I sent up these sorrowful cries: "How long, how long? Tomorrow and tomorrow? Why not now? Why not this very hour make an end to my uncleanness?"

29. I was saying these things and weeping in the most bitter contrition of my heart, when suddenly I heard the voice of a boy or a girl—I know not which—coming from the neighboring house, chanting over and over again, "Pick it up, read it; pick it up, read it." Immediately I ceased weeping and began most earnestly to think whether it was usual for children in some kind of game to sing such a song, but I could not remember ever having heard the like. So, damming the torrent of my tears, I got to my feet, for I could not but think that this was a divine command to open the Bible and read the first passage I should light upon. For I had heard how

Anthony, accidentally coming into church while the gospel was being read, received the admonition as if what was read had been addressed to him: "Go and sell what you have and give it to the poor, and you shall have treasure in heaven; and come and follow me." By such an oracle he was forthwith converted to thee.

So I quickly returned to the bench where Alypius was sitting, for there I had put down the apostle's book when I had left there. I snatched it up, opened it, and in silence read the paragraph on which my eyes first fell: "Not in rioting and drunkenness, not in chambering and wantonness, not in strife and envying, but put on the Lord Jesus Christ, and make no provision for the flesh to fulfill the lusts thereof." I wanted to read no further, nor did I need to. For instantly, as the sentence ended, there was infused in my heart something like the light of full certainty and all the gloom of doubt vanished away (*Confessions,* book 8, chapter 12. From The Library of Christian Classics, vol. 7, Westminster, 1955, pp. 175-176).

Bernard of Clairvaux (c. 1090-1153)

I think myself that the command to love the Lord our God with all our heart and soul and strength will not be perfectly fulfilled until the mind no longer needs to think about the flesh, and the soul ceases having to maintain the body's life and powers. Only when she has been relieved of these encumbering cares will she be fully strengthened by the power of God: she cannot concentrate her faculties on God and fix her gaze upon his face, while they are being both absorbed and dissipated in caring for this weak, rebellious frame. But in the spiritual and immortal body, the body perfected, at peace and unified, the body made in all things subject to the spirit, there she may hope to reach the fourth degree of love—or, rather, to be taken into it, for it is not attained by human effort but given by the power of God to whom he will (*On the Love of God,* chapter 10. From The Library of Christian Classics, vol. 13, Westminster, 1957, p. 65).

Francis of Assisi (1182-1226)

Most high, omnipotent, merciful Lord,
Thine is all praise, the honor and the glory
   and every benediction.

To thee alone are they confined,
And no man is worthy to speak thy name.

Praised be thou, my Lord, with all thy creatures,
Especially for Sir Brother Sun.
Through him thou givest us the light of day,
And he is fair and radiant with great splendor,
Of thee, Most High, giving signification.

Praised be thou, my Lord, for Sister Moon and the stars
Formed in the sky, clear, beautiful, and fair.

Praised be thou, my Lord, for Brother Wind,
For air, for weather cloudy and serene and every weather
By which thou to thy creatures givest sustenance.

Praised be thou, my Lord, for Sister Water,
Who is very useful and humble, precious and chaste.

Praised be thou, my Lord, for Brother Fire,
By whom thou dost illuminate the night;
Beauteous is he and jocund, robustious, and strong.

Praised be thou, my Lord, for our Mother Earth,
Who sustains and rules us
And brings forth divers fruits and colored flowers and herbs.

Praised be thou, my Lord, for those who grant forgiveness
    through thy love
And suffer infirmities and tribulation.
Blessed are they who bear them with resignation,
Because by thee, Most High, they will be crowned.

Praised by thou, my Lord, for our sister bodily Death,
From whom no living man can ever 'scape.
Woe unto those who die in mortal sin.
Blessed those who are found in thy most holy will;
To them the second death will bring no ill.

Praise and bless my Lord, render thanks to him
And serve him with great humility.

(*The Canticle of Brother Sun.* From The Library of Christian Classics, vol. 13, Westminster, 1957, pp. 124-125.)

Thomas Aquinas (c. 1225-1274)

The distinctive function of a mediator is to bring together those between whom he acts as mediator; for extremities are united in the middle point. Now to unite men with God in the manner of a self-sufficient agent is the office of Christ, through whom men are reconciled with God, *God was in Christ reconciling the world with himself*. It follows that Christ is the self-sufficient mediator of God and men by reason of his having reconciled, through his death, the human race with God. Accordingly, after saying, *mediator of God and men, the man Christ Jesus*, the Apostle adds, *who gave himself a redemption for all* (*Summa Theologiae*, 3a.26. McGraw-Hill edition, vol. 50, 1965, pp. 207-208).

Thomas a Kempis (1380-1471)

1. The glory of a good man is the testimony of a good conscience. Have a good conscience and thou shalt ever have joy. A good conscience is able to bear very much and is very cheerful in adversities. An evil conscience is always fearful and unquiet. Sweetly shalt thou rest if thy heart reproach thee not.

Never rejoice but when thou hast done well. Sinners never feel true joy nor interior peace, because There is no peace for the wicked, saith the Lord. And if they should say, —We are in peace, no evil shall fall upon us, and who shall dare to hurt us?—believe them not; for upon a sudden will arise the wrath of God, and their deeds shall be brought to nought and their thoughts shall perish.

2. To glory in tribulation is no hard thing for him that loveth; for so to glory is to glory in the cross of the Lord. That glory is short which is given by men and received from men. Sorrow always accompanieth the glory of the world. The glory of the good is in their consciences and not in the tongues of men. The gladness of the just is of God and in God, and their joy is of the truth (*The Imitation of Christ*, book 2, part 6. Macmillan edition, 1938, pp. 83-84).

Martin Luther (1483-1546)

Many people have considered Christian faith an easy thing, and not a few have given it a place among the virtues. They do this because they have not experienced it and have never tasted the great strength there is in faith. It is impossible to write well about it or to understand what has been written about it unless one has at one time or another experienced the courage which faith gives a man when trials oppress him. But he who has had even a faint taste of it can never write, speak, meditate, or hear enough concerning it. It is a living "spring of water welling up to eternal life," as Christ calls it in John 4.

As for me, although I have no wealth of faith to boast of and know how scant my supply is, I nevertheless hope that I have attained to a little faith, even though I have been assailed by great and various temptations; and I hope that I can discuss it, if not more elegantly, certainly more to the point, than those literalists and subtle disputants have previously done, who have not even understood what they have written.

To make the way smoother for the unlearned—for only them do I serve—I shall set down the following two propositions concerning the freedom and the bondage of the spirit:

A Christian is a perfectly free lord of all, subject to none.

A Christian is a perfectly dutiful servant of all, subject to all (*The Freedom of a Christian.* From *Luther's Works,* vol. 31, Muhlenberg, 1957, pp. 343-344).

Ulrich Zwingli (1484-1531)

The Word of God is so sure and strong that if God wills, all things are done the moment that he speaks his Word. For it is so living and powerful that even the things which are irrational immediately conform themselves to it, or to be more accurate, things both rational and irrational are fashioned and despatched and constrained in conformity with its purpose. . . .

. . . The whole teaching of the Gospel is a sure demonstration that what God has promised will certainly be performed. For the Gospel is now an accomplished fact: the One who was promised to the patriarchs, and to the whole race, has now been given to us, and in him we have the assurance of all our hope . . . (*Of the Clarity and Certainty or Power of the Word of God.* From The Library of Christian Classics, vol. 24, Westminster, 1953, pp. 68, 72).

John Calvin (1509-1564)

Whoever is utterly cast down and overwhelmed by the awareness of his calamity, poverty, nakedness, and disgrace has thus advanced farthest in knowledge of himself. For there is no danger of man's depriving himself of too much so long as he learns that in God must be recouped what he himself lacks. Yet he cannot claim for himself ever so little beyond what is rightfully his without losing himself in vain confidence and without usurping God's honor, and thus becoming guilty of monstrous sacrilege. And truly, whenever this lust invades our mind to compel us to seek out something of our own that reposes in ourselves rather than in God, let us know that this thought is suggested to us by no other counselor than him who induced our first parents to want to become "like gods, knowing good and evil" (*Institutes of the Christian Religion,* book 2, chap. 2, part 10. From The Library of Christian Classics, vol. 20, Westminster, 1960, pp. 267-268).

John Wesley (1703-1791)

14. In the evening I went very unwillingly to a society in Aldersgate Street, where one was reading Luther's Preface to the Epistle to the Romans. About a quarter before nine, while he was describing the change which God works in the heart through faith in Christ, I felt my heart strangely warmed. I felt I did trust in Christ, Christ alone for my salvation; and an assurance was given me that he had taken away *my* sins, even *mine,* and saved *me* from the law of sin and death.

15. I began to pray with all my might for those who had in a more especial manner despitefully used me and persecuted me. I then testified openly to all there what I now first felt in my heart (*Journal,* vol. 1, pp. 475-476).

Dietrich Bonhoeffer (1906-1945)

Cheap grace is the preaching of forgiveness without requiring repentance, baptism without church discipline, Communion without confession, absolution without personal confession. Cheap grace is grace without discipleship, grace without the cross, grace without Jesus Christ, living and incarnate.

Costly grace is the treasure hidden in the field; for the sake of it a man will gladly go and sell all that he has. It is the pearl of great price to buy which the merchant will sell all his goods. It is the kingly rule of Christ, for whose sake a man will pluck out the eye which causes him to stumble, it is the call of Jesus Christ at which the disciple leaves his nets and follows him.

Costly grace is the gospel which must be *sought* again and again, the gift which must be *asked* for, the door at which a man must *knock* (*The Cost of Discipleship,* Macmillan, 1959, pp. 36-37).

John XXIII (1881-1963)

The Catholic Church . . . considers it her duty to work actively so that there may be fulfilled the great mystery of that unity, which Jesus Christ invoked with fervent prayer from his heavenly Father on the eve of His sacrifice. She rejoices in peace, knowing well that she is intimately associated with prayer, and then exults greatly at seeing that invocation extend its efficacy with salutary fruit, even among those who are outside her fold (Opening Speech to the Second Vatican Council. From *The Documents of Vatican II,* Herder and Herder, 1966, p. 717).

Karl Barth (1886-1968)

In virtue of God's dispensation man is Christ's property, not in spite of but in his freedom. For what man knows and lives as his freedom, he lives in the freedom which is given him and created for him by the fact that Christ intercedes for him in the presence of God. That is the great good action of God, signified in this, that Jesus Christ is the Lord. It is the divineness of this good action, the divineness of the everlasting mercy which, before we existed or thought of Him, has sought and found us in Him. It is this divine mercy which is also for us the basis of Christ's lordship and which delivers us from all other lordships. It is this divine mercy which excludes the right of all other lords to speak and makes it impossible to set up another authority alongside this authority and another lord alongside this Lord and to hearken to him. And it is this eternal mercy, in which this dispensation over us is included, which makes it impossible to appeal past the Lord Jesus Christ to another lord and to reckon once more with fate, or history, or nature, as though these were what really dominated us. Once we have seen that Christ's *potestas* is based on God's mercy, goodness and love, only then do we abandon all reservations. Then the division into a religious sphere and other spheres falls out. Then we cease to separate between body and soul, between service of God and politics. All these separations cease, for man is one, and as such is subject to the lordship of Christ (*Dogmatics in Outline*, SCM, 1949, pp. 91-92).